D0655155

A Most Dangerous Woman?

To Anne Boyle, my secretary,
for whose patience and commitment I am more grateful
than I can say and to John Beyer, Organizing Secretary
of National VALA, whose loyalty and resourcefulness
make such a great contribution to the work

Mary Whitehouse

A Most Dangerous Woman?

A LION BOOK

Copyright © 1982 Mary Whitehouse

Published by
Lion Publishing
Icknield Way, Tring, Herts, England
ISBN 0 85648 408 3
Albatross Books
PO Box 320, Sutherland, NSW 2232, Australia
ISBN 0 86760 410 7

First edition 1982

All rights reserved

Phototypeset by Input Typesetting Ltd, London
Printed and bound in Great Britain
by A. Wheaton & Co. Ltd, Exeter

Contents

Author's Foreword

I am very conscious of two things about this book.

First, many of its early pages cover events which appeared in my autobiographical *Who Does She Think She Is?* (1971). But that book has been out of print for the last ten years and some understanding of the events it covered is, I think, essential if this one is to be put in perspective.

Secondly, I am aware that within these pages very little is told of the many relaxed and happy times with our children and grandchildren or about the hours I spend working in our lovely garden. Without the joy that they have all brought I doubt if the book would ever have been written or the experiences it contains actually have happened.

Mary Whitehouse

Chapter 1

'Who does she think she is?'

'How did it all begin?' That's the question I've been most often asked over the years. Of course, the thing about 'beginnings' is that one does not often recognize them as such at the time. But at least this one is quite clear in retrospect.

Driving into school one Monday morning early in 1963 I was met at the gate by a group of fourth year girls. Had I seen the *Meeting Point* programme the night before, they asked excitedly? 'It was about pre-marital sex, miss and ever so interesting.'

Quietening them down I promised we would discuss it later in the morning and as soon as the bell rang for change of lessons the girls came rushing in, as one of them cried, 'I know what's right, now, miss.'

'Good, well now you tell us,' I said hopefully – this had been a religious programme after all. So Susan told me that when her father had heard what the programme was to be about he insisted that she and her two sisters should stop what they were doing and watch it. By the end they were all quite sure, she told me, 'that we shouldn't have intercourse until we're *engaged*'. And the other girls who'd watched the programme had come to the same conclusion.

So what was this programme which had made such an impact on them? 'What Kind of Loving?' (8 March 1963; BBC1 *Meeting Point* series) was a classic example of the way in which the BBC was then allowing itself to be used as a launching platform for the so-called 'new morality' – though why it should ever have been called the *new* morality when it was as old as the serpent in the Garden of Eden I'll never know. But it was, of course, a very clever turn of phrase.

Anything *new* was bound to attract the young, not to mention some of the not so young who still hankered after their adolescence.

As Paul Johnson of *The New Statesman* said about that particular programme:

> Amazing the advice young people get nowadays. I switched on BBC television to hear a panel of experts talking about pre-marital sex. They consisted of a psychologist, a bishop's wife, a headmistress and a clergyman . . . Although none of them dare say it outright, they all seemed in favour of sex before marriage if certain conditions were fulfilled.
>
> Nobody was prepared to take the orthodox line of traditional Christian morals. The clergyman was twice pressed to say whether or not fornication was a sin, but declined to give any direct answer.

Because I had the time and the opportunity to discuss the programme at length with these particular children I don't think much harm resulted, though there would be the inevitable damage that is done to the innocent when elders are more concerned to be 'with it' than to give the guidance which every younger generation has a right to expect.

We spent the whole of that lesson talking about the implications of this particular broadcast, and it was in this relaxed and open atmosphere that one of the girls, shy and withdrawn, began to talk. With the wisdom of hindsight I realized that this particular child had previously taken no part in the discussions which were part of our sex education scheme, but now, suddenly, she started to talk.

She'd watched one of the international films then being shown by the BBC. Fortunately I'd seen it myself. In the course of the film two men had chased a young woman out of a brilliantly lit fairground into the surrounding fields, thrown her to the ground and roughly made love to her. Whether it was with or without her approval I can't now remember. Standing in the shadow of the hedge were two young teenage children, a boy and a girl. As the boy watched what was happening his face changed, and he turned to look at the girl at his side with a strange expression on his face. The girl, startled by what she saw in him, turned and fled.

By now the child's words were pouring out of her – 'and I was so frightened, miss, by what boys might do to me that ever since then I've been too scared of them even to sit alone in the same room with my brother'.

Later on I talked quietly with her and I could tell that she had certain emotional and family problems, so whenever the opportunity arose I tried to help her to develop a more natural and healthy attitude to the opposite sex both in her home and out of it. I'm not suggesting for a moment that all television programmes should be limited by the sensitivities of such a child but surely there's a lesson to be learnt here somewhere, if only in relation to the power of television.

1963 was, by any standards, an extraordinary year. It was the year in which Dr Peter Henderson, then Principal Medical Officer of the Ministry of Education announced that he did not consider it 'unchaste' to have pre-marital sex; in which Dr Alex Comfort defined a chivalrous boy 'as one who takes contraceptives with him when he goes to meet his girlfriend'; in which the BBC gave the 'full treatment' to the exponents of the New Morality while at the same time censoring by exclusion the protagonists of established morality. 'Kitchen sink' plays and late night satire were at their peak and it was the year of the Profumo[1] affair and of the publication of the then Bishop of Woolwich's book *Honest to God*[2]. ' "God is dead" says Bishop,' shouted the newspaper headlines.

'Homosexuality', 'prostitution', 'sexual intercourse' became, via the television set, the routine accompaniment of family tea and the subject of excited conversation in the school cloakrooms and playgrounds as the Profumo affair unfolded before our eyes. Suddenly 'they' were seen to have feet of clay, and a totally different way of life became suddenly visible and accessible to the children. How 'accessible' I was soon to discover.

[1] The Rt Hon. John Profumo, Minister of War, and his relationship with the call girl Christine Keeler.
[2] SCM Press, 1963.

Not much goes on at school without it coming to the ears of the staff by one means or another, and it wasn't long before I, as Senior Mistress of a large mixed secondary school, found myself talking to five fourteen-year-old boys and girls who had, according to other children in the class, 'been doing things they shouldn't'.

'But *why*?' I asked them.

'Well, miss – we watched them talking about them girls on TV, and it looked as it was easy, and see how well they done out of it miss, so we thought we'd try.'

Shamefaced and rebellious, but little more than children.

These incidents made a tremendous impression on me. If the normal, unsophisticated children I was teaching had been affected by these programmes in the way they had, wasn't it logical, I asked myself, to assume that impressionable teen-agers all over the country could have been affected in a similar fashion?

During that strange summer of 1963 an even more telling example of the immediacy of television came my way.

A mother visited me at school in great distress. Her daughter had 'gone off with a boy' a night or two before. I knew the girl as lively and headstrong, always 'after' the boys, but I'd never been seriously concerned about her behaviour. So I tried to find out more of the background to this story.

'What time does she come in at night?' I asked.

'But I don't let her out, miss, because she's too young to be going off with lads.' Then she burst out: 'But, I can't stop her doing everything, can I? I can't stop her watching television.'

'But why should you?' I asked, and the story came out.

'She was sitting right in front of the TV screen watching one of those plays, and when it got to the sexy part I could see her getting redder and redder in the face, she was so worked up. Then she got up and ran straight out of the house and went off with this boy.'

I tell this story again, just as it was told to me nearly twenty years ago. Reactions to it may vary enormously, but it seems to me now, as it did then, that those who scoff do not begin to be honest. The purpose of much of the sex we see on television and elsewhere *is* to titillate, and the young are a great deal more open about its effects than are adults. As one of the girls admitted in class discussion, 'When I go to bed I think about doing the same thing with my boyfriend.'

Naive as I then was I couldn't believe that the BBC would persist in its policy of giving *carte blanche* to new writers because they were new, and irrespective of their genuine talents, or that its Governors would fail to take action over the Corporation's bias towards humanism and 'South Bank' theology, if they realized the effect it was having upon young people. So I decided that I would go to see the BBC and the IBA (or ITA, as it then was) and tell them of my experience with the children I was teaching.

I wrote to the then Director-General, Mr Hugh Carleton Greene and I received a reply from his Deputy, Mr Harman Grisewood, brother of the late and much loved Question Master, Freddie Grisewood. He informed me that Mr Hugh Carleton Greene was out of the country. If I cared to postpone my visit until late September I could see the Director-General when he returned. Otherwise he himself would be very happy to meet me and hear what I had to say. Since by September I would have been back at school I accepted with alacrity the invitation to go to Broadcasting House to see him. I went the following week.

Mr Grisewood was courteous and concerned. It was obvious that he also was deeply troubled about some of the things which were happening at the BBC. I told him of the effect of the *Meeting Point* programme on the girls' attitude to pre-marital sex. But, he asked me, 'is it not true that the majority of young people now accept pre-marital sex as normal?'

'No, I don't think it is, certainly not amongst the young people I know,' I replied.

Then, very tentatively, I told him how much I wished he could meet some of the youngsters I was talking about, and to my great surprise and delight he said that he and his wife would be very pleased to do so.

It was, in Mr Grisewood's words, 'a most memorable evening'. But nothing moved him more than Pauline's story.

The child of a broken home Pauline was mature beyond

her years. She and her younger sister, for whom she felt greatly responsible, had been left in the care of a grand-mother. She sat at one end of the settee, with the Deputy Director-General of the BBC at the other, in the small London flat where Mr and Mrs Grisewood had come to have supper with us. And she told him in her simple and natural way how 'Daddy came back to see Mummy four times to try and sort things out. I don't think they wanted to separate really, but they're both very proud people and I don't think they knew how to talk out their troubles'. She leaned forward to ask him earnestly and quite spontaneously, 'Don't you think it would be wonderful if the BBC could put on plays which would help families like ours to stay together instead of ones in which, whenever there's trouble, people fly for a cigarette or a drink or out through the front door?'

Besides Pauline there was her friend Anne, our son Richard, then at Birmingham College of Art, a Rhodes Scholar from Oxford and several other young people, all of whom made it quite clear that the standards of 'swinging' London were not theirs.

Mr Grisewood wrote to me afterwards saying how much the whole evening had meant to both him and his wife, that he would always remember what Pauline and the others had said to him and would bear it very much in mind in the months ahead. But it wasn't long before Harman Grisewood resigned. He was, to my mind, too sincere and too gentle a Christian to be at ease amongst the demolition men who frequented the BBC at that time.

I returned to school that autumn feeling pretty satisfied with my vacation activities, and hopeful – would you believe it? – that there might be some improvement in television standards. But I was 'up from the country' all right. For, far from improving, the 'kitchen sink' plays reached an all-time low, and the late night satire[1] shows three nights a week continued their trail of destruction, doing as great a disservice to genuine satire as they did to the nation at large. Sir

[1] '*That Was The Week That Was* was watched as an obsessive ritual by millions of people with its huge team of writers earning comparatively astronomical sums for mass producing personal abuse and bitter attacks on every kind of authority.' Christopher Booker, *The Neophiliacs*, Collins.

William Haley, a former Director-General of the BBC and then Editor of *The Times* described the BBC as being engaged 'in a panic flight from all decent values', 'televising insanities' and showing 'a sick, sniggering attitude to life'.

Throughout 1963 the whole country was in an uproar. Women's organizations, magistrates, church leaders, feature writers, public and private figures joined in the chorus of protest which the Director-General was to dismiss as the voice of 'the lunatic fringe', while being forced for the first, but by no means the last, time to bow to its intensity. *That Was The Week That Was* was taken off the air at the end of the year with Carleton Greene still defending it. 'I enjoyed it. It was very good. It was positive and exhilarating. I have no objection to the language used.'

It was not until March 1965 that the Director-General was finally forced to make a full public apology following Bernard Levin's references to Sir Alec Douglas-Hume as 'a cretin and an imbecile'. The late night satire shows had destroyed themselves.

What had Greene been defending and enjoying and approving? A show 'as smutty as a train window in a Crewe railway siding' (*Daily Sketch*); which was 'adding a new quality to its irresponsible offensiveness – it is now sinister' (*Time and Tide*) and which week after week 'raised questions of taste, fairness, propriety and even libel' (*The Daily Telegraph*), and enabled its scriptwriters to disseminate personal abuse, and bitter attacks upon authority of every kind.

In January 1964 the Charter of the BBC was renewed for another twelve years and Jasper More, then MP for the constituency in which I lived and taught, rang me from the House of Commons to say that the additional safeguards which we'd hoped might be built into it had not materialized.

'What are you going to do now?' he asked. (He knew all about the activities of the past few months.) And out of the depths of my disappointment I replied, 'Well, there's nothing left, is there, but for the parents of the country to rise up and say that we haven't borne our children and built our homes to have them undermined like this.' I've always remembered Mr More's reply. 'I'm sure you are right. Parliament is powerless to do anything in this situation unless it has behind

it a massive and continuing expression of public opinion.'
Mind you, it hasn't done much now, eighteen years later!

It was at that moment that the grass-roots movement
which was to be known first as the 'Clean Up TV Campaign'
and later as the 'National Viewers' and Listeners' Association' was born, though I hadn't the faintest conception of
how it was to lead my life and the lives of those closest to me
into strange and sometimes dangerous areas.

Norah Buckland and I were old friends and had often
discussed the problems created by television in her parish
work as wife of the Rector of Langdon, West Staffs. When it
became clear that not much help was to be expected from
Parliament, she and I, with the assistance of our husbands,
put our heads together and produced what became known as
the 'Clean Up TV' Manifesto, the wording of which was
built into the Petition read to Parliament by Sir Barnett
Cocks in 1965:

1. We women of Britain believe in a Christian way of
   life.[1]
2. We want it for our children and for our country.
3. We deplore present day attempts to belittle or
   destroy it,[2] and in particular we object to the
   propaganda of disbelief, doubt and dirt that the BBC
   projects into millions of homes through the television
   screen.
4. Crime, violence, illegitimacy and venereal disease are
   steadily increasing, yet the BBC employs people
   whose ideas and advice pander to the lowest in
   human nature and accompany this with a stream of
   suggestive and erotic plays which present
   promiscuity, infidelity and drinking as normal and
   inevitable.
5. We call upon the BBC for a radical change of policy
   and demand programmes which build character
   instead of destroying it, which encourage and sustain

---

[1] In later editions 'men and women of Britain'.
[2] The wording of points 3 and 4 was later adjusted to pay tribute to the many
excellent programmes presented on the BBC and to take note that there was
some improvement in BBC drama.

faith in God and bring Him back to the heart of our family and national life.

How many times have we been told by 'inside' people that 'the BBC was very hurt' by what we said in that document! It should be said, also, that no mention was made of ITV because in those early days it gave little cause for offence. Times change!

None of us had any experience whatever of campaigning. But having decided on the wording we had two thousand copies printed, convinced that if we could get twenty signatures on each the BBC would be *bound* to listen to 40,000 people. So we thought; but in any case we had no idea how to launch this great campaign.

'Why not try *The Birmingham Evening Mail* – they've been carrying a great deal of correspondence about all this?' a friend suggested. So we rang them up.

Much more alert now to the ways of 'inky men', I doubt if I should fall quite so easily today for the reporter's enquiry as to whether we proposed to hold a public meeting, especially as we hadn't even thought of it. But then: 'Yes, certainly,' I replied, on the spur of the moment.

'And will you be holding it in the Birmingham Town Hall?' he asked.

'Yes, indeed,' I said, thinking 'I may as well go the whole hog', but certainly not knowing that the Town Hall held 2,000 people! So there we were, the four of us, with a Manifesto and a commitment to a massive public meeting and nothing else – except our determination.

'Mothers Campaign for Higher TV Morals' was the headline on the front page of *The Birmingham Mail* next evening. The following day the national papers picked up the story and we were away. Twenty letters came in the post next morning, building up to a climax of 322 in one delivery just prior to the Town Hall meeting.

'Perhaps never before in the history of the Birmingham Town Hall has such a successful meeting been sponsored by such a flimsy organization. There are no committee members, no officers, and no hard plans for the future, except for the hope that the people at this meeting will go out and spread the word in other parts of the country.'

So said *The Times* correspondent the morning after the mass meeting to which we had so recklessly committed ourselves three months before.

But that glorious night was the culmination of some very anxious weeks. We had neither the means nor the organization to mount a great publicity campaign. All we could do, apart from sticking up one large poster outside the Town Hall, was to send tickets and leaflets to all those who were writing in support, in the hope that they would come and bring their friends.

As 5 May 1964 drew near we felt as though we were living on a precipice. 'What,' we kept asking ourselves, 'is the smallest number of seats which need to be filled if the press are not to report that the huge hall was nearly empty?' Our hearts sank at the thought of only 200. Five hundred, we thought, might just get us by.

When I rushed home from school on the fateful day I found two telegrams on the floor. One was from the then Archbishop of Canterbury, Dr Michael Ramsey, expressing 'interest'; the other was from Dr Donald Coggan, who was then Archbishop of York, giving 'support'. Then we set off for Birmingham to be met by a BBC television crew who asked for permission to televise the meeting with a 'silent camera'. They would not, they assured us, be recording any sound or interviewing anyone – an assurance that lasted no time at all.

I shall never forget walking out on to the huge stage of the Birmingham Town Hall, with over 300 people stacked behind us, to look across the sea of 2,000 faces. (Many others, we were told afterwards, were turned away.) The whole of the front of the platform was decorated with banks of hydrangeas and flowers of every kind, tied with huge cellophane bows. These had all been given by a complete stranger who had rung up the week before to say she would like to be responsible for the flowers at the meeting. We'd expected a few pot plants for the table in the centre of the stage! We never discovered who this generous person was or heard from her again, except when she sent beautiful bouquets to Norah

Buckland and me on the first anniversary of the launching of the campaign.

And the hats! No fuddy-duddies here. 'I'd expected to find a little gathering of rather weird old ladies', a reporter from one of the national papers told me later, admitting rather shamefacedly that he'd really come for a laugh. The meeting was a sensation, outside as well as in. Thirty-seven coachloads of people from all over the country, as well as carload after carload poured unexpectedly and all at once into the busy centre of Birmingham where the Town Hall stands – and we hadn't even thought to notify the police!

Inside the BBC cameras were being fixed up and the lights arranged (coincidentally?) alongside various dubious looking characters who, immediately the signal was given by the ringleader on the platform behind us, attempted to break up the meeting.

As I was speaking, this young tough strode across the platform to grab the microphone and grappled with my husband who, along with two of our sons and several of the platform party, had come to my assistance. As the hecklers beat out a chant of 'We want sex' the BBC men rushed madly around the hall and on to the platform to give maximum coverage – in *sound* as well as vision – to the disturbance. Meanwhile a group of young people, incensed at the publicity being given to the hecklers, turned off one of the TV lights while the great mass of the audience set up a slow handclap – ably supported by a row of nuns who stamped on the floor with the thick soles of their shoes.

The whole disturbance was over in a few minutes and the meeting went ahead with enormous enthusiasm from the body of the hall, and considerable conviction from the platform, building up to a grand climax with the singing of 'Jerusalem'. A wonderful and most memorable night; but we went home to one phone call after another from anxious relatives all over the country. The BBC television coverage of the event with its emphasis on the fracas had given the impression of a near-riot. And indeed one camera man was heard to say, 'Blow it up – we can soon ditch this lot!'

Up to this point the policy of the BBC had been to ignore our campaign in the hope – and belief – that it would burn itself out. But the Birmingham Town Hall meeting, which we had originally seen as the climax, turned out instead to be a launching-pad! We had set out to get about 50,000 signatures on our Manifesto and had collected 500,000. We had hoped for an audience of 250, and over 2,000 people came. In its attempt to destroy the campaign the BBC had given us nationwide publicity. So now there was apparently only one thing to do. We as an organization must be discredited and I, in particular, had to be exposed as an 'interfering busybody'. Who on earth did I think I was? Well, who indeed was I?

Chapter 2

Scholarship girl

My Dad was a Scot – one of the Hutcheson family whose forebears, George and Thomas, founded the Hospital for Poor Boys in the Gorbals area of Glasgow which is now the famous 'Hutchies' Grammar School.

His father, Walter, was a well-known Scottish artist. But it was a by no means lucrative occupation and he and his wife Jeannie had to struggle hard to bring up their seven children on his salary as illustrator for *The Glasgow Herald* and *Chatterbox*. As children we used to hear fascinating stories of how grandfather would be called from his bed in the middle of the night to rush to a fire in the streets or the docks and then hurry back to do his engraving ready for reproduction in the morning paper.

The artistic talent which is so characteristic of the Hutchesons – still – springs from his modest genius. But it didn't work out well for all of them. My father, Jamie, desperately wanted to follow in my grandfather's footsteps, but he would have none of it and packed his son down 'south of the border' where he started a gentleman's outfitters in Nuneaton. It was there he met my mother.

It was in the autumn of 1981 that I – consciously – saw my birthplace for the first time. I visited Nuneaton to speak at the Sixth Form College there and having met me at the station the master responsible for my visit took me round to see it – not least because, I was given to understand, it was now a sex shop, or something very near it! I didn't stop.

Shortly after I was born (I already had an elder sister very severely affected by the polio epidemic of 1910) my father went bankrupt, sold his shop and left Nuneaton. Poor

Dad, he was never a businessman and his genuine artistic talents never found their adequate outlet, though he loved helping me with illustrations for my school work and did a great deal to help my sister with the handicrafts which later became her very successful livelihood.

No one we knew had ever heard of my mother's maiden name of 'Searancke' and no one could spell it, either! As children we heard vastly intriguing stories of the origins of this family, no doubt much embroidered in the telling. However, many years later my cousin, Esme Searancke, traced our lineage back to a yeoman family living in the town of Hatfield in the early 1500s. In a history of the area published by the Hatfield WEA, the Searanckes are described as 'one of the leading families and employers. Their brewery was probably Hatfield's main industry'. The biggest landowners after the Earl of Salisbury, the Searanckes owned 'some forty houses and shops, with yards, gardens, orchards, barns and farm premises, a smithy, cooper's shop, pot kiln and some fifty-five acres of land. This was in addition to the brewery estate, the brewery premises, maltings, about eight inns and public houses and eight acres of land'.

There followed generations of apothecaries, surgeons, clergymen, maltsters, bakers and brewers. There were three mayors of St Albans and a High Sheriff of Hertfordshire (1777).

When, in 1979, I was given a copy of Lord David Cecil's beautiful book *The Cecils of Hatfield House*, I could not resist the temptation of writing to its author and telling him of my forebears' connection with Hatfield. In his typically charming way he wrote to say that he liked to think of them living in Hatfield and concluded his letter: 'I am so pleased you liked my book and especially the passage at the end about the sense my father had and my brothers and sisters conveyed, of their awareness of a Divine Reality – nor do I think this awareness is lost nowadays. (Actually the Church in this village[1] is more alive than when I was a child here.)'

In the nineteenth century the family broke away from Hatfield and many of them emigrated. One of them, William

---

[1] Cranborne.

Nicholas Searancke, eighth child of a naval captain who lost an arm fighting with Nelson at Copenhagen, trained as a surveyor, went out to California in search of gold (though there's no record that he ever found any!) finished up in New Zealand and married a daughter of the Maori King Tawhiao. Princess Te Puea Harange, CBE, born in 1882, was the child of their eldest son. Like her father and grandfather before her she fought to protect Maori lands, culture and institutions, while at the same time accommodating the best of European influences. Only with the publishing of her biography[1] in 1977 was it possible, so the blurb tells us, for the people of New Zealand fully to understand what she did, not only for the Maoris but for New Zealand itself. When she died in 1952 'the funeral ceremonies were the largest seen in New Zealand outside those for Prime Ministers who had died in office'. I found her whole story quite amazing.

Grandfather Searancke was a master builder in a small way, but he died as a comparatively young man just before the birth of his twelfth child, leaving his wife destitute and without any of those supportive social services which would ease the lot of any such mother today. Grandmother sought help from the other branch of the Searancke family, but they, so the story goes, were 'not interested in poor relations'. The only assistance forthcoming was from a wealthy maiden aunt who offered to adopt my mother, lavishing upon the child everything that money could buy, but cutting her off from her large family of brothers and sisters. Her loneliness and the fact that Aunt Fisher wanted her to become a Roman Catholic – 'the smell of the incense made me feel sick' – caused her to run away and return home. She never became the heiress she was meant to be but, in spite of the fact that she was one more mouth to feed, Grandmother was very glad to have her back – a story she told us countless times and which we children never tired of hearing!

The eldest boys of the family had to earn coppers where they could. One of them stood as a little lad of ten selling shoe-laces and tins of blacking in all weathers. The tale of his 'runny nose' as he 'shivered in the bitter winter weather'

---

[1] Michael King, *Te Puea*, A Biography, Hodder & Stoughton NZ 1977.

outside the local shoe shop, which he was later to manage until he retired, is another nostalgic memory. Two of the others started as brickboys and made their way until they became very well known in the East Midlands as master builders and sand merchants and I remember very vividly the fun we children had in those sandpits when we went to spend holidays with our indulgent uncles.

When, during the First World War, my father moved from Shrewsbury to Chester with his family of four young children, the only accommodation he could find was an old house high on the city walls. To my mother and father it was dark, depressing and, worst of all, damp. But to us children it was exciting and very special. The house was large, square and flat-roofed, and boasted five blank windows – relics of the window tax of 1696. It had its own little chapel lying right back from the city wall, approached by a long path at the side of the house. This was at that time occupied by two quaint old ladies who seemed to us children to sit permanently and very still at the top of the steep steps which led directly into the chapel itself, which was their only room.

Our playground was the city wall and although this meant that we could not play many of the games other children played we had special ones of our own, like chasing up and down the 'wishing steps'. We believed if we could do it three times with one breath our wishes would come true. But balls would bounce cheerfully over the wall to be lost in the tall conifers which grew alongside, or roll across the road into the River Dee before any passer-by could stop them for us!

'Dropping' was our speciality. We would scramble through the side rails which were built on the wishing steps, lower our legs through and hang on with our fingers before dropping down on to the path below. The higher the step from which we started, the greater the drop! There was always much 'daring' but I do not remember anyone actually suffering the broken leg our elders always prophesied.

Our greatest joy was the river itself, with its weir, its swans and, in season, its jumping salmon. We loved the stories of how, not so many years before it seemed, the river had frozen over for six long weeks. Horses and carts were driven on it and every night there were bonfires and feastings

on the deep ice. The old suspension bridge, long since replaced, fascinated us and we jumped up and down on its
broken planks, terror-struck by the sight of the fast-moving
river below. Incredible, when one thinks about it, that people
were ever allowed on that bridge. But we were and the more
we could make it swing the happier we felt.

But in the end it was the river which caused us to move
from the old house. The rising mists were bad for my mother
and so my father found a house in another part of the city.
Though small and cramped after the freedom of our house
on the wall, we were lucky to find one at all in the acute
housing shortage which followed the First World War. None
of us liked it very much and I spent as much of my time as
I could away in the fields nearby. We 'haymaked' in the
summer, blackberried in the autumn, made slides on the
ponds in the winter – and I still remember the joys of dis-
covering the first wild flowers in the spring. We really *could*
go out in the country on our own in those days without anyone worrying about us, as long as we got home in good time
for bed. We took our sandwiches and made our little fires.

But life was not all bliss by any manner of means, even
for children too young really to understand much of what
was going on in the minds and hearts of our parents. It was
only when I was married and had children of my own that
I came to understand something of the burden my mother,
in particular, had carried.

Four young children, with the eldest badly handicapped
by polio and frequently in hospital, put tremendous strain
upon her. As the second eldest in the family, with two
younger brothers, I was expected to help a great deal, which
I by no means always did with a good grace. I know I was
often self-willed and difficult. One of my jobs was to scrub
the front path and whiten the steps of the house before I
went to school. This particular task didn't worry me very
much, as long as I could get it done before my friends passed
by. But I was by no means always so accommodating.

My sister and I can laugh now, she still rather ruefully,
at the tricks I got up to when I was made to take her out in
her bath chair just when I wanted to do something else.
While I chased at great speed along the pavements, leaving

other people to watch out for their heels, my poor sister frantically steered the Bath chair's wobbly little front wheel among the startled passers-by feeling, as she has told me since, terribly upset if we bumped into anyone. To me it was a childish game, but not to her!

My father's job was really quite a good one, bringing in anything from £10–£20 a week, a lot of money in those days. But the demands of my sister's medical treatment, my mother's frequent illnesses and a number of unfortunate business transactions which drained his resources for years, meant that our financial situation was always precarious. So I learnt very early 'to make do and mend' and accept with grace the clothes which were handed on to me.

Looking back I think quite the worst time of my childhood was during the dreadful 'foot and mouth' epidemic of the 1920s which went on for many weeks. My father would go out day after day, riding his push-bike – no car then – for mile after mile in all weathers down the Cheshire lanes, tramping the muddy fields, only to be met over and over again by a large 'No Admittance' notice. I can still feel his total despondency as he returned hopelessly day after day, and see him collapsing in a chair by the fire, as he held out his legs, one at a time, without a word, for me to take off his muddied leggings and pull off his boots. This was the time when my mother sat up through the night making little dresses for the neighbours' children. One night she stitched on and on until the needle of her handturned sewing-machine went through her finger.

We all went to the council school at the end of the road and everyone left at fourteen unless clever enough to win a scholarship. My parents, and particularly my father with his Scottish passion for education, were very anxious indeed that I should pass and the teachers encouraged them by saying that I stood a good chance if only I would be 'more careful and less slapdash'. However, careless and slapdash as I'm sure I was, I still did well enough to move to a very good central school. From there, at thirteen, I was awarded a bursarship which carried a small grant and a commitment to become a teacher. So from then on there was never any question about what I should be. All I had to do was work hard, get a good matriculation, go to college and qualify. The wonderful thing was that I never ever wanted to do anything else and when the time came I dearly loved teaching, and the children I taught – or most of them!

My years at the Chester and City County School (Chester City Grammar School now) were more full of fun and games of one kind and another than of hard work. Although 'scholarship girls' always started with a bit of a disadvantage socially we made up for it in other ways. We were supposed to have 'brains' and were much in demand for checking homework early in the morning. There were three 'schols' in our class and two of us became firm and lasting friends. The third was altogether too good to be true, and her conscious virtue, hard work and tidiness were a constant thorn in my flesh. 'Mary, why can't you be more like Martha?' haunted me for years, even into my college days, for Martha arrived there a year before I did and gave me a fine reputation.

However, being ladylike held no attraction for me, and I was a rebellious child who resisted pleas to 'speak nicely' and to keep the hair ribbon at the end of my long thick plait properly tied.

Constantly in trouble for mischief of one kind and another I redeemed myself, in the eyes of some members of the staff at least, by my insatiable interest in geology and love of wild growing things, by the goals I scored as right wing in the 1st XI hockey team and my prowess in tennis. And even the Head came over to pat my back and help me recover my breath when I won the quarter-mile, in record time, at the annual sports.

Being 'proper' was mandatory for a schoolgirl who wanted to 'get on' in the 1920s and I fear I was a sore trial to our Headmistress, Miss Footman. Certain things were expected of the 'gels' in her school. We must never eat sweets in the street, always wear gloves when in school uniform and carry a clean 'hankie' in our pockets. To fail in any of these was to court trouble. To break the three rules at once was to invite disaster. And one Saturday morning I did just that.

Surreptitiously biting a bar of chocolate I'd just bought at the newly opened Woolworths, I wandered into the famous Rows to feast my eyes on Browns of Chester's window

display. This shop was patronized then by the Duchess of
Westminster and her friends, and had such an aura of gran-
deur that very few of the natives of Chester, the ones I knew
anyway, ever seemed to go inside. 'County' girls were not
supposed to stand and stare anywhere, least of all outside
Browns.

But here was I, munching away, without my gloves on,
entranced by the beauty of the gowns displayed in the great
windows, oblivious of everything – until I felt, rather than
saw, a presence towering above me. The pained, almost
strangulated, voice of the Headmistress boomed out. 'Mary!
. . . what are you doing here? . . . eating sweets in your school
uniform!' And, final indignity as I hurriedly wiped my mouth,
'Your handkerchief is far from clean!'

First thing on Monday morning the Deputy Head, a large
gaunt woman, swept into 4A's classroom.

'Girl called Mary Hutcheson here?'

My hand went up.

'Then stand at the end of the second form line when you
go into Assembly,' she ordered, and swept out again.

Everyone was agog. 'What have you done, kid? Won a
scholarship?' – though no one really thought I could have
done anything right. So what was this all about?

It never entered my head that it could be anything to do with
the previous Saturday's escapade. I had supposed that the
stern 'on the spot' homily had been the end of the matter. In
the deathly hush that always accompanied the entrance of the
Headmistress I was called on to the platform and stood there
– hopefully – while she quelled the school with her glance.

Then she spoke, and I suddenly realized I was to be
'made an example of' – for having been found 'feeding'
outside Browns. 'Feeding?' I often thought afterwards – 'feeding', indeed!

Miss Footman was in many ways extraordinarily kind,
particularly to my mother, for whom she felt both admiration
and compassion. But I remained a total mystery and embarrassment to her. She once told me, without I am sure meaning
to be unkind in any way, that she 'would never understand
how a nice woman like your mother came to have a daughter
like you!'

Even when I left school and went to ask her for a testimonial her only response was to tell me to 'write one out for yourself and if I approve of it I'll sign it'. So I did. And she did. I have often wondered since whether the sense of humour she seemed so sadly to lack during my years at school suddenly surfaced in the end, perhaps at the thought of getting rid of me!

I became a Guide – leader of the Scarlet Pimpernel patrol. Several years ago I was invited to go to Chester to speak at Hoole Church, which was the one I had attended as a child. At the end of the meeting a short, plump, grey-haired woman came up to me and said excitedly, 'You remember me Mary? . . . don't you . . . I'm Louie!' The blankness of my memory must have shown in my face until she reminded me eagerly, 'You know, Louie – Patrol Leader of the Robins!' And we stood grinning at one another as though the fifty years between had never existed!

My bicycle was my passport to quiet roads and luscious fields. Taking with me a bottle of 'pop', a hunk of Cheshire cheese and a bag of apples I would pick my grasses, my leaves and my flowers, folding them carefully between sheets of paper ready for pressing. Sadly, of course, they inevitably lost their colour and it was a pale and crushed shadow of a periwinkle which found itself duly labelled and fastened in my book. So always I had to go back, walk barefoot in the wet grass and discover my flowers again. If it rained as I pedalled my way home so much the better. I can still feel the stinging drops as they hit my hot cheeks and taste the freshness as they ran over my lips.

When my first baby was born I would put his pram under the trees so that he could watch the dancing leaves. And I would let him roll on the grass, to discover for himself the tiny creatures which inhabit the earth. I'm not sure that he actually did at that stage, but all his life he too has loved growing and living things. I well remember the sad little boy who, when we had to leave the country to live in the town, was found walking on a neighbour's uncut lawn with his shoes off, 'just to feel the grass on my feet, Mummy'. But I anticipate.

Chapter 3

Living in the
expectation of miracles

I was a very good tennis player, even while I was still at
school. My parents were asked if they would agree to me
being trained as a 'county' player. But although they were
very proud that I was considered that good, we did not have
the necessary money and I was in any case committed to
teaching. The lost opportunity didn't really bother me; I
joined a tennis club and played for the team. And, of course,
for the first time I was *free*! Sometimes now, when I am
speaking to young people I tell them how they have been
conned over this 'generation gap' business, as they have in
so many other things. The real generation gap came between
our generation, which as teenagers in the 1920s reaped the
benefits of the emancipation of woman that followed the First
World War, and our parents' generation who were Edwar-
dians with a Victorian overhang.

I still lived at home, but many of my friends were already
in flats of their own and there we would meet, young men
and women together, to eat and drink and talk until the early
hours of the morning. No subject was taboo, though I suspect
that our conversation was a great deal less obsessed with sex
than is usual today. 'Free love', like communism, was fearlessly dissected, solemnly assessed and, in the great majority
of cases, discarded in practice. My poor parents, lying awake
night after night, waiting to hear me walk up the path
and put my hand through the letterbox to pull out the front
door key, were worried to death. But they needn't have been.

My old school friend, Martha, who preceded me to the
Cheshire County Training College in Crewe had painted
such a lurid picture of me and my antics, that when I finally

arrived there no 'Senior' wanted me for her 'daughter'. Ultimately, a pale timid girl, too unsure of herself to choose from among the new arrivals, was landed with me. She was the only one left 'childless' and I was the only one not yet 'adopted'!

The college was fortunate to have as Vice-Principal at that time a very remarkable woman, quite famous in educational circles, particularly for her work in the field of child psychology. Margaret Phillips was prepared to spend endless time with individual students and I blossomed under her guidance and in the warmth of her faith in me. That, in itself, was quite a novel experience! It was she who introduced me to the work of Cezak, the great Austrian teacher, who in the days between the wars opened up a completely new approach to children's art. It was she who helped me to understand the symbolism of Epstein's work and to see beyond the controversy which raged around the controversial sculptor at that time. I was one of those who moved slowly in the great queue which filed for days past his 'Genesis'. And when I finally stood in front of it, how poignant it seemed, how innocent the emptiness and littleness of the woman, as her energy drained into the child in her womb. The promise within that great carved stone still lives with me, still touches me.

I enjoyed my college days immensely even though, half way through them, my father went bankrupt and I had to undertake to pay back my college fees as soon as I started teaching. Because of my special art qualifications I was offered a choice of jobs and to this day my Chester relatives find it difficult to understand why I should have chosen to spend most of my teaching life in the Industrial Midlands, so very different from the countryside I love so much, and indeed from Chester itself.

Yet, I felt instantly at home in the little Black Country town of Wednesfield, where steel traps of every kind were then still made in the little back-street workshops for export all over the world. In spite of its closeness to Wolverhampton, the community was very introvert and inbred but to be accepted by one family was to be accepted by all and there was a great warmth and friendliness which was very welcome after the cliquishness which characterized Chester's social life at that time. The children too were open, unsophisticated and appreciative, so that I look back on my first years of teaching as some of the happiest in my life. I made a lot of friends in Wolverhampton, joined a tennis club and went to dances and altogether had a very good time.

It was at this time that a friend invited me to an Oxford Group meeting in the old Wolverhampton YMCA. As we entered that Sunday night in 1932 we saw a group of young men laughing together. One face particularly impressed itself upon my mind. It was the face of the man I was later to marry and, though it was to be more than two years before I spoke to him, I have never forgotten the scene when I opened the door at that first meeting.

The sincerity, vitality and commitment of the Oxford students was tremendously impressive and I was intrigued by what they told us.

'If you listen,' they said, 'God will guide you day by day and transform your whole life.'

However, interesting as all this was, it did not touch a very deep chord in me at that time. I had no desire to change for I'd found an intellectual freedom from the religious ideas which had been so much a part of my upbringing, and I was determined to discover what life was all about for myself.

It was not long before I did. I fell deeply in love with a man who was already married and as my unhappiness and conflict grew I thought again of the message of the students. I went back to the Oxford Group meetings and Ernest was among the half dozen or so of us who travelled together around the Midlands speaking in church and public meetings. I remember very well how upset some of the elders of one church were when Ernest said that he 'would put his shirt on God'! These were immensely exciting and satisfying times. The real thrill of seeing people give their lives to God and commit themselves to his way is something I still remember with gratitude, not least for the fellowship and fun we had together.

It is nearly fifty years since I asked God to take my life and use it and, although they have held many experiences of sorrow as well as joy, the sense of release and joy which came to me then has remained as living experience in the years since. Ernest and I still get up every morning soon after 6 o'clock to have our 'quiet time' of Bible study – and in my case of writing up my diary. Nothing has altered the conviction that came to me all those years ago that God could and would work miracles in the big and little things in life if I lived in the expectation of them. Time and again in the years since, and in particular in the strange and unknown ways of recent years, I have been upheld by that knowledge and experience. And this transformed not only my personal life but my professional life too.

Would I take on the job of training the choir for the Staffordshire Musical Festival, the Headmaster asked one day. I was appalled at the very idea. Music – the one subject I'd vowed never to teach at all.

'How could I possibly? . . . I can't sing . . . I've no idea how to conduct . . . I play very little and, anyway, how could I conduct the choir, and play at the same time?'

Quite unmoved, even by the poignancy of this last anxious plea, the Head asked me to think it over. I promised I would, but in my own mind there was no doubt what my answer would be, for I felt I would only make a fool of myself and everyone else. But next day, when I'd had time to think about it, I realized that my decision was governed by my own anxiety and self-consciousness, and that this was no basis on which to work. 'I must live in the expectation of miracles,' I said to myself, and hoped that everyone else would too! So I told the Headmaster that if he were prepared to stand by the consequences I would agree.

I began by telling the choir that I knew as little about the whole business as they did – should we tackle it together? Would they be as open and frank with me as I intended to be with them?

'Yes, miss,' shouted the delighted children, and off we went – me rushing over to the piano to strike a note, them holding it till I could get back to the front to conduct. The great thing, I felt, was to get the tempo right and the spirit, and to enjoy ourselves. But I still had no pianist and I waved my baton more with energy and high spirits, than with any kind of musical expertise.

Then one day a very well-known Midland pianist and friend of the Headmaster offered to come into school three times a week, really more to train me than to train the children. 'Keep your foot still, girl,' she'd shout at the top of her voice.

It was at this point, too, that one of my friends, a musician whose health was too uncertain at that time for him to follow his profession, offered to come to school each day. The time fled by – Stephen at the piano, Miss Cluely in the body of the hall, and me and the choir on the platform, as likely to be told off from the one place as the other! The children loved it all and I still remember vividly the thin, rather scruffy little boy – Johnny was his name – who stood in the front row with his eyes following my every movement. As I tried to get the children to put some soul into the line 'Come O my love prepare thee in dreamland to wander with me', I pleaded with them, 'Come on . . . *Think* of your love, *dream* of your love. Who's your love, Johnny?' The reply came back like a shot – 'You, miss!'

The day came, the school closed, and some of the staff came too. They told me afterwards how they sat on the edges of their seats gripping one another's hands as we walked up on to the platform smiling cheerfully and ready for – what?

The first song was a sea shanty, and as 'the raging sea did roar and the stormy winds did blow' the whole proceedings seemed to me to become airborne. All fears and anxieties were left behind and the children sang with tremendous zest and polish. So it was with the other 'classes'. They really did have the mood to fit the song, and everything they had been taught, by all of us, blossomed on the day. We were given 'A minus' or 'B plus' in each group and were 'Highly Commended' for the 'relationship between conductor and choir' and for the spirit with which we sang.

Only a tiny miracle, but I have no doubt that it has meant as much to the children who were part of it as it has to me in the years since.

In the meantime Ernest and I were feeling more and more drawn to one another and began to feel that part of the plan that God had for our lives was that we should marry. I suppose most people would feel that we had a very strange courtship indeed as we travelled from meeting to meeting, spending far more time with other people than we did alone together. But what an immovable base our decision to put God first gave to our relationship. We were very young in the ways of the Spirit, but we gradually learnt how greatly God honoured the sacrifice and turned it into a blessing.

If, in saying these things, I give the impression of a drab and pious relationship, how badly I write! For these were days of great spiritual adventure together and we were increasingly certain that, when we married, our life together would have a deeper and more secure foundation than just sexual attraction or compatibility, important though these were. As indeed it has. Many years later, in the middle of the Clean Up TV Campaign, a Fleet Street man was to say to me, 'You must have a remarkable marriage for it to be able to stand up to a strain like this.' I do. I have a remarkable husband, too, who in his quiet and self-effacing way has always been so ready to sacrifice his ease and comfort and to advise and support. For instance, who does all the shopping and the planning ahead of the meals? Certainly not me. Who thinks about the money I shall need when I set out on a journey? Not me either! Who prays for the family, for the work, for me when I'm too exhausted to do anything but put my head on the pillow and fall asleep? Ernest.

Ernest was working with his father when we were married at Easter 1940. He had been taken away from Wolverhampton Grammar School – one of whose most illustrious old boys was Norman Brook, later Lord Normanbrook, Chairman of the BBC – to help his father found an industrial coppersmith's business in a little workshop measuring only twelve by eighteen feet, in one of the back streets of Wolverhampton. Together they adapted a method widely used by brewers to cool beer to produce a simple means for dairy farmers to cool their milk. This device proved to be a most successful method of preserving it from rapid souring. It was later made a compulsory routine for all milk producers and, although John Whitehouse and Son held no patent on the model, the business slowly flourished as it ventured successfully into wider fields of milk refrigeration and the manufacture of copper hot water cylinders.

Our first son was born in 1941 and since, war or no war, we wanted a sizeable family we were delighted in the following year to be told by the doctor that I was carrying twins. But this was the beginning of a sad and difficult time for us, as I had to spend many of the following months in bed. We were warned by a specialist that the babies were likely to be very delicate and he recommended that I should have an abortion. But neither of us wanted that and although I spent the last three months of my pregnancy in bed, which wasn't easy with our first child still so very young, and even though my babies did not live, I've never regretted the decision we made. My twin sons remain part of our family and I am very grateful for what they gave to me in courage and maturity.

It was nearly three years before our next child was born and eighteen months later came our third son. Then, when he was eighteen months old, my brother's wife died in South Africa at the age of only twenty-one, leaving a baby girl just three months old. It seemed best that she should come and live with us, to be brought up with our young family, and her maternal grandmother flew out to bring her to us. She was a bonny little thing and we had a rare time with three children under four, with a mature seven-year-old always ready to help with any crisis that arose.

In the early years of our marriage we lived in one of a group of four houses designed to be part of an estate. But because the war had stopped all civil construction we and our neighbours – all with small children like our own – found ourselves living in the middle of fields! The children, constantly in the open air, had all the 'natural' play materials to hand and were a lively, adventurous bunch. My husband, an experienced climber, took our eldest son with him into Snowdonia when he was still a very small boy. By the time he was four years old he had climbed 2,000 feet and he eventually became a very skilled rock climber. But, as a little one, he not infrequently put my heart in my mouth. On one occasion I heard him calling me as I stood in the garden, but I couldn't see him anywhere – until I spotted him on the top of the chimney stack of a house which was being built nearby.

We only tried a boarding-house holiday once. As the rain

fell day after day and the proprietor came into the room every half hour to wipe the children's finger-marks off the piano, I would look longingly at the caravans on a nearby site. From that year on, until the children left school, we spent our holidays near the Barmouth estuary in a converted bus, close to the shore where the children could play safely and happily. And I would sit – for odd minutes at least – soaking in the sun and the sea, and occasionally scribble.

> I found here the quiet place
> The still and elemental place –
> No noise of people, not a trace
> Of voices, cars and hurried pace
> Of feet, feet, feet.
>
> Just to sit.
> While children play –
> Far enough,
> Their voices sound
> Like seagull cries.
>
> Honey coloured creatures, fair,
> For once slow moving,
> Engrossed in eels
> Slithering swiftly
> Between dun stones with seaweed hung.
>
> How still.
> Winter days of rush and strain
> Will quietened be,
> As closed eyes, softly,
> Longingly,
> Reach for the shore again.

Things began to go wrong with the baby when she was about ten months old and after several anxious weeks coeliac disease was diagnosed. (It was for this illness that the BBC broadcast an almost daily SOS for bananas during the war, as this was the only food such patients could assimilate.) But we were immensely fortunate in that Wolverhampton came under the

Birmingham Group of Hospitals which was, at that time, engaged in research into the disease and on the basis of this research I was told she must be taken off all other food and put on a diet composed solely of soya flour and glucose! I must 'starve her' and withhold all other food until, in desperation, she would eat the soya flour biscuits I had to make, whether she liked them or not. For ten days she refused to touch them. Her condition deteriorated in a frightening fashion until our youngest son decided to try one of these new 'bikkies' for himself. Mercifully – how mercifully! – he liked them and the problem was solved. For the two of them, always inseparable, would feed one another with obvious though incredible relish with those unappetizing, hard little objects.

So long as she was kept on her diet the baby flourished. Miss a day and she wilted like a flower without water. She had to be taken regularly to hospital for check-ups and I would push the pram as far as the bus-stop, go into town, then walk to the hospital with the baby on one arm, the two-year-old in the other and a fretful just-four-year-old – then suffering temporarily and painfully from flat feet – hanging on to my skirts.

The increase in our family, the distance from town and the up-hill, unmade road over which I had to push the prams, made us decide to move. So we bought a large Victorian house quite close to Wolverhampton town centre. With plenty of room inside, it had the additional blessing of a very large garden – a lawn big enough for cricket, an orchard of not very special fruit trees under which the bluebells blossomed in the spring, and an old fountain which our eldest son turned into a fine pond for his plants and aquatic animals. It took him the whole of the first summer to dig out and remove the concrete fillings, but it was only that pond which reconciled him to the loss of the fields and friends he had just left behind.

For the others this house was joy untold: attics and cellars for secret games, long passages for tricycle rides on wet days and a huge playroom, later to have its ping-pong table and its dart board, but now with its lower walls covered in rolls of wallpaper (plain side out) and little tables stacked with jars of tempera paint and long thick brushes. And there were supplies of hammers, big nails and bits of wood so dear to the hearts of small boys.

In this garden, as in the earlier one, spring always saw the delivery of a ton of sand. It was the best and most inexpensive 'toy' we ever bought, that and the long pipe through the kitchen windows so that little naked bodies could splash to their hearts' content.

The trouble was that the little naked bodies did not always stay in the garden. And I well remember the horrified voice of a rather charming old lady who lived opposite, when she rang to tell me that the three youngest ones were through the front bedroom window and standing on the little outside balcony 'without a stitch of clothing on' waving at the passers-by and the traffic on the busy road beneath.

Next door but one to us, in Merridale Road, lived Mr Enoch Powell and his family. His two daughters were then very tiny and could be seen at their nursery window watching our children build their 'tree house' in the big old apple tree at the edge of the lawn. Mr Powell had only a tiny garden but we observed with fascinated interest and respectful awe the care with which he planted out his lettuce seedlings. We felt he must be almost counting the specks of soil between each, so meticulous was he. However, we weren't so impressed with the way he treated the fruit which grew on his one apple tree, half of which hung over our garden wall.

I well remember the three workmen who were doing some alterations for us, sitting in the garden eating their lunch and making almost unprintable remarks about 'that chap on the wall shaking the fruit off the tree'. They didn't know who 'that chap' was, sitting astride the dividing wall, and we didn't share their dismay because to us the falling apples simply demonstrated the direct Powellian approach to the immediate problem.

Although we have been fortunate in many ways we've had perhaps more than our share of illness, and our years at Merridale Road were marred by one calamity after another. One of the children picked up a streptococcal infection when he was six years old which left him with chronic – and sometimes acute – rheumatism. He was nearly twelve years old before he went back to full-time schooling, and was in bed for many months at a time in the intervening years. One of his problems was that his eyes, because he had chorea, did not focus properly. So he couldn't read or draw, or play with anything which demanded any kind of close attention. The great stand-by was plasticine and, with his budgie pecking at his ear, he would mould and press and pull for hour after hour as he watched the passers-by. We had brought him down into the front room and put him by the window, so although his bed was invisible his little head was not, and the 'regulars' would wave to him as they went about their business.

We learned later that the view into the room from the top of passing buses became something of a land-mark. As the bus drew up to the stop opposite the conductor would call out, 'Anyone for the little boy in bed?' From time to time some kind stranger would knock on the door and bring a present for him and the neighbours would pop in to tell him stories. But they were long, long days.

It was while this illness was at its height that near-disaster struck our youngest son. He was playing in the outhouse when a spirit level exploded in his face and he came rushing in with his right eye filled with blood. Within minutes we had him at the Eye Infirmary, mercifully only at the end of the road. The specialist, who operated immediately, could offer no hope that the sight or the eye itself could be saved. But as the child lay under the anaesthetic we telephoned our closest friends, who in turn rang others, so that very many people held the little boy, and the brilliant surgeon who operated on him, in their constant prayers during the next hours and in the weeks that followed. His eye was saved. So was a considerable portion of his sight. And it was the specialist himself who said to us when the child was finally discharged from hospital three years later, 'this has been the most remarkable case I have ever handled'.

It was in 1953 that I made my first, and for very many years my only, broadcast. I had been deeply moved by the Queen's first Christmas broadcast, shortly after the death of her father King George VI. She spoke simply and with deep sincerity of her forthcoming Coronation, of her dedication to her people, and she asked us all to pray for her.

During the next weeks and months I thought a great deal about what the Queen had said, and wondered how someone like myself, so far removed from her as a person, could really help her. I knew I could pray, day by day, that she be given the health and strength and courage to fulfil her duties, but was there nothing else? Was there no small dedication that I, too, could make?

Gradually I put my thoughts down on paper and when they were sufficiently 'polished' I sent them off to the BBC, unaware that the plans for the Coronation broadcasts had been completed long before. I was also unaware that the programme planners, realizing how deep an impression the Queen's speech had made, had sent our researchers to try to find a woman who, in their own words, 'had been changed' by the broadcast. Apparently they'd been into pubs, talked among their friends, put out feelers in many directions, but all to no avail – until my script arrived just a fortnight before the Coronation itself.

I received two telegrams within an hour. The first asked if I would go for a voice test. The second said 'Script accepted. Please contact immediately'. I collapsed on the bottom stair, shaking like a leaf. All the times I had been working on the script I had never thought of what it would mean actually to do the broadcast! However, I did it, and 'A housewife's thoughts on the eve of the Coronation' went out live as the last item on *Woman's Hour* on the afternoon before the Coronation. My first venture into broadcasting.

Although by this time my brother's little girl had gone to live with my sister, the strain of the past few years had begun to tell on me. Each winter saw me in bed for several weeks at a time with chronic kidney trouble. This finally culminated in an infection which kept me in bed for fourteen weeks and doctor's orders for a complete break from my family responsibilities. So my mother took me away to the sunshine of the Canary Islands where I spent the next six weeks.

The sun has always been the most wonderful tonic in the world for me and I came home tanned and fit. I can still see the little faces, torn between tears and laughter, which crowded the front door as I walked in again. There was so much for me to see. The marks on the wall which showed how each child had grown; the 'wash' 'dry' 'put away' rota at the side of the sink; and of course I had to taste the gravy! From that day on my gravy was never quite as good as the thick, dark brown concoction that the boys had learned to make while I had been away.

Although the doctors had given me the 'all clear' I never seemed fully to regain my physical stamina, and the polishing, lifting and cleaning which are so much part of the day's work tired me excessively. I really needed more help in the house, but this we found difficult to afford. So, for the first time, we wondered whether I should take a part-time job which would enable us to pay for daily help.

I went to see the Wolverhampton Education Officer. Would he be interested in my services? But when I said that I was really only interested in teaching art, that I would not wish to leave home until I had seen the children off to school and would want to be back before they returned, the enthusiasm which my original question had aroused somewhat evaporated.

'Wasn't that asking rather a lot?' Indeed it was, but I couldn't go back to teaching unless those conditions were met. So we left it at that.

Less than a fortnight later I was offered a job as a part-time art teacher in a school just around the corner. The new pattern of life worked out so well that in the course of a few years my part-time work became full time, and I enjoyed it all tremendously.

One day I saw advertised a post for Senior Mistress at Madeley Secondary Modern School in Shropshire, with responsibility for art throughout the school. I went to see the Headmaster and would love to have applied for the job, had it not meant a journey of sixteen miles each way – too early a start in the morning and, with the special duties involved, far too late a return at night.

But not much more than a year later we moved to the beautiful village of Claverley, six miles out of Wolverhampton. By now our eldest son was at university and the second son at Birmingham College of Art, and I had more time on my hands. One day I said to my husband: 'You know, if that job at Madeley ever came vacant again I think I would apply.' Account for it how you will, the situations vacant column that weekend carried another advert for the same post. I applied and was appointed.

Chapter 4

Whatever happened to innocence?

So how did Mrs Whitehouse of all people come to be involved with sex education? I can always sense the faint waves of shock which pass through an audience at such a thought!

Just before I started teaching in 1960, in what was then Madeley but is now part of Telford New Town, the Head-master had decided to invite marriage guidance counsellors to give a series of sex education lessons, complete with film-strips and films on 'Human Reproduction' to the fourth year girls. As I was Senior Mistress responsible 'for the moral welfare of the girls' – amongst many other things! – I was immediately involved in this project and became, as far as the girls were concerned, primarily responsible for it.

My feelings about the whole business were very mixed. Ernest and I had always been quite frank with our own children, answering their questions as and when they were asked. I was quite convinced of the need for such openness in the home but much less sure of what I felt about sex education in school. However, I was as they say 'landed with it'.

All the staff involved were agreed that we would be in a better position to judge whether or not this was a good idea when we'd seen the marriage guidance counsellors at work. The very first hurdle we had to get over was the unwillingness of the marriage guidance doctor and her colleagues to have any staff in the room while they gave their talks and showed their slides. But we were there all right! Their approach was entirely factual. No moral questions were raised or answered. This made us even more convinced that we'd been right to insist on being present, especially as the newly published Newsom Report on secondary education had made it clear that sex instruction must be given on a basis of 'chastity before marriage and fidelity within it'. That had to be the basis of *our* teaching but it certainly didn't enter into the visitors' presentation.

It is difficult to believe that this Report is still the most recent one on secondary education – how strangely those words fall on the ears these days. I may say that our decision to stay in the hall with the children was more than vindicated when, during one of the talks and while I was watching the reactions of a group of girls I knew to be rather more mature than the rest, another girl at the end of the row fell off her chair in a faint. I found when I talked to her afterwards that she was in a considerable state of anxiety because of difficulties between her parents and the tensions this created in the home. No doubt she was to some extent an exceptional case and one could not judge the efficacy of the lessons by the impact they had on her, but that experience served to pinpoint for us the dangers of teaching the intimacies of sex to a group of adolescents on the hit-or-miss principle – something which is surely fundamental to the wise handling of a sensitive subject.

At the end of the series of visits we took stock and decided to dispense with the services of the counsellors and to take complete responsibility ourselves for whatever sex instruction was to be given at school. One of our most important and genuinely progressive moves was to offer parents the opportunity to become fully involved with everything that went on under the banner of 'sex education'. We invited them to come to school in the evening and see for themselves the filmstrips and slides that we proposed to use and – very revolutionary! – we left the choice of whether their children should participate in the lessons entirely with the parents. It was a case of 'opting in' rather than 'opting out' of sex education (attempts to do the latter have caused much heartbreak in recent years). We had evening meetings in which mothers came to school with their daughters and fathers with sons, though it has to be admitted that the mothers were very much more in evidence than the fathers.

Some wonderful things happened through these classes. The mother of one girl who had got into serious trouble with a local boy had been to school to see me about the matter, and the bitterness and hurt between the two of them were dreadful to see. But a considerable and rather wonderful change came over this relationship as they attended the evening classes together, and I will always remember watching them go through the door at the end of one of our sessions with their arms around one another. The girl herself altered out of all recognition as the months passed by, and all because mother and daughter could at last talk to one another. That is what they *both* told me. An experience to treasure.

It became very clear as the experiment progressed that children of the same age-group vary enormously in their emotional and physical development. 'Can we come and talk to you on our own, miss?' the more sophisticated would say and I would make myself available whenever they wanted to come and chat after school. The interesting thing about these discussions was that it was the relationship with *Mum* rather than with their boy friends which troubled the girls the most, and the one who asked me rather poignantly, 'What do you do with a mother who doesn't trust you?' was very typical. And the mother who said to me, with a touching anxiety to do the best she could for her daughter, 'I *want* to talk to her, miss, but I don't know the words to use' responded with obvious relief when I replied, 'Well, come and we'll teach you the words to use.'

We decided, in the end, to take 'sex education' as such off the timetable. We replaced it with a rather ponderously titled 'Education for Living' which in practice made sex education just one aspect of a syllabus which spread over many aspects of school life, from the domestic science department, to biology, to social studies, to religious education and even to my art room, where the aesthetics of home building gave rise to many imaginative projects and, I may add, much fun.

It was these experiences which made me react partly with relief but also with considerable sadness when I read recently an interview with Dr Keith Taylor, the newly appointed Director-General of the Health Education Council. He was asked, 'Do we need more and fuller sexual and contraceptive information to counter the tragic consequences for so many of premature sex? Or will this, as its opponents fear, simply encourage carefree experimentation?' He replied, 'We are concentrating on the wrong target – parents, not children, are where sex education should begin.' He went on to say that he wanted to see 'classes' for parents where couples can 'swap ideas, problems and solutions, with professional medical and educational help present to give guidance, teaching know-how – and the right words'. And he added, wisely, the warning that many of those officially concerned in teaching our children on sexual matters or helping them with consequences also need a little re-education.

'They start off,' said the doctor, 'by saying, "If you can't talk to your parents. . ." Well, I want to encourage the attitude which says, "Try talking to your parents." For all our sakes we *must* re-affirm the role of parents.'

Surely this is precisely what we were saying and doing twenty years ago!

So what happened to turn back the clock? Why did the work we were so successfully pioneering disappear almost without trace? (Perhaps I should say *public* trace, for much quiet, responsible and enlightened sex education has continued in schools up and down the land but always subjected to extreme pressure from the libertarians and the money grubbers and those ideologically committed to change course into more permissive paths.)

In this matter, as in so much else, what happens in Britain has its origins elsewhere. The tidal wave of permissiveness which hit our children in the 60s was no exception. For instance, the Head of Sexual Education in Sweden announced, 'We don't care at what age children start going to bed with each other as long as they are prepared. We don't tell them that they've got to wait until such and such an age to start their sex life. . .'

By 1971 the new guidelines were being prepared for Swedish teachers. They were told not to advise abstinence for teenagers. On the contrary, it was suggested that contraceptives should be provided in all schools since it was reckoned that 50 per cent of all teenagers over fifteen had intercourse. Indeed the Swedish Association for Education mounted a campaign to persuade girls to carry condoms in their school satchels. (In fairness it should be said that those same sex radicals – for example Mr Hans Nestius, Chairman of the National Swedish Association for Sexual Instruction – who twenty-five years ago were fighting so hard for 'liberation' are now wringing their hands and saying, 'What have we done? What can we do about it in the future?'[1] and are determined to find the answer.

In Germany much the same thing was happening. Anyone who has seen a copy of the German sex education manual *Zeig Mal*, as I have, could only be appalled by its photographs of tiny tots playfully engaged in oral intercourse, mutual masturbation and homosexual activities. Its highly professional presentation would no doubt have recommended it to the elite of the sex 'educators' (it was only our threat of legal action that kept it out of Britain) but one suspects that it was meant not so much for the 'education' of children as for the gratification of adult voyeurs and paedophiles. Incredibly, the German sexologist Helmut Kentler was at the same time demanding that children be 'exposed to pornography at the age of three'.

So the tidal wave originated elsewhere. But things had been happening in Britain ever since the war which had been destroying our moral and intellectual defences. Various so-called 'progressive' educational philosophies were gradually taking hold, and although A. S. Neill's Summerhill School was virtually a one-off case, its influence was pernicious in the extreme. James Dobson, the American psychologist, had this to say about the Summerhill philosophy:

> Please note how many of the following elements of the new morality can be traced to the permissive viewpoint represented by Neill: God is dead; immorality is wonderful; nudity is noble; irresponsibility is groovy; disrespect and irreverence are fashionable; unpopular laws are to be disobeyed; violence is an acceptable vehicle for bringing changes; authority is evil; everyone over thirty is stupid; pleasure is paramount; diligence is distasteful.

[1] *Sweden Today*, Spring 1981.

And, of course, it was a very small step indeed from Summerhill to 'children's rights'. The Children's Angry Brigade Communique No. 1 warned its readers that 'education can damage your mind'. It went on: 'We are tired of being a repressed generation. Our generation is repressed by censorship laws, age regulations, school, and sadly our own parents. No longer shall we accept this repression. We are angry. . . We shall not limit ourselves to non-violent acts if the school situation persists. . . All sabotage is effective in hierarchical systems like schools – smash tannoys/PA systems, paint blackboards red, grind the chalk to dust.'

Barking up the same tree, but more elegantly, were the BBC and ITV schools broadcasts of the autumn of 1970, with their prevailing mood of doubt, confusion and depression. 'Moral principles should be decided by me' was what the children were encouraged to believe. 'The morality of work is the morality of slaves' they were told, while family life was invariably shown as unpleasant, mothers as selfish and incapable, the home as a place of strife and boredom, Christianity as a mixture of boring symbolism and difficult theological ideas, and Jesus Christ as a humanist.

Then throughout the 70s there was the manipulation of the family planning propaganda, which tried to persuade one and all that teenage pre-marital sex was inevitable and that the only answer was easy access to contraceptives – a hugely lucrative business. There were publications like *Make it Happy* which explicitly described for its teenage readers a whole range of perverted abnormal sexual practices (group sex, communal masturbation, oral and anal intercourse, etc.). There has also been the irresponsible and distorting effect of so many of the teenage magazines.

So how could 'chastity' and 'fidelity' possibly survive, even as words, in this maelstrom of atheist humanist claptrap? Especially as so many church leaders, politicians and media people lacked the courage to expose the irrationality of its so-called logic and the dangers to mind, body and spirit this posed, particularly to the vulnerable young. One's heart bled for them, giving added impetus to the efforts which had to be made to protect them. Not least among these efforts were those undertaken to ensure that Dr Martin Cole's infamous sex education film *Growing Up* should not be shown to school children and that *The Little Red School Book* should not be read by them.

It is impossible to understand the values of many young adults today without taking into account the type of 'education' which was being given (and those who were giving it) in the field of sex and morals by BBC and ITV schools broadcasting in the late 60s and early 70s. Because we were receiving quite unsolicited letters from individual parents expressing anxiety about the content of some programmes, we carried out a Schools Broadcasting Monitoring Report in the autumn of 1970 and very revealing and disturbing it was.

The series *Apes and Men* (BBC TV) constantly reiterated the theme that man is merely a superior ape likely to be guided only by instinct and emotion – no sign of a soul. The radio series *Inquiry* (BBC Radio 4) majored on the humanist philosophy that 'moral principles should be decided by me'. *Living with Authority* taught that 'major social changes and great leaps in social progress can only be achieved through militant action' – a statement which, today, would certainly hit the headlines. As far as *Work* was concerned, well, that was a bore and 'the morality of work is the morality of slaves', while life itself, not to mention home, was a terrible bore too.

The series *Sexual Feelings* boasted Dr Martin Cole. Masturbation for both boys and girls was described in great detail and, in the following programme *Falling in love*, a precise description of sexual intercourse with 'partners', with no reference to husband and wife.

Throughout the series, which set out to clarify personal values, the programmes made no reference to high standards of behaviour, to ideals or unselfishness, gave no suggestion of the type of hero or heroine that the children could benefit by emulating. They did, however, contain a very strong indication that most parents cannot, and do not, understand.

The BBC television series *Growing Up* gave rise to enormous controversy. The criticisms were well aired: the lack of any reference to 'love', 'husband and wife' or marriage; the possibility that such explicit visual material presented to eight- to ten-year-olds might precipitate adolescence and rob the child of its 'latency' period; the woman without a wedding ring in the 'from the waist up' copulation slide.

We were greatly concerned that parents should have the right to preview any sex education material being given in schools. The controversy surrounding the BBC programmes brought many deeply concerned letters to us from parents all over the country. I quote from just one of them:

My eldest daughter, who is now thirteen years old, shared my pregnancy when I was expecting her little sister, seven years ago. Jane was six years old when Katherine was born. When she was eight or nine I told her about the father's part in making a baby, because I believe that sexual love is a very personal thing and I wanted her to learn about it in a personal way, and I knew that the time was imminent for the school to begin their programme. So Jane was fully conversant with sex education when one day, when she was ten years old, she came home from school in tears, complaining about a 'horrible film' that her class had been shown at school that day. The film had shown naked pregnant women being 'prodded about' by a doctor, and Jane claimed that the man teacher had been so engrossed in the film that he had failed to notice that the boys in the class were sniggering and gesticulating at the girls, and making fun of them.

I went to see the headmaster, complaining bitterly that I was not consulted or even informed that my child was to be shown this film, explaining that Jane was not ignorant about sex and that even if she were, I would never approve of *visual* sex education, and demanding that she be excused from any further films of this sort. I had to be firm and aggressive because this otherwise excellent headmaster was so proud of his frank programme of enlightenment that he refused to see my point of view at all, and even told me that, if it were up to him, this programme would start in the infant classes!

Going on to her secondary school, Jane then had to submit to five double-lesson periods of Human Sexual Reproduction presented to an all-girl class in an all-girl school by a young man teacher. Drawings were seen, and had to be faithfully copied into workbooks, of the internal and external sexual organs of the male and female of the species; every aspect was investigated in the fullest detail until there was no mystery, no beauty, no tenderness, romance and, for goodness' sake, certainly no trace of *love* anywhere in sight. Jane now has a serious psychological hang-up about sex.

Towards the end of last term I received, from the headmaster of Jane's old school (which is now Katherine's school), an invitation to attend a PTA meeting after which films would be shown which were to be shown to our children as part of their sex education. The general theme of the headmaster was: that sexual ignorance in youngsters was a crime, that anyone who didn't agree was either ignorant themselves, a prude, a moral fanatic to the degree of absurdity, or just plain sexually hung-up themselves. Anyone being stupid, petty or ordinary enough to *demand* that their child should not see these films, would just have to suffer, along with their child, the consequences of that child being ostracized by the rest of the class, and being told or questioned, probably in some mixed-up fashion, about the film which they had not seen.

Now I have watched Parts 1 and 2 of the new *Merry Go Round*. I freely admit that Part 1 was very good; I would love to have been able to view it with either or both of my girls here at home, and I should not have objected too strongly if I had been informed that it was intended to show it to them at school. . .

But having watched Part 2 this morning I am again in the 'anti' camp.

What concerns me is this: why, why, why the need for *visual* sex education? The children are shown a man's penis, and then its erection diagrammatically; today, watching the particularly messy birth, we were then shown (again unnecessarily) a long clear shot of the mother's stretched and swollen pubis. After this, is it such a very big step to saying: 'we have been so very frank up to a point, lest anyone still be in any doubt or ignorance at all, shouldn't we be totally frank and show coitus, just in case any poor dim-witted child might still think that Daddy puts his penis into the gooseberry bush and Mummy eats the gooseberries in order for the seed to get into her tummy?'

Secondly, what is the motive behind school sex education? If the powers that be really had the child's welfare at heart, would they not agree that everything to do with sex is a wonderful, special, personal thing that should ideally be taught in the home, and would they not see that trouble is taken to ensure that such a home-teaching programme were not interfered with or imposed upon by the school? Would they not ensure that a less ready child than the rest of the class, or an ultra-sensitive child, be treated in a way that his/her individuality demands, and not just lump them all in together and throw the lot at them?

What can be done about this? I know that I can personally demand that my youngest child be totally excluded from the school programme, but if, after that demand, she were included anyway, is there anything that I could do? Such as bring a law suit? Maybe I should mind my own business and not concern myself with other people's children. One mother, at the PTA meeting, confided in me that she had only come to ensure that the penis was shown erect, because she felt that it would not be totally honest if it were not shown. I could cry for her and her children! Ignorance can be a crime, yes. Most people would agree. But what happened to the belief that innocence should be protected? Other people's children are my business and I want to protect their innocence too, if only because I can see no happiness in the future for my (hopefully) sensitive child in a desensitized and brutalized society.

Well, we've got that now, haven't we? And how I echo that mother's concern. As I said in my earlier book:[1]

> Children have a right to their fantasies. They need to be free to interpret words and ideas in terms of their own imaginings and at a speed dictated by their personality and experience. Total visual imagery – the product of adult minds and experience – presents children with detailed actualities which can destroy their own curious searchings. Explicitness reduces the need and opportunity for fantasy so that there is a danger that 'too much, too soon' is a stealer of dreams. The joy of discovery and the mastery of a developing understanding are important elements in healthy psychological development. If creative fantasy is stifled, emotional life is stunted. Children are so often denied the right to reach out towards a new discovery in their own way and in their own time, and the privacy which is so necessary to their human development and to the growth of a rational and unselfconscious attitude to their fellows is destroyed.

[1] *Whatever Happened to Sex?* Hodder & Stoughton, 1977.

Chapter 5

Not the man for the job?

This Temple of the Arts and Muses is dedicated to Almighty God by the first Governors of Broadcasting in the year 1931, Sir John Reith being Director-General. It is their prayer that good seed sown may bring forth a good harvest, that all things hostile to peace and purity may be banished from this house and that the people, inclining their ear to whatsoever things are beautiful, and honest and of good report, may tread the path of wisdom and uprightness.

Translation of the inscription on the dedication panel in Broadcasting House

'Whatever happened to Blousie?' the front page headlines trumpeted on the day after the latest episode of *Swizzlewick* (BBC1). That's a very long time ago – 1966 to be exact. But the effect of the omission from the programme of a shot in which the city councillor is seen coming out of the prostitute's room, zipping up his trousers, was to last for very many years.

Swizzlewick was a calculated skit on our campaign. The Chairman of our Committee was Birmingham City Councillor Pepper – the councillor in the programme was named Salt. There was a 'Mrs Smallgood' who was launching a 'freedom from sex' campaign. She wore a hat very similar to the one I'd worn at the Birmingham Town Hall meeting. And there was a character called Ernest, the postman. The inspiration for this, considering that our house at that time was called 'Postman's Piece' from the name given to the land on which it was built, was not far to seek!

It really was in every way, as the papers said, 'a sordid and salacious' piece of work, 'a new low in tastelessness'.

And when at the end of a public meeting I was offered the script of the following week's episode containing the details of the *Blousie* episode – which had already been reviewed very critically – I decided to send it straight to the Postmaster-General, who was then the Minister responsible for broadcasting. It got it into his hands within a matter of hours by a special arrangement with the Post Office.

When the programme was transmitted it was two-and-a-half minutes short and the offending episode had been omitted. And what a fine old row that caused! Sir Hugh Greene, then the Director-General of the BBC was in Australia at the time but returned, it was said, 'in a fine fury', determined to find out how I got hold of the script. He didn't. I've never told anyone the name of the person who gave it to me. Following that episode an order was issued by the Director-General that, under peril of losing his job, no employee of the BBC was to have any contact with me whatsoever. And indeed for eleven years I was never invited to appear in any capacity in a BBC programme.

Things got so bad that one BBC personage, finding himself at the same private party as me, slipped quickly away through the back door! Others working for the Corporation would attend meetings at which I spoke, then wait behind till everyone had gone before coming over to speak to me, saying they felt sure I would understand why they did not give their name. Indeed I did. Letters addressed to me care of the BBC would be sent to a newspaper to redirect. No one at Broadcasting House was apparently allowed to admit that they even knew where I lived.

Ah, well, those days have long since passed. The *persona non grata* mould was broken when I was invited to participate in a BBC2 discussion on the Annan Report on the Future of Broadcasting in 1977. Robin Day, in the chair, laughingly stopped me after one comment, saying, 'We mustn't let you say too much, Mrs Whitehouse!'

The same year the BBC Religious Affairs Department did a documentary on the Gay News blasphemy trial which, in the event and with a production team working under considerable difficulties because an Appeal was pending, was very fair and indeed, 'compulsive television', as everyone agreed.

Since then, notably with the *Person to Person* programme in 1979 when David Dimbleby and his team joined us here in Ardleigh from Monday morning till Thursday night (mercifully a lovely week in early summer, so we were able to do most of the filming out of doors), and with a very happy late night chat between Sue Lawley and myself a couple of years later, the early resistance to my appearance on BBC television seems to have largely disappeared. Though I was told even as late as 1981 by someone working with the Corporation that there are only two people whose names have to be 'referred up' before a producer can invite them to appear on a BBC television programme: 'One is Enoch Powell and the other is you.' And a quite recent invitation to take part in a programme was cancelled – when the referral 'up' was made – on the grounds, I was told, that insufficient time had elapsed since my last appearance. At least I'm not likely to suffer from over-exposure.

However, to return to the 60s, Sir Hugh Greene ploughed on in his 'progressive' way, while we on every possible occasion challenged his philosophy and his policies. So great was the Corporation's anxiety and indeed anger over our activities that the whole of the introduction to the *BBC Handbook* for 1966 (eight pages of it) was devoted to an attack upon our work. But, of course, we weren't alone. The Church of Scotland published a report on 'The New Impuritanisms' as a result of which, according to *The Scotsman*, Sir Hugh was 'carried kicking and screaming' up to Edinburgh to answer the criticisms made against his director-generalship. A first leader in *The Times* joined in too and declared that the BBC was engaged 'in a panic flight from decent values'; it 'televised inanities' and had 'a sniggering attitude to life'. However, Sir Hugh Greene was not one to bow to public opinion and he went on his way unrepentant – glorying, one felt, in all the controversy.

A kind of tug-of-war had developed between viewers and the BBC. On the one hand, public anxiety; on the other, the apparent determination of the Director-General to ignore it. I think it is very difficult for people nowadays to remember the measure of public controversy which surrounded the BBC during the reign of this particular Director-General, so different in just about every way from his predecessor Sir William Haley and the founding father of the BBC, Sir John Reith.

Thursdays, Fridays and Saturdays saw the late night satire shows, *That Was The Week That Was*, etc. Sunday evenings produced *Meeting Point*, a platform for the 'new morality'. Monday was the night for *Till Death Us Do Part*. And Monday to Friday inclusive there was the current affairs programme *Tonight*, eventually taken off, so it was claimed, because of its heavy left wing element. *The Wednesday Play* week after week roamed clumsily, even subversively, amongst the more sensitive areas of human, social, political even international affairs, in a way which I do not believe could happen today. Take for example *Fable*, screened in January 1965, which took as its theme Britain under Negro rule, with coloured strong-armed police carrying off whites into concentration camps. *For the West* was a vicious and divisive play set in what is now Zaire, known then as the Congo, and screened at a time of great political sensitivity in that country. Milton Shulman described it as 'an ugly little effort, mean, shrill, deceitful in aim and tone . . . events distorted into leering, vicious, crude propaganda that one used to associate with the less edifying techniques of Streicher and Goebbels'. Philip Purser, writing about the play in *The Sunday Telegraph*, declared: 'The white flag jerks to the top of this column. I concede victory to all those hon. members who have been attacking BBC drama. . . There is nothing that can be said in defence or mitigation of *For the West*.'

Propaganda was the name of the game throughout *The Wednesday Play* series. How much of the anti-American feeling which surfaced in the 60s can be attributed to plays like *The Good Shoemaker* which screened violent armed robbery and murder in the States and presented American justice as evil and corrupt, and to plays like *The Pistol*, which depicted US soldiers as cowardly, having no sense of duty, lacking in integrity and moral courage – in short as a 'dirty, thieving, undisciplined rabble, panicking at the prospect of the Japanese invasion'?

Religion came in for it too. *The Bachelors* showed practising homosexual Roman Catholic priests importuning teenage members of the congregation at the church door. In the same play a family doctor gave advice to the husband of one of his woman patients on how to murder her! Comedy, too, had its own very sick interpretation. In *And Did Those Feet* one of the characters, following the gruesome murder of a child, was heard to say, 'God is just an idiot with a tape recorder playing back into my mind.' Controversy raged. *The Wednesday Play* invariably made headlines in the national press every Thursday morning. Lady Laycock writing in *The Daily Telegraph* at that time most aptly and movingly expressed what so many people felt, and her letter has I think some lasting significance in the story of the BBC drama:

After watching *The Wednesday Play* on BBC1 on 5 January [1966] I slept on my wrath, anxiety and indeed unhappiness for several nights, hoping that with reflection would come some understanding or excuse for showing *The Boneyard*, advertised as the first of a series of 'comedies'. No such enlightenment has come and my anger has fermented.

Even in these days of popular sick humour, how can anyone laugh at the tender performance given by Neil McCarthy standing bewildered at the feet of Christ crucified? And even the most hardened and scornful of the irreligious can surely find no merriment in a woman crazed with grief at the death of her child.

Perhaps *The Boneyard* has a 'message'. If so, it does not surprise me that it passed me by, since I count myself lucky if I understand half the plays I see on television. (I will not accept that this lack of comprehension is due to advanced middle age or stupidity. I admit to the former but utterly refute the latter and share my perplexity at TV drama with almost all my friends of a very wide age group.) But that this Wednesday Play should have been advertised as a comedy has not only shaken me, it has also frightened me . . . when I am invited to laugh at the

fundamental agony in men's souls I can keep silent no
longer.

Take care, BBC, or we may one day all be asked to
split our sides at a farce called *The Goons of Buchenwald*.

So great was the tide of anger involving viewers, politicians,
clergymen, in fact practically everyone except the 'trendies',
that Mr Sydney Newman, then head of BBC drama, was
driven to issue a directive to drama producers and directors.
They were told 'to exercise stricter control over the use of
violence, sex and bad language in their productions'. In
practice it meant not a thing – it was, after all, the second
such directive to be published that year and was really intended as a warning to his producers not to rock the boat *too*
hard in case of reprisals from the Government.

Behind all this lay the 'liberating' hand of Sir Hugh
Greene who seemed, as we said in a telegram to the Prime
Minister, 'determined to provoke and insult the viewing public'. That public finally revolted and the late night satire
shows, with their often bitter ridicule of almost everything
and everybody that people in Britain respected, collapsed
and died. So did *The Wednesday Play*.

However, that was not the end of the anti-establishment
propaganda which the BBC, with the special encouragement
of its Director-General, churned out during his years of office.
The viewers, having rejected political satire and drama, were
to be seduced with humour. Johnny Speight centred his *Till
Death Us Do Part* on a ludicrous right wing villain whom he
reckoned we would be bound to hate – or so he thought. But,
of course, as everyone knows, the idea misfired. People *didn't*
hate Alf, the series' loud-mouthed 'hero'. They actually identified with him and felt sorry for him. In desperation his
creators made Alf more and more extreme in his coarseness
and vulgarity in the hope that viewers would be alienated
not only from him as a character but from all those people
– such as the Queen – to whom Alf was devoted, and from
all those Christian principles in which he said he believed.

The characterization and acting in the series was brilliant,
but Johnny Speight, its script writer, clearly believed that if
a word or an expression was used in real life that was

sufficient justification for him to use it over and over again on television. He seemed unable to understand that to describe a coloured person as a 'coon' was offensive, or that to talk about the Bible as 'bloody rubbish' would be regarded as blasphemous – and not only by those who would consider themselves 'religious'.

But there was one episode of *Till Death* . . . which I still vividly remember with a mixture of amusement and incredulity. Alf's son-in-law Mike was sitting on the settee reading a boy's book about football. Alf was reading too and, although it was not possible to see the title of the book, his head was nodding up and down in self-righteous approval as he shot contemptuous glances at his son-in-law. 'You should read this,' he told him. 'She's got the right ideas; she'd clean up the place.' Although the camera had still not shown the cover of the book he was reading, I guessed! And I was right – it was my newly-published book *Cleaning Up TV* (Blandford Press, 1966). The whole episode was built around the book and before very long, and not for the first time, the fascist implications were there again, not only as far as Alf was concerned but, by implication, involving me too.

The whole country needed 'cleaning up', particularly of the 'coons', Alf ranted. (Can anyone imagine that happening now?) And with the usual loud-mouthed flourish he marched off to the lavatory taking my book with him.

The twist to the story came when the old man was found to be a carrier of the very germs that he blamed the coloured people for bringing into the country. How else could he have contracted them but by reading my book? So what was the best thing to do with that? Burn it, of course. And the programme ended as it was dropped on to the fire to a chorus from the rest of Alf's family of 'unclean', 'unclean'. Well, at least I have the dubious distinction of being the only British author to have a book publicly burned on television – in this country at any rate.

There was, however, nothing at all personal behind the 'open letter' which we sent to the Director-General in March 1968, though I must admit looking back that I'm a bit surprised at our temerity. But the truth is that by this time the situation had become so urgent, the threat to the national

well-being so great, that we felt nothing could be gained by
mincing words. However, I'll let the letter speak for itself:

Dear Sir Hugh,
    It is a long time since we corresponded. This is not
to say, I am sure, that we have been unaware of one
another's existence. There have been many signs that
you are very conscious of the activities of the movement
which now represents over a million people. And
certainly we have studied your public speeches and
policies at home and abroad with the greatest interest.
    Why, you may well ask, have I decided to write to
you now? The answer is quite simple. More and more
people, of whom I am one, are questioning your
suitability as Director-General of the BBC. It is only
right therefore that you should understand why.
    Four years ago we called for your resignation. The
cry was echoed in many quarters. You weathered the
storm.
    Indeed you did more. You developed a strategy of
'defence by attack'. Far from adjusting your policies in
the light of your obligation 'not to offend against good
taste and decency' and 'not to give offence to public
feeling', far from taking into account the vast amount of
public cricitism – in spite of your duty to do so – you
seemed to work from the assumption that the 'public'
could be conditioned to accept anything if they were
given it often enough, if the boat could be pushed out a
little further each time, and if – most important of all –
you could make us laugh, not only at programmes but
at people and ideas.
    It has been a hard fight, with, apparently, all the
odds on one side. You were in a position to tell the
world that you were 'glad to offend' those who took
exception to certain episodes in *Till Death Us Do Part*
and you were able to use every technique and platform
to ridicule those who would not pipe to your tune. The
cheap satirists basked in the security of your approval.
Only you can know how many of the 'conservatives'
within the BBC have been eliminated or persuaded to

change their approach, how many creative men and women have been denied the opportunity of broadcasting because they wished to present ideas about life which did not fit in with the atheist drift – or shall I say compulsion? – so apparent in the 'growing points' of television. And I must admit that I am astounded at your comment (Canberra, 17.2.68) that the communists within the BBC are 'none of my business', for they will certainly make the BBC their business.

But we have weathered the storm too, and now the mood of the country is changing. The laughter is ringing hollow as we realize the cost to our children of the mass-produced giggle. We're haunted by the failing bodies of our young drug addicts. We're shocked to know that the growth rate of addiction is greater in this country than anywhere else in the world – and then we remember how we dallied with the 'flowers' you presented to us night after night last summer through. As we hear the chorus of 'bloodies' from the infant playground we wonder at our credulity – wonder that we should ever have been taken in by the idea that it needed endless expensive university research to prove that children (and the rest of us) copy what they see and hear. I often ask myself, Sir Hugh, whether you would rank the establishment of the word 'bloody' as common parlance in the English language your greatest single achievement during your period as Director-General?

But new days call out new ways. In the hard light of its present situation the country is growing up fast. It has outstripped you, Sir Hugh. Your professionalism is unquestioned. Your vision is. We know that you honestly feel you are leading – or rather dragging – a reluctant, even unintelligent, public into new, more enlightened ways. Your recent advice to Australian Broadcasters 'not to tag along with public opinion' underlines your own contempt of those who will not tread the Greene line. But this contempt has built a wall around you and you seem unaware of what constitutes real value for our money. The truth is that the days when Britain was prepared to flirt with the 'new' morality you did so much to launch are passing, and the philosophy of the men-without-God is being seen for the empty sham it is. Faith, discipline, patriotism and self-control are coming 'in' again.

Your idea of 'reality' is too small. The life we want to see reflected is so much brighter, more compassionate and more stimulating than the world in which you seek to contain us.

If I had the opportunity to talk to you face to face I would ask you the question so many people are asking themselves – 'What kind of man, what sort of values does Britain most need today?' The answer to that question gives us the key to another – 'What type of leadership does the BBC most need today?' And the answer to *that* means that we have to begin our fifth year where we began our first, by saying 'You're not the man for the job, Sir Hugh'.

It was Brian Walden, then an MP but now well known as presenter of Thames TV's *Weekend World* who went out of his way at that time to persuade us – out of genuine concern I'm sure – that our continued demand and other people's too for the Director-General's dismissal was a complete waste of time.

'You could not have taken on a more hopeless task. Sir Hugh Greene *is* the establishment,' he told us and there was nothing we or anyone else could do to move him. He had 'put the Labour Party in power and the Government will see that he stays'.

This last remark no doubt reflected the effect which the late night satirists had had on the political scene in the middle 60s and, in particular, their role in discrediting the Tories in the run-up to the 1964 election. That was in 1967 and I did not meet Mr Walden again until 1970 but by that time a new Director-General *had* been appointed at the BBC. How it came about is really quite an extraordinary story and what part, if any, our 'open letter' played in the whole saga one can only surmise.

Chapter 6

All change at the BBC

'I'm not asking so much for your comment at this point, Mrs Whitehouse, but what *do* you make of it?' 'It' was the appointment of Lord Hill of Luton as Chairman of the BBC. 'That'll put the cat amongst the pigeons all right!' I said. And it certainly did. 'This is preposterous – the only person who is going to be pleased about this is Mrs Whitehouse' was the spontaneous reaction of a senior BBC personage.

As far as the public in general was concerned I'm sure it's true to say that the reaction to Hill's appointment was one of hope and relief. The press came to the conclusion that it was a calculated attempt to curb the powers of Sir Hugh Greene, upon whose expected resignation bets were laid.

Lord Hill was clearly going to take time to play himself in, as it were, and possibly give Greene – not to mention Johnny Speight – enough rope with which to hang themselves. *Till Death* . . . was still, as James Thomas of *The Daily Express* said, 'raising the hackles of half the nation' with its blasphemous and foul language. The original script of one episode contained the lines, 'You and your bloody brimstone and fire God. If we don't agree with everything he says he bungs us in the fire – he's worse than Hitler.' But the BBC's legal advisers decided those words were blasphemous and most of them came out.

There was so much in *Till Death* . . . which was highly entertaining. But once its progenitors entered, as they did, into a trial of strength with the viewers the programme was doomed. And the verdict? James Thomas of *The Daily Express* summed up for all of us: '*Till Death* . . . was lost for the silliest motives – the battle to get past a more and more anxious

BBC lines and words which could be considered offensive and without which the series would not have suffered at all.'

Johnny Speight never, as far as I know, had any regrets except one imagines that the series was taken off. He claimed that Alf 'was created by a vile society. I wrote this thing knowing that Garnett is true of people living in this country'. Well, he may have been true of *some*, though I doubt if many others would use up 121 'bloodies' in half an hour.

In the meantime our campaign for the resignation – or, at a push, the sacking – of Sir Hugh Greene never slackened. But perhaps one of the most effective things we ever did was done without any sense that it could turn out to be the last straw as far as the Director-General's term of office was concerned.

Early in December, in a cutting from one of the pop music periodicals, I read the words of a song which was included in the Beatles' film *Magical Mystery Tour* to be shown on BBC television in the early evening on Boxing Day, 1967. It contained the line 'you been a naughty girl, you let your knickers down'.

I drew Lord Hill's attention to the song and hoped he would agree that it was most unsuitable for children's viewing. He acknowledged my letter and said he would look into the matter, so I listened on Boxing Day to see whether or not the song was still included. It was, and I was disappointed. But to be truthful I quickly forgot about it until one Sunday in March the following year.

The Sunday Times had that day published the first episode in the saga 'Take-Over At the BBC' by Kenneth Adam, Director of BBC Television, 1961/1968. For years Adam had worked side by side with Greene, but by then he was visiting Professor of Communications at the University of Temple, Philadelphia. He claimed to tell 'the whole fantastic story . . . from the inside, passionately and provocatively'. Well, that was a good start. And I must say he was as good as his word.

Mr Adam told of the 'polite, but guarded' first meeting between Lord Hill and Sir Hugh Greene; of the moving of Lord Hill's private secretary, Mrs D. H. Fenton, from the ITA to the BBC; of a new suite constructed at the top of

Broadcasting House; of Lord Hill's cautious geniality towards his new colleagues, and of Greene's own determination 'not to rock the boat'.

'Apparently a *modus vivendi* was established on the basis of a desire to avoid clashes; and at management meetings Greene went out of his way to report promising signs in the Chairman's attitude and actions. Would he, after all become one of us?'

But then Kenneth Adam went on to tell of how, at Christmas 1967, 'an open breach was only narrowly averted'. He spoke of the crisis which developed between Lord Hill and Carleton Greene over 'an indecent line in the song "I am the Walrus".' This was the line I had referred to in my letter to Lord Hill!

'Hill wanted it to be taken out or the film cancelled altogether,' said Adam but 'Greene declined to do either. Hill asked what would happen if he gave an instruction. Greene said that regretfully he would be unable to accept it.'

Could it really be, we asked ourselves when Adam's article was published, that our letter had played a key part in triggering off the palace revolution which was to follow? We have been told – by someone in a position to know – that in the moment when Greene declined to respond to the Chairman's wishes he sealed his own fate. And certainly Hill was not the man to play second fiddle to the man who was, in the last resort, second fiddle to him.

Be that as it may, the 'Greene must go' campaign culminated in his resignation in July 1968. It's a funny thing – he came and went without us ever having met face to face even though he spoke of 'the lynching party led by James Dance MP[1] and Mrs Mary Whitehouse' which he was always expecting!

Mr Charles Curran, the Secretary of the BBC was appointed as his successor and his path was by no means an easy one. As far as programme standards were concerned it had already been ploughed for him by his predecessor, and whatever changes he might personally wish to make these would clearly have to come gradually unless he was to have

---

[1] First Chairman, National Viewers' and Listeners' Association.

a palace revolution on his hands. The 'young turks' whom Greene had brought into the BBC and to whom he had given so much licence were now climbing up the ladder into positions of considerable power.

One of the biggest controversies Curran ever faced was over Ken Russell's *Dance of the Seven Veils*, an orgy of sex and violence based on the music of Richard Strauss, and described in a House of Commons motion as 'vicious, savage and brutal'. *The Times* (17 February 1970) said that 'the film was remarkable, if for nothing else, for showing such items as rape, violence, copulation and nudity to an extent never seen on television before'. Desmond Shaw Taylor, then music critic of *The Sunday Times* described it as 'a deliberately crude, hysterical caricature, executed without conscience and without taste'.

Offence of a different kind was given by *An Act of Betrayal* in the *Play of the Month* series (3 January 1971). This purported to be the story of the spies Helen and Peter Kroger who were repatriated to Russia in exchange for several Britons held by Russia. The play not only presented them in a most sympathetic light but did the reverse for the young couple who were instrumental in their arrest. The real villains of the play were the security men who arrested the spies. It certainly seemed to many who watched it that the play itself was 'an act of betrayal'.

It was only a few days after this that I went to see Mr Enoch Powell. He was very relaxed and friendly and we chatted for a while about the time when he and his wife and family had been next-door-but-one neighbours in Merridale Road, Wolverhampton. But then we got on to the purpose of my visit, which was to seek his advice about the BBC. I wrote in my diary that night:

> We talked for ¾ hour about the problem of the BBC. He agreed entirely with our assessment, feels the situation is parlous and not very hopeful. Thinks there is no chance in present circumstances of tightening up the obscenity laws. Says the only real answer is to replace Lord Hill with someone who is prepared to go through the great crisis which would arise if he really

came to grips with irresponsible producers. 'He would only need to sack one,' said Enoch. But says Hill won't do it. Enoch thinks he's too near retirement – doesn't want to do anything which will 'rock the boat'.

That was true enough.

It was in mid-December 1970 that I received a reply from Charles Curran to my request that he would receive a deputation from National VALA. Although we had by this time met and talked with Lord Hill we were anxious, after all the years of difficulty with his predecessor, to establish a good relationship with the new Director-General.

In his letter Curran said that he saw 'no immediate prospect' of us meeting officially but that 'if the occasion arose when we could meet personally and talk' he would be very pleased to do that so, in due course, I wrote and suggested a date. However, his secretary rang to say that the day I had suggested was not possible, but went on, so my diary records, to say:

The Director-General was very enthusiastic about the idea of meeting me with Bishop Butler. 'And who is Bishop Butler?' I asked somewhat taken aback. 'Don't you know about this, Mrs Whitehouse?' she asked, sounding as surprised as I felt. 'Not a word,' I replied. Later in the day she rang back to tell me that she'd found out that Bishop Butler was a former Abbot of Downside and was now Cardinal Heenan's second in command and President of the Social Morality Council – a body in which I do not have a lot of faith!

Shortly afterwards the Bishop's secretary rang to say that Bishop Butler would like to invite me to lunch privately at his home with Charles Curran, Director-General of the BBC. I said I was grateful for his courtesy and a date was fixed.

The pressure was on me to agree that a member of the Social Morality Council should also join us, but I wrote to the Bishop, sending a copy to Charles Curran, to tell him, very politely I hope, that who he invited to his house was, of course, entirely his affair, but I was not happy for the

Director-General's original idea of the private meeting between him and myself to be extended in this way. Actually I thought it most strange and suspected that the idea was to outmanoeuvre me in whatever matters were raised.

However, in a very nice personal letter to me Charles Curran said that he agreed entirely with what I had said, that he was very grateful indeed to Bishop Butler for making it possible for us to meet in his home and would be 'very sorry indeed if any extraneous circumstances' were to prevent this happening. I guessed that he and Bishop Butler had discussed the situation together and come to the conclusion that if they continued to press the matter of the Social Morality Council representative the meeting would not materialize at all. And indeed as far as I was concerned it would not have done.

How odd it felt on that lovely May[1] morning to be setting out, all on my own, from our Worcestershire home to meet the Director-General of the BBC at a secret rendezvous in Hertfordshire. All very hush-hush and too far away from the beaten track of broadcasting for anyone to spot us – and it has been hush-hush ever since, till now.

St Edmunds College, of which Bishop Butler was principal, provided an elegant and refined setting for our meeting. The Bishop and I chatted together before Charles Curran arrived and I found him very friendly and very interested indeed in our work. I remember very vividly how, during the meal, he sat, silent for the most part, as host at the head of the long empty refectory table, with Charles Curran on his left and me on his right. I told my diary:

> I was very conscious of the uniqueness of the occasion and felt very appreciative of the fact that Charles Curran had been prepared to come so far to meet and talk with me though, to be honest, there did not seem to be much meeting of minds and our conversation, on the surface at least, did not seem very profitable. He seemed to me to be both shy and defensive. How defensive he was became very apparent as time went on

[1] 18 May 1971.

– extraordinary how these BBC people have their own jargon and it acts as a barrier between them and lay people like myself.

What was most disturbing was Curran's implication that the BBC no longer has a commitment to Christianity.

He kept repeating that the Corporation had 'no principle' – clear that 'situational ethics' have taken over there. Martin Cole's sex film was mentioned and Curran told us why the BBC had refused to show it – first because they were annoyed at him pinching the title of the BBC's own sex education series *Growing Up*; secondly because they felt that 'Martin Cole was publicity mad' and they didn't want 'to satisfy his ego'!; thirdly because they felt that the film, *'at this moment'* did not add anything to sex education as such. No suggestion from the Director-General of any moral or ethical reason – such as the film's advocacy of pre-marital sex, the display of masturbation, etc. What was more he added very ominously I thought – 'I am not going to say we will never show it' – (no principle here either).

I found it very difficult throughout the meeting to make any considered point because, as the Bishop said afterwards, Curran would wait without really listening to what I was saying, then come in with one of the usual cliches (my phrase rather than the Bishop's). I came away feeling really rather disappointed and wondering if it hadn't been something of a waste of time.

Sometime later I mentioned my disappointment – very confidentially – to a friend of mine much involved in broadcasting. He said he would have been very surprised if I had felt otherwise. 'Having seen Curran so often at press conferences I'm in no doubt that he would be very afraid of saying anything at all which would seem like "giving" anything to you. He would be extremely wary of saying anything that you might use in an article or speech.' The Director-General, he said, was *bound* to be very defensive, being in the position he was and with the whole history of our relationship with the BBC, and with his predecessor in particular, very much in his mind. My friend felt, as indeed Bishop Butler did, 'that the important thing was that you met one another'. I'm sure it was. It is extraordinarily difficult for me to assess precisely.

I met Charles Curran a number of times at Royal Television Society Conventions, and once in his office before his retirement in 1979. He always seemed a very shy and withdrawn man with none of the *bonhomie* of his colleague Sir Hugh Weldon, for instance, or the natural charm and friendliness of Sir Michael Swann, who was for years his Chairman of Governors. But he was a good man. I can well imagine that there must have been, from time to time, considerable conflict between his own personal standard of rectitude and his role as defender of the Corporation against all comers.

Chapter 7

A Broadcasting Council?

Whether television is to make for better men and a better society or whether it will be another factor in the decline of spiritual values depends on the co-operation of the men of learning, the support of the public authorities, the quality of the programme directors and finally, the good sense of the public.

Marcello Rondino, former head of Italian Television

'Whatever happened to the idea of a broadcasting council?' those with long memories sometimes ask us. It's a good question and an interesting story which may yet have a happy ending.

The National Viewers' and Listeners' Association was launched on 29 November 1965 at a press conference in Fleet Street. It was to replace the Clean Up TV Campaign which had no organization but was simply a grassroots pressure group, by then so strong that our parliamentary advisors felt we should re-form into a properly constituted body. At its first meeting it announced its intention of pressing for the setting up of a Viewers' and Listeners' Council.

When I re-read now the statement we issued at the time I am struck by two things. First, how visionary and sound – or perhaps just plain commonsensical – our ideas were and, second, how naive we were to imagine that amateurs like ourselves could ever have got such a revolutionary concept effectively established in the face of the antagonism of the hierarchy of the BBC and ITV and of the broadcasters themselves. What were we proposing the powers and responsibilities of such a Council should be?

1. The Council to be composed of elected representatives of the churches, women's organizations, magistrates, doctors, educationalists, parents, youth, social workers, police, political parties, local government and writers, none of whom shall be serving on the advisory councils or as employees of the broadcasting authorities.

2. The function of the Council to be to represent the opinions, ideas and experience of the whole country to the broadcasting authorities. It would not make its own judgements but would simply reflect the reactions and opinions of the country as they have expressed themselves through individual and collective representations.

3. A member of the Viewers' and Listeners' Council to be co-opted to the Board of Governors of the BBC and of the ITA and a member of each broadcasting authority to be members of the Viewers' and Listeners' Council.

4. The Council to establish a secretariat into which viewers' and listeners' letters regarding the whole range of broadcasting would flow.

5. The Council to establish a comprehensive monitoring system.

6. The Council to promote research into current trends in broadcasting and suggest specific ways in which television and radio can best serve the interests of the country.

7. The Council to issue reports at regular intervals and an annual report to be debated in Parliament. It would issue special reports as need arises, giving public reaction to specific programmes.

And we added: 'The public must be in a position to know what it, collectively, feels. Correspondence from individuals and groups is the only certain way of knowing public reaction to both individual programmes and broadcasting policy. Hence our demand for a separate secretariat. The monitoring system would enable the Council to support the complaints and suggestions of viewers and listeners with accurate information and the Council would be in a position to supply the Governors, Public, Press and Parliament with the detailed picture of public reaction.'

That such a Council was not the mad idea many professionals claimed it to be is evidenced by this quote from an article by Ralph Bettinson in *Television Mail*:[1]

> There is surely a proper function for a Viewers' and Listeners' Association as distinct from the Advisory Councils with which the BBC and ITA are already furnished. It can serve a constructive purpose having nothing to do with censorship. It can bridge the gap between the public and the authorities. . .
>
> Such an Association could make a valuable contribution to the future development of television in this country, always provided that it represented the broadest possible cross-section of public, political and religious opinion. It should elect from among its members a Council on which both the BBC and the ITA are represented. For it can never be effective unless it understands the difficulties of those it seeks to help.

All this was happening against the background of constant controversy and public anger over what was being screened almost nightly, on the BBC in particular. The Clean Up TV Campaign had gone from strength to strength, with a daily post of up to 350 letters in one day, and much support from a number of organizations, churches and MPs. Now we were talking about a broadcasting council.

National VALA's Chairman at that time was the late James Dance, MP for Bromsgrove. One day in December 1966 he rang to ask whether Ernest and I would go to see him at his home that afternoon.

'I've something very important to tell you. I can't talk about it on the telephone.'

We went, and heard how Mr Gibson-Watt, then Conservative spokesman on broadcasting had been approached by Lord Normanbrook, Chairman of the BBC, who'd told

[1] 16 July 1965.

him that he wished to meet Mr Dance privately in his capacity as Chairman of National VALA.

Gibson-Watt passed this message on to Jimmy who told us how he and Lord Normanbrook had had lunch together at Broadcasting House that week and had talked alone together for over two hours. The 'alone together' is vitally important, for when we eventually published this story[1] the BBC denied that the Chairman had ever spoken in the terms he did to Jimmy.

As Jimmy told the story to us – and I have never doubted his integrity either in this regard or any other – Lord Normanbrook spoke of the 'total rift' between himself and Sir Hugh Greene, then Director-General of the BBC, of his deep concern about the country in general and the BBC in particular. He confessed also to the deep hurt he had felt when we had described as 'arrogant' his refusal to meet a deputation from the mass meeting at Birmingham Town Hall eighteen months previously.

Jimmy said how sorry he was that Lord Normanbrook had taken it as a personal slight, but hoped he would 'agree that we'd had a fair amount of aggravation!'

'We both laughed at that, and the atmosphere became much more relaxed and friendly,' Jimmy told us, and after a certain amount of general discussion Lord Normanbrook came to what he described as his 'main purpose in proposing the meeting'. He was, he said, most anxious to do everything possible to bring about an improvement in standards and re-establish public confidence in the BBC. He shared our belief in the need for much closer liaison between the Corporation and the public, and was very interested in our suggestion of a Viewers' and Listeners' Council. Did Mr Dance think that Mrs Whitehouse would be prepared to set up such a Council?

They discussed the matter at some length and, when Jimmy left, Lord Normanbrook asked him to put the proposal to me with the request that, should I decide to accept his invitation, I would ensure that such a Council would be composed of a representative cross-section of society, rather

[1] *Who Does She Think She Is?*, 1971.

than exclusively of members or supporters of National VALA. He in return gave an assurance that there was every likelihood that such a Council would be able to meet regularly with the Governors of the BBC, and, once that was established, no doubt with the Governors of the ITA.[1] Lord Normanbrook was anxious that all these arrangements should be carried out in complete secrecy so that no word of what was happening should leak until we were ready to present it *fait accompli* in an appropriate manner.

'Will you do it?' asked Jimmy. I was completely dumbfounded by the proposition but said that 'I would certainly try'. It took me several weeks to get adjusted to the idea that the Chairman of the BBC should have approached me in this way, and I would sometimes shake Ernest awake in the middle of the night to ask if it was really true. 'Yes, of course it is. Go to sleep!' he'd reply with some exasperation.

The more I thought about it the more difficult the exercise appeared, especially as it had to be so secretive, until I remembered again one of the great lessons I'd learnt from the experience of the recent past. Always go through 'open doors' to particular people. I was determined, after the intrigue[2] which followed the launching of National VALA, not to get involved with representatives of official bodies of any kind.

During the following months an impressive and representative group of men and women, all eminent in their own spheres of life, agreed to serve on the Council. But it was a very slow process, since every approach had to be made personally – I couldn't trust my telephone – and this meant a great deal of travelling in addition to all my other commitments.

But shortly afterwards Lord Normanbrook became seriously ill and by the following June, and before the Council had time to get itself established, he was dead. Before long Lord Hill had been brought from the ITA to take his place. So where did we go from there? We felt the best thing to do was to discuss the whole situation with the new Chairman of

[1] Now the IBA.
[2] See *Who Does She Think She Is?*

the BBC, so several of us met him early in October 1967.

By this time I had begun to see that Lord Normanbrook's proposal could never work. As he saw it the Broadcasting Council would be – to put it bluntly – appointed by *me* and that was not what we had in mind at all. It would inevitably and rightly have been accused of special pleading. What we had in mind was a Council which could genuinely be the vehicle of public opinion as a whole.

And it was clear from our meeting with Lord Hill that he too had his doubts. I see that I wrote in my diary on the day we went to see him (9 November 1967): he 'was not prepared to have any kind of "special relationship" with us, which is not what we wanted anyway. After we'd talked generally about programme standards he said he would certainly be willing to hear the views of any council we like to set up and the more serious research it did the better'.

And indeed, as the years have gone on, National VALA has published many monitoring projects and pieces of research including:

'Schools Broadcasting', 1969/70
'Recommendations as to how viewers' and listeners' views can best be represented': published at the request of the then Minister responsible for broadcasting, Sir John Eden MP
'Recommendations to Annan Enquiry into the future of broadcasting', 1974
'Children's Viewing Habits', 1977
'The Hastings Report': monitoring of all programmes on all channels for one week, 1978
'What Price Annan?', 1978: a report on what, if any, response the broadcasters had made to the Annan Report
'Law & Disorder', 1979: report on the depiction of police officers on television
'£34 for this!', 1980: monitoring of television programmes by student teachers and graduate students
'A Public Disservice': report on programmes over the period 1977–80
'Direct broadcasting by satellite', 1981

'It makes you wonder why you bother': a report on viewers' letters to the BBC and IBA and on the replies received

As time went on I had found myself with less and less enthusiasm for the kind of Council Lord Normanbrook had envisaged. While I would not in any way question his motives, it had become increasingly clear to me that a Council of the type envisaged by him would have become part and parcel of the BBC 'establishment' – just another Advisory Council. And we would have been as silent and sadly ineffective as the present Advisory Councils appear to be, certainly as far as standards are concerned. This did not mean that we ceased to fight for the *principle* of an independent body to represent the public. But it did mean that we had to change our strategy.

Almost invariably the justification for foul language, smutty jokes, not to mention violence and explicit sex, offered by the broadcasting authorities was that such things 'reflected life'; that such realism was essential; that this was 'adult' viewing; that compared with the 15, 16, or however many million viewers it happened to be, the complaints that had been received were minimal – as, indeed, they were bound to be. And, of course, the TV critics, objecting viewers were told, thought that particular programme splendid.

At the same time the BBC in particular turned its back on the concept of public service broadcasting and on any relics that remained of that early dedication to 'whatsoever things are pure . . .' (chapter 5) and opted for 'moral neutrality', a moveable feast if ever there was one!

Clearly, if the lowest common denominator was to be the guide – as in many cases it seemed to be – then we had to try and lift it up somewhat. It was at this point that we broadened our activities to include the whole spectrum of the media and, it seems in retrospect, almost every moral issue! Certainly the press encouraged us to do so.

This widening of our strategy was important also because there was a limit to the number of programmes and the kind of comment that I, as Honorary General Secretary of the Association could make, especially as our theme remained basically the same. The great thing was to encourage *others* to write or express their reaction to programmes. Wherever I spoke I made this a major theme and, since for the vast majority of the time I was speaking at public rather than National VALA meetings, I emphasized that I was not asking people to agree with what might be our view of any particular programme. They should simply make their personal view heard wherever it might be on the spectrum of public opinion.

The Annan Committee into the Future of Broadcasting received recommendations not only from National VALA but from other bodies who saw the necessity for some kind of *independent* council, call it what you will. We couldn't help but feel encouraged by the submission of Mr Anthony Smith on behalf of the Standing Conference on Broadcasting, which had proposed a National Broadcasting Centre to 'create an open body representing the public as a whole and to bring about a change in the behaviour of the broadcasting institutions'. Although the Standing Conference and ourselves were in some regards strange bedfellows, we shared its conviction that 'British broadcasting is run like a highly restricted club – managed exclusively by broadcasters according to their own criteria of what counts as good television and radio'. And indeed its recommendations were not by any means dissimilar to our own recommendations for a Broadcasting Council made more than a decade earlier.

However, it was not to be, although Annan did recommend a Public Enquiry Board[1] independent of the Authorities (whatever happened to that?) and a Complaints Commission, which was duly established. Its function was twofold: to adjudicate on complaints of 'unjust or unfair treatment' in radio or TV programmes and of 'unwarranted infringement of privacy'. Even these very limited terms of reference didn't

[1] 'We therefore recommend a Public Enquiry Board for Broadcasting should be set up, with the safeguards we shall set out, to be responsible in the course of holding public hearings for taking a general view of broadcast services in the public interest. The main instrument for doing so will be public hearings every seven years on the way each Broadcasting Authority has discharged its responsibility. . . . In this way, people would have an opportunity to express their views about the performance of each Authority. . . . If there was strong evidence that services were unsatisfactory, or that the remit was out of date, this could call for action by the Home Secretary and possibly by Parliament.'

please 'the left' at all, one of whose spokesmen, Geoffrey Robertson, who was defence lawyer in the blasphemy trial, bitterly attacked the proposal in the columns of *The Listener*. Paul Johnson sharply responded by asking whether Mr Robertson opposed the idea because 'the left is satisfied with their penetration of TV and with the general slant of its programmes and therefore wishes to leave well alone?'

During November 1980 the Broadcasting Bill, which gave legal status to the fourth channel recommended by the Annan Committee, was debated in the House of Lords. But the terms of reference of that Committee extended well beyond the implications of an additional channel, as the following quote from the Annan Report illustrates:

> In the view of most of us, the concern which people express about certain topics is justified: and the broadcasters have failed to consider seriously enough the objections raised to certain programmes. In our view people are right to object to the glorification of violence when its depiction may possibly, even probably, do positive harm, especially to the most vulnerable with the fewest defences. We agree with those who deplore the brutalization of sex and the craven disinclination to judge a sexual problem against a sense of what is right and wrong in the world. Most of us, like the nation at large, feel that the gratuitous use of bad language, which shocks some and bores others, tends to destroy the nuances of feeling which language exists to express. We do not accept as a comprehensive defence the argument often put forward by producers, writers and critics, that the action and language objected to is like life, or is artistically necessary, or that objections are at best irrelevant and at worst destructive of high art.

That was in 1977. We had been concerned to find out to what extent – if at all – the broadcasting authorities had taken note of, and implemented what Annan had to say, and had produced a pamphlet entitled 'A Public Disservice'. This illustrated very vividly not only the lack of response to the above strictures but the extent to which both Authorities had been prepared to push back the bounds of acceptability in spite of them.

Before the debate we distributed sixty copies of this publication amongst their Lordships. During the debate on that section of the Bill which provided for a Broadcasting Complaints Commission[1] Lord Nugent of Guildford proposed that its terms of reference should be extended to include 'unwarranted infringement of the integrity of family life, in connection with the material broadcast as regards violence, indecency or profanity, irrespective of subject matter'.

It was a fascinating debate to listen to! Lord Nugent was making a very powerful case about the way in which television adversely affects family life, referring particularly to the threat to a young mind when television presents 'brutal and licentious behaviour as if it were normal', when Lord Ted Willis sprang up from the opposition benches. He asked Lord Nugent to give him 'one example of a programme in the last six months containing brutal and licentious behaviour'. Lord Nugent replied, holding our publication in his hand, that he would 'be very pleased to give the noble Lord plenty of examples'. Lord Aylestone, himself formerly Chairman of the IBA, and very defensive of the broadcasters, also referred to our brochure, saying that it contained extracts from ITV and BBC programmes which were 'smutty', 'sexy' and 'salacious'. In fact he said 'the whole publication was pornographic'. Amazingly he went on to criticize, not the fall in standards, but us for 'sending it through the post'!

It was a powerful debate which put very great pressure on the Government. But while it did, in the end, say 'No' to Lord Nugent's amendment it nevertheless conceded that in the light of the debate 'the Home Secretary considered that it would be desirable for the broadcasting authorities to include in their annual reports an account of the volume and nature of the complaints they receive each year and any action taken in consequence. This would enable Parliament

[1] The Commission's members are all government appointments and it has legal power to control unfairness and invasion of privacy by broadcasters. The television companies will also be obliged to broadcast the Commission's findings.

and the public to take stock each year of the exact position regarding complaints. Accordingly, my right honourable friend has asked the Chairman of the BBC and the IBA to include this information in their annual reports, and they have indicated that they will do so.'

Much of our time in the office during the first three months of 1982 was taken up with assessing copies of viewers' letters to the BBC and the IBA, and the replies they received. Altogether we looked at about 250 letters and this was indeed a mammoth task since this was in addition to all the other work of the office; the finishing of this book; the trial of *The Romans*; the fight against sex shops and for tighter obscenity legislation; the visit to this country of the Solicitor General of Fulton County, Georgia, USA, Hinson McAuliffe, whose successful fight against sex shops in his State meant that he had much to share with us; not to mention, as far as I was concerned, the disability of a broken rib!

As I write, the full report[1] is not yet finalized but certain conclusions are clear for all to see. Most striking, perhaps, is the reluctance of the Broadcasting Authorities, especially the BBC, to admit that they ever make a mistake. The onus is always on the viewer for having taken offence, not on the broadcasters for having given it.

Nothing more clearly illustrated the attitude of the BBC to viewers' reactions than its response to complaints about the series *Triangle*, which was transmitted in the early months of 1981 at the early hour of 6.55 p.m. It received most critical notices and as Richard Last, *The Daily Telegraph* TV Critic, said[2]: 'As a contribution to the Beeb's well known concept of family viewing it must have raised a few eyebrows.'

As I wrote to Mr George Howard,[3] Chairman of the BBC: 'It is difficult to believe otherwise than that the titillating near nudity and the seductive "zipping down" in the first episode was intended to hook the male voyeur early in the evening, while talk of "rape", "whorehouse", etc are such an affront to the concept of family viewing at that time – how

---

[1] *It makes you wonder why you bother!*, obtainable from National VALA, Ardleigh, Colchester, Essex, price £1.50.
[2] 8 January 1981.
[3] 20 January 1981.

does one explain them to the very young children still viewing? – as to raise the question as to how the series came to
be placed in such a slot in the first place.' And I drew the
Chairman's attention to the extraordinary statement made
by Bill Sellars, producer of the series, in *Feedback*[1] to the effect
that the programme was 'meant for adults' and that he 'was
under no instruction' to consider that children might be
viewing at that time.

It has to be said that Mr Howard, quite unlike his predecessors, Sir Michael (now Lord) Swann, Lord Hill and
Lord Normanbrook, has shown himself singularly unwilling
to respond personally to such letters. The task of so doing
fell upon Mr David Barlow, who at the time of the *Triangle*
debacle was the Secretary of the BBC. In his letter to me he
said, 'Your reference to the concept of Family Viewing Time
intrigued me since it was not one I recognized either by name
or description.' This I found quite incredible and in my reply
I drew his attention to page 11 of the BBC's publication
Children as viewers and listeners (May 1974) which states: 'Programmes placed in the early evening – and especially between
6 p.m. and 8 p.m. – are thought to be suitable for family
viewing.'

He then went on: 'However, we appreciate that a series
such as *Triangle*, whose dramatic plots concern difficult adult
relationships may make it less suitable than some others for
viewing within the family circle. Even so, children, in any
case, are as much individuals as adults; what one 9 year-old
can watch with equanimity, another may find disturbing.
Our view has long been that only someone who knows a
child intimately and is thoroughly acquainted with his or her
circumstances can judge what he or she can assimilate. What
we try to do is to provide parents in advance with enough
factual information about the content of a programme on
which to base a judgement. In the case of the series *Triangle*,
the billing in *Radio Times* for the first episode read: "Who is
the scantily-clad, attractive female on the crew's private sun
deck? Matt Taylor, Chief Engineer, assumes the task of telling her she shouldn't be there." Thus parents had a clear

[1] 9 January 1981.

indication of the nature of the drama in the billing, and also in a feature article contained in the same publication.'

Just how parents were to know that the 'scantily-clad attractive female' would turn out to be quite so deliberately seductive or that the conversation would be so 'adult' we are not told. And as for the assumption that for some *nine* year-olds this would be suitable viewing, one is lost for words.

As for action taken as a result of complaints, Parliament will, I think, be hard put to it to discover precisely what its nature – or even its existence – is. But the question of whether and how seriously the Broadcasting Authorities take the Government's instruction has yet to be answered. One thing's for sure – *only* an annual debate on the Reports of the IBA and the BBC, something which we called for all those years ago, will ensure that the Home Secretary's words mean more than, or as much as, the *Hansard*[1] they were printed in.

I must say that I have a feeling that when the Broadcasting Authorities come to give their account 'of the volume and nature of the complaints they received in 1981/82' the IBA are going to be even more hard pressed than the BBC. Certainly at the time of writing the programme output of ITV is giving more concern than that of the Corporation, which makes a startling change from how things used to be.

There is now an abandonment, which reflects a weak IBA, amongst the ITV Companies. How else could the stream of violent, obscene films screened during the Autumn of 1981, which culminated in the showing of *The Gambler*, have been transmitted? The fact that this film was withdrawn to be 'cleaned up' a couple of days before it was due to be shown, reappearing a fortnight later *still* containing a round dozen of *the* four-letter word used in the most aggressive, even blasphemous way, tells its own story about the judgement of those responsible.

The IBA actually saw and approved the Central Television series *Over the Top* (*OTT*). The first episode[2] according to a doctor who monitored the programme for us contained a sequence in which 'three entirely naked men danced about

[1] 3 November 1980.
[2] 2 January 1982.

the stage each holding two small balloons. At one point, one of the men, twisting the balloon, simulated a swollen, bulbous penis and a pair of large testicles. The scene was juvenile and extremely vulgar'. Our colleague noted that the second episode 'was much less offensive than the first, no doubt due to protests from outside ITV', which just goes to show. But of course, the improvement was by no means maintained.

If the BBC has lost its commitment to public service broadcasting the IBA has certainly thrown away its (legal) obligation 'not to offend against good taste and decency'.

The Broadcasting Authorities' insensitivity to their obligation in this regard reached an all-time peak in 1980/81 with films such as *Chato's Land*,[1] *Smile*,[2] *Serpico*,[3] *La Premier Fois*,[4] *Strosjek*,[5] *An Investigation of Murder* – all monitored for us by a medical consultant.[6]

In *Chato's Land*, in the context of a very violent film 'a woman had all her clothes torn off and her private parts exhibited. Her screams while she was being raped were dreadful to hear. She was shown again all trussed up and exposed. No attempt was made to hurry these scenes so as to minimize the effect'.

In *Smile*, 'full of foul language', there was a scene in which 'fabricated beaks were used as penises in disgusting gestures that could only have been simulations of sodomy. At one point a large roast bird (chicken?) was brought in on a dish, held in front of a recruit, its legs separated and its vent then pressed against the recruit's mouth. The bird was squeezed and a white creamy froth came out plastering the man's nose and mouth. What this obscene antic was meant to simulate I cannot imagine'.

In *Serpico* there was 'a distressingly violent scene in which a young black was kicked with sickening reality in the genital area by a burly policeman and then badly beaten up. A close-up is shown of his bruised, swollen face. The violence

---

[1] 7 July 1980, BBC1.
[2] 12 October 1980, BBC2.
[3] 16 August 1980, BBC1.
[4] 1 August 1980, BBC2.
[5] 17 May 1980, BBC2.
[6] 1 September 1980, BBC1.

continues. A specially bad feature of the film was the unremitting use, by all parties, of a particularly vulgar and distasteful four letter word'.

In *La Premier Fois*, under the specious pretence of enlightening teenagers, the film began with a middle-aged 'Cousin Leon' selling pornographic books to curious adolescents. It went on to show 'Cousin Leon' masturbating the 16 year-old youth beneath the bed-sheet. After an unsuccessful love scene with a girl friend, the film continued with the youth's first encounter with a professional prostitute, her washing of his private parts (mercifully not a full frontal view), her questions re the possibility of his being diseased'.

In *Strosjek* 'foul language was used by a group of ruffians, bullying thugs of the worst type. At one stage a girl was brutally dragged by her hair up a stair, along a landing into a room. Her face (close-up) was shown badly bruised. The atmosphere of the first part of the film was very brutal'.

An Investigation of Murder 'was a film of violence and disgusting language and of obnoxious scenes in sex clubs that almost defy description. The scenes in sex clubs are appalling. In one the viewer is shown a black girl, naked, lying on her back with legs stretched up and parted, masturbating in full view of the audience whose attention is riveted to the spectacle. Granted the viewers' picture is from behind the girl's head, but not a lot is left to the imagination. The violence is frightful, a sex maniac shoots the passengers in a bus, close-ups are given of the victims and their wounds dwelt upon. All the while the disgusting language continues, four letter words are used virtually non-stop, while blasphemous expletives are shouted everywhere'.

The BBC's otherwise extremely good *Sons and Lovers* was spoilt for many by the last episode[1] in which was shown a crude and explicit scene of sexual intercourse between two completely naked people, complete with grunts and moans and panting for breath.

ITV was following a similar path in its choice of films.

In *Death Wish*[2] 'the obscene language used by the police, newspapermen and the muggers was foul in the extreme'.

[1] 28 February 1981.
[2] 16 May 1981.

In *Marathon Man*[1] the foulest of language again characterized this film, with four-letter words used in the grossest
manner and obscene violence.

In *Deliverance*[2] 'the photography was certainly first class
and the filming of the action in the rushing and turbulent
waters of the river was superb, but the film was spoiled and
degraded by two things, the disgusting language and a quite
unnecessary episode when two of the canoe party are "sexually assaulted" by two mountain men. One of these had a
gun, the canoeists were unarmed. The mountain men im-
mobilized one canoeist by fixing his belt tightly round his
neck and a treetrunk, anchoring him completely and then
forced the other at gunpoint to take his clothes off. The
subsequent attempts at sodomy left nothing to the imagination! The language throughout was disgusting, endless use
of four-letter words'.

In *Going Out*,[3] the story of a school leaving party, 'the
language used by the children was foul and blasphemous,
there was a violent fight between groups of boys and girls
and much very coarse sexual talk'.

And, of course, there was *The Gambler*.[4]

It appeared to us that the time had come to consider an
option we had long thought available but which we considered to be the last resort. Namely the possibility of some
legal action. One difficulty is that broadcasting is specifically
exempt from Obscene Publications legislation. So in the summer of 1981 we took Queen's Counsel's opinion in the matter,
presenting to him details of the programmes referred to
above. He advised that it *would* be possible to make an application to a judge in Chambers for a declaration that the
BBC was in breach of its Charter and its now legal obligations
not to 'offend against good taste and decency', not to 'encourage crime and disorder' or transmit anything which
would be 'offensive to public feeling'. As far as the IBA was
concerned, Counsel advised that 'in his opinion there is sufficient evidence to show that the IBA in permitting the trans-

[1] 1 September 1980.
[2] 27 June 1981.
[3] 1 November 1981.
[4] See Chapter 10.

mission of such programmes was failing in its duty to comply with the terms of the Television Act and that National VALA would be able to apply for a High Court declaration to that effect'.

But by this time (November 1981) *The Romans in Britain* case had still not come to the Old Bailey and it was clearly neither possible nor advisable to have two legal actions running concurrently.

It has to be said, moreover, that since that appalling sequence of films on both BBC and ITV nothing quite as bad has been transmitted.

However, Queen's Counsel's advice still stands to be acted upon in the future should we see fit to do so.

In all our deliberations on such matters the fact that many children are watching such material is paramount. The BBC and IBA defend their policy of showing these films by stating that their responsibility effectively finishes at 9 p.m. when all children and young people, they appear to claim, should be in bed. But the PYE Research into Children's Viewing Habits (1978) finally destroyed whatever credibility such a claim may ever have had:

Who's watching?

7–10 years old:	45%	up to 9 p.m.
	9%	up to 10 p.m.
11–14 years old:	42%	up to 9 p.m.
	42%	up to 10 p.m.
	9%	up to 11 p.m.
15–17 years old:	46%	up to 10 p.m.
	42%	up to 11 p.m.
	6%	12 p.m. or after

Chapter 8

Malaria – and a visit to Australia

Looking back I'm tempted to say we should have had more sense! We ought to have known that all the cards were stacked against us. With Christmas looming, our comments on Chuck Berry's presentation of 'Ding-a-Ling'[1] were a gift to the cartoonist, the comic and the critic alike. But nothing of this entered our heads when we despatched a letter of protest to Sir John Eden, then Minister of Posts and Telecommunications.

We told him of the complaints we had received from 'young people, as well as older ones, including two doctors', about the pop singer's obscene interpretation of lines like 'I like to play with my Ding-a-Ling' and 'Most of all with your Ding-a-Ling' and about the way in which Chuck Berry told the cameramen to pick out some obviously embarrassed young girls who were not joining in all the so-called fun and games. But at no time did we object to the song *itself*, a fact which was completely and deliberately ignored by the media in the furore which resulted.

Two days later Ernest and I left for a couple of weeks in the USA, returning just in time for Christmas. So we missed the full impact of the resulting notoriety as it occurred. Whether it would have been easier to take it on the chin day by day or, as we did, reap the full impact in one blow on our return, it's difficult to say. Be that as it may, a huge pile of press cuttings, human excrement amongst my post and a Christmas card with 'F... You' scrawled across it, awaited me.

[1] BBC1 *Top of the Pops*, 23 November 1972.

Apparently the filmed sequence about which we'd complained had been cut out in subsequent transmissions and had even been replaced by delightful little animal cartoons which made the words sound no more than the harmless little ditty which, on their own, of course they were.

By so doing the BBC tacitly admitted the validity of our complaint. But its action had the effect of persuading viewers who had not seen the original programme that we must possess a very dirty collective mind. And, indeed, I did feel increasingly burdened with the realization that it was *we* who seemed to be destroying the innocence of children by drawing attention to Chuck Berry's grossly indecent interpretations of words which very young children would otherwise have taken on their face value.

So it was that I felt tired, dispirited, and sick at the pit of my stomach when I left with Ernest, early in 1973, for our long planned 'away from it all' holiday in The Gambia in West Africa – a holiday which, it turned out, was to have far-reaching and quite serious consequences.

But there's one story I must tell about that holiday. It has nothing to do with our campaigning but everything to do with the kind of man my husband is.

It was really quite foolish of us to go into the sea at all because the little wooden sign – admittedly roughly painted, old and tatty – did warn us that bathing on that part of the beach could be dangerous and there was no one else about. However, in we went and were generally splashing around and enjoying ourselves when I was suddenly knocked clean off my feet by a huge wave and down I went. I gurgled and struggled my way to the surface and on to my feet but then, to my horror, realized that I couldn't see further than the end of my nose! My specs, which I wear from the time I get up until I go to bed – even when I swim! – had disappeared.

Panic-stricken shouts of 'My glasses – they're gone!' brought Ernest running over to take my hand and lead me out of the water on to the beach. But my sense of desolation at their loss quite overcame my feelings of relief that I was safely on terra-firma, for I knew that without them my holiday was ruined.

Ernest quietly told me to stand just where I was while he

walked back into the waves. There was no way he could know where I'd actually been when I'd gone down and, in any case, the powerful undercurrent and heavy breakers had churned up the dark sand so that it was impossible to see anything through the water. As I stood anxiously watching, even my myopic eyes told me that Ernest had stopped, and then that he'd disappeared below the surface of the sea. But seconds later there he was up again, waving his arms and shouting excitedly, 'I've got them!' What a relief it was to have them back on my nose without even a scratch on them! Ernest told me afterwards that with every step he took he'd prayed that he'd be led straight to them – and so he was. He didn't even tread on them – the frames came up between two of his toes.

It turned out to be a lovely holiday, mostly spent quietly on our own. But on the very last day, again when I was swimming – though this time in the hotel pool – I suddenly felt very peculiar indeed and quite ill. I only vaguely remember the doctor murmuring something about 'sunstroke' and the kindness of the couple in the chalet next to ours who helped Ernest pack our bags and look after me at the airport.

Within a day or two I was feeling better, which was just as well, since in the first few weeks after our return, I talked about our visit to The Gambia for the World Service of the BBC; did an hour-long programme for Belgian TV; did a phone interview for a Fleet Street agency to syndicate to the States; agreed to write an article for *The Church Times*; was interviewed by *The Observer*; made the first approach to No. 10 Downing Street over the presentation of the 1,350,000 signatures on the Nationwide petition for Public Decency; heard with delight that the British Board of Film Censors had denied a certificate to *Oh, Calcutta*; attended the High Court to hear Counsel for the Independent Broadcasting Authority defend his client against the late Ross McWhirter's application for an injunction to stop the transmission of the Andy Warhol programme; went up to Manchester for an 'Open Night' with Granada Television; had lunch with the Minister of Posts and Telecommunications, Sir John Eden; spoke at Middlesex Polytechnic; took a delegation to meet Mrs Margaret Thatcher, then Minister of Education; wrote an article for *Cosmopolitan,* and was invited to take part in *Start the Week* to discuss the Code on Broadcasting Standards (cancelled because 'The Hierarchy' had decided that 'it was not the moment for me'!).

I mention all this to give some idea of the pressure of events which built up and which eased not at all during the succeeding months. In the middle of it all Dr John Court, Associate Professor of Psychology at Flinders University in Adelaide, telephoned on behalf of the Festival of Light there, to ask whether I would consider going to Australia in the Autumn. I said I would be delighted.

Then there was the *OZ* trial, Martin Cole and his sex clinics, *Last Tango,* and a legal case over a magazine called *Curious.* But way above and beyond it all was the disastrous plane crash over France which killed Ernest's brother and sister-in-law, making orphans of their three teenage children.

None of us were therefore the least bit surprised that from time to time during these early months of the year I had bouts of ague and drenching sweats – 'overstrain' said everyone. I thought so too and took it more or less in my stride, until one day in early May. I had been up to Preston to speak to an Inspectors' Course at the Headquarters of the Lancashire Constabulary, and had enjoyed myself, as I always did when I went there. I arrived home in the early evening not feeling in any way tired and as it was such a lovely day I went for a quiet little stroll around our peaceful meadow, with its lovely views across the Clee Hills. It was just as I walked back across the yard into the house that, suddenly, all my strength seemed to drain away.

'Oh, dear, I've begun to feel so exhausted,' I said to Ernest as I came in.

'You've been doing too much again,' he replied. 'Why not go to bed and have an early night? I'll not disturb you when I come up.'

But no sooner had I lain down than I started the most dreadful ague. The sweat just poured out of me and in what seemed only a few seconds I was lying in a pool of water. To move the bedclothes even a fraction was to send what felt like a blast of icy air down my neck. I felt too ill to get out of bed and though I called and called Ernest did not hear –

he was listening to music with his earphones on! It was only when he came to bed several hours later and found me still shaking and sweating violently that he realized what had been happening. He got into bed beside me and held me tight until gradually my body quietened down and in the early hours of the morning I finally fell asleep.

At about 7.30 our great friend who was then Chairman of National VALA's Executive Committee (the late Dr David Sturdy) rang as usual. But when he heard what had happened and how exhausted I felt, he said, 'You're thoroughly overtired, so stay where you are for today and rest.'

At about ten o'clock my phone rang – it was David again.

'Mary, tell Ernest to get the Doctor at once. You've got malaria!'

'Oh, David,' I said unbelievingly. 'How on earth *could* I have?'

'Don't argue, just do what I say,' was his reply.

David told me afterwards that, in the middle of his surgery, he'd suddenly remembered our visit to The Gambia a few months before and realized that my bouts of shaking were very probably not overstrain at all but malaria. He'd been in Africa with the army during the war.

Before the day was out I was isolated in Kidderminster General Hospital with 'suspected malaria and typhoid'. Within hours tests were being sent to the School of Tropical Medicine in Birmingham and the verdict came back – no typhoid but malignant tertian (MT) malaria. I was told later that this disease normally kills in three out of four cases unless treated within the first forty-eight hours. And here was I, having carried the bug around for over three months!

Only one thing could be done for me apparently – just one massive injection. And how long that operation seemed to take. I can still see the kind face of the consultant who, very gently, took charge of proceedings and reassured me as I muttered clumsily, 'My lips are all swelling up'. I was under constant surveillance all that night, but by next morning my temperature was down and the danger had abated.

I was discharged from hospital several weeks later and although the malarial infection had been dealt with I was desperately tired and lacking in any sort of vitality. Ernest was advised to take me to Liverpool to see Professor McGrath of the School of Tropical Medicine there. He explained to us that MT malaria germs attack and destroy one's red blood corpuscles. It was the resultant anaemia which accounted for my exhaustion, and that he was able to treat, thank goodness.

But at least one very good thing came out of my illness. Len Matthews, Managing Director of ATV and a long-time friend, was not only personally concerned about my illness and the reason for it – not taking anti-malarial tablets! – but realized its importance in the field of public health. He asked the producer of *Crossroads* to come and see me and together we went again to see Professor McGrath. As a result, a story-line based on my experience was built into the series and the Professor described it as 'far and away the most effective propaganda there has ever been for malaria control'. So that was something!

Mercifully this particular type of malaria does not recur. But it did leave me with one small but permanent disability – it paralysed the pupils of my eyes so that they are permanently distended and do not contract in the light. This means that I find strong light extremely trying and I can no longer drive at night, since car headlights pierce my eyes like knives. My only defence is to shut them!

The 'You can't possibly go to Australia' which I'd heard so many times during these summer months changed, as I got stronger but was still not entirely fit, to 'You can't possibly go alone'. And though I gradually regained strength through the summer the organization of the tour went ahead only on the understanding that Ernest would accompany me to make sure that I 'didn't overdo it'. We were both looking forward to it immensely when, just ten days before we were due to leave at the end of September 1973, the doctor shocked us all by telling Ernest, 'No flying for you'. The strain of the past months had pushed his blood pressure too high for safety.

So there I was, not yet getting up for breakfast, and about to be launched all on my own into what I felt was the nearest thing to outer space I was ever likely to experience. And it was months since I'd done any speaking. What would it feel like to stand on a platform again? Would my memory, which had been so affected by my illness, function as it needed to? And how would the 'Aussies' react to what I had to say, even if it did? Suppose I wasn't strong enough to cope, all those many miles from home? The prospect was well-nigh over-whelming. But it was now altogether too late to cancel the many arrangements which had been made for my visit. Phone-calls backwards and forwards to Australia during the next few days changed many things – not least when the cost of Ernest's fare was added to mine and my tourist ticket was changed to a first class one!

It was suggested by my friends 'down under' that I should have a short break *en route*. Where would I like to spend it? Singapore or Hong Kong? It so happened that a friend stay-ing with us when the call came had a married daughter living in Singapore.

'I'll ring her up now,' she said. And so it was arranged there and then that her daughter would meet me at the airport and look after me during my stay. So everything that could be done was done. All the same, I shall never forget leaving Ernest at Heathrow. I had no confidence at all that I'd ever see him again, and I have a feeling he was thinking much the same thing about me as I disappeared through the barrier.

No sooner did I arrive in Singapore than I heard my name called on the intercom. And for the next few days it seemed that everyone back home who knew anyone in that city had made up their minds that I would be well cared for and generously entertained.

The question, 'What would you like to do?' brought, among other delights, a night under the sky watching the Filipino Ballet, and the first of those almost unreal experi-ences which were to characterize the whole trip. I was sitting having supper with some of my new friends when to my delight and astonishment who should walk in to the res-taurant but the kind couple who had been so good to us when I was taken ill in The Gambia!

'I don't believe it!' we all exclaimed. We spent the rest of that evening together and met again before I left. I had pretty much the same reaction from one of my old sparring partners at the BBC who spotted me getting out of a taxi next day outside the British Club.

'Good God, what's *she* doing here?' he asked his companion.

'Having lunch with me' was the reply! What memorable and delightful days those were.

The other side of the world's not so far away after all, I thought with wry amusement when I arrived in Darwin. For I'd flown straight into an airport strike, an electricity strike, a postal strike – what had we said about writing every day? – and into three of the most hectic and rewarding weeks of my life.

I was still apprehensive about what would happen when I stood up to speak, so I was very relieved when my host told me that they didn't have many public meetings in Darwin.

'So how many are you expecting tonight?' I asked cautiously.

'Maybe as few as six. Fifty will be good.'

That will give me a chance to break in gently, I thought.

In the event there were about 300 of them – warm, friendly Australians, predominantly young parents, many of them civil servants working in the outposts of administration. But it soon became clear that we spoke the same language and shared the same concerns. By the end of the evening my wobbly legs felt stronger. I had addressed my first public meeting for five months.

I managed to get from Darwin to Brisbane without too much difficulty over transport and spent a very happy couple of days there. But the Great Adventure – as I still think of it – began when I tried to move on from Brisbane for the official launching of my visit in Sydney. No scheduled flights whatever were leaving Brisbane and my friends worked tirelessly trying to find some means of getting me on my way. Then, just as they despaired of success they were introduced to a young pilot who had brought a couple of Sydney businessmen up to Brisbane in his little Cesna plane earlier that day. He had intended to fly back immediately but was persuaded to stay overnight and take me back with him, starting at 5.30 in the morning. I well remember wondering whatever

Ernest and the boys would have said if they could have seen me climb into that tiny plane standing all by itself on the huge deserted airport in the cold clear dawn!

Because of the strike there was no radar, no airport controls or safety devices of any kind and I was instructed to keep my eyes wide open to spot anything which might be coming in our direction. My head went round and round like a helicopter propeller! The great question in the pilot's mind, and mine, was whether or not we would be allowed to *land* in Sydney, presuming we got there. Try as he would, he could not get an assurance over his radio to that effect, so my companion told me he would have to land half way at Port Macquarie and take in enough fuel to return to Brisbane if the final verdict was 'No'.

The name Port Macquarie had conjured up in my mind an image of a sizeable town. But far from it. If there was a house anywhere, let alone a port, I certainly didn't see it – only a single, very short airstrip on the copper-stained ground, with a single petrol pump standing alongside a tiny shed at the end. No other sign of life at all. We taxied slowly along and stopped in front of the pump. Out jumped the pilot and picked up the nozzle, only to discover that, because of a *petrol* strike, the pump was empty! So for the next three quarters of an hour I walked round and round that barren place to the accompaniment, it seemed to me, of endless argument between my pilot and a Sydney air traffic controller about whether or not we would be able to land if we went on.

Finally, the answer came. 'No.' The only other possibility, I was told, was to fly to Sydney and land on a private aerodrome twelve miles out of the town. Mercifully, we got the OK from there but were instructed to fly below the clouds (lying low at 500 feet) and to follow very closely the edge of the coast. I even found myself flying round a lighthouse at one point. Occasionally the clouds were so low that we were only just above the sea. I had a feeling that if we hit a sizeable air pocket we would drop neatly into the water.

However, greatly to my surprise at the time, and even more so in retrospect, I enjoyed every minute of what turned out to be a most exhilarating and exciting experience – as long as I could keep my mind off the rather strange noises and even stranger silences from the engine.

I reckon I saw more of Australia that day than many Australians do in a lifetime and the sight of the line upon line of waves breaking on the beaches below us remains a vividly beautiful memory. I was almost sorry when I spotted the little reception committee below us, so tiny in the middle of the deserted airfield. But how relieved they were to see us. And how warmly they thanked the pilot as they invited him to come for a meal with us.

'No, thanks very much,' he replied quickly. 'I don't like the sound of that engine at all and I've got to check it over before I do anything else.' So I'd been right after all.

As I was rushed off to the press conference which had already been postponed three times, I was told how the radio commentator had been giving a 'blow by blow' account of my adventures. 'Mrs Whitehouse down at Port Macquarie,' and half an hour later, 'Mrs Whitehouse *still* at Port Macquarie,' etc., etc. Four TV interviews, and a very tough – and cheeky! – radio interview followed the press conference. Then, after a cup of tea and 'a bite' I set off for the TV Centre to do two current affairs programmes which were nationally networked. By the end of *that* day I knew I'd got my health and strength back again.

Six-and-a-half thousand people turned out to hear me speak in Sydney Town Hall, so that overflows had to be arranged in the cathedral and the square outside. ABC TV reckoned there were 20,000 at the Adelaide Rally and 5,000 young people at the Apollo Stadium Rally. But throughout the whole tour, exhilarating and immensely worthwhile as it was, there was always the awful question hanging over my head – would I actually make it to where I was supposed to be?

The various strikes – postal, petrol and airport – added an unexpected dimension to a trip which was in any event quite unique as far as I was concerned. And nothing better illustrated the constant dilemmas we faced than the problem of getting from Tamworth to Adelaide.

At the end of a long day of one disappointment after another, spent in the cold and rain of the empty Tamworth airport, it became obvious that the only remaining hope was for me to fly back to Sydney in the plane which brought the newspapers and was scheduled to return empty as soon as it had unloaded and refuelled. Once there, I would catch the overnight train to Adelaide on which a suite had been reserved for me by the Minister of Transport, the Hon. Milton Morris, who had introduced me at the Sydney Town Hall meeting the previous Sunday.

We stood, a tiny group in the middle of that barren airport, and waited as powerful gusts of wind sent the clouds scudding just above the tarmac. Still the plane didn't appear. It had been diverted because of the appalling weather conditions. Then, at about five o'clock, it came down out of the clouds and we all watched with growing anxiety and dismay as the grey, square metal box of a thing shuddered onto the ground. Two of the men went to speak to the pilot and look inside. They reported back that there were no passenger seats. I would have to sit on the hard, dirty metal floor.

We didn't like the look of this at all, nor, if the truth be known, of the very rough, tough-looking pilot, either. I didn't *really* fancy going up into the clouds all alone with him! Everyone was very sure that I shouldn't and that there was nothing left to do but go home, have something to eat and pray for another miracle – I'd been living by them – which would somehow ensure that I would be in Adelaide in time for the lunch-time reception planned for the following day. Thoroughly exhausted, I went to lie down for a couple of hours. When I awoke I was met by the news that the strike was off.

So, the next morning, I stepped off the plane in Adelaide just as originally planned, only to be greeted at the bottom of the steps by a policeman who warned me that as soon as I entered the reception area I would be met by a solicitor with a writ to subpoena me as a *defence* witness in a forthcoming obscenity trial. I spotted the dark-suited gentleman straight away as he approached me very purposefully. But I walked sideways, saying 'Hello' to all the people who had gathered to welcome me, and ignoring the demanding 'Mrs Whitehouse! Mrs Whitehouse!' in my ear. Just as I reached the press conference room he pushed the writ into my hand

and immediately the press, who'd obviously been forewarned, wanted to know what I intended to do about it. 'Absolutely nothing,' I said. And indeed the judge decided that I didn't have to.

Chapter 9

Children at risk

Of *course* it was not the sort of thing a more-than-middle-aged lady normally says to a 'gentleman of the cloth'.

The Rev. Paul Oestreicher, witness for the defence in *The Little Red School Book* case, came striding across the Old Bailey Court at the end of the trial with his hand outstretched to shake mine. The words were out before I could stop them – even if I'd wanted to.

'Do you know what I was thinking when you were in the witness box?' I asked him, ignoring his hand: and, in the pause that followed, 'Better a millstone be hung around your neck,' I said – referring to Jesus' words about those who cause 'little ones to stumble'.

The almost ingratiating smile with which he was greeting me fell from his face. '*You* are the millstone,' he shouted and stalked away across the Court.

So why should I have behaved as I did? Looking back now I have no regrets and I'm sure I would react in precisely the same way were I to find myself in the same position again. My response to his apparent gesture of friendliness – and I use the word 'apparent' judiciously – sprang from months of battling against one of the worst threats to children and young people which the 'permissive' society had produced. And to see a clergyman in the witness box defending it! Well, that was more than my equanimity could stand.

Looking back now, the first six months of 1971 was, I think, the most concentrated and in many ways the most difficult period of all our years of campaigning. During that time my mother, who had been bedridden for some years, suffered most terribly in her long-drawn-out last illness. Ernest and I spent many weekends going backwards and forwards to Chester to see her and my sister. I wrote the 65,000 words of *Who Does She Think She Is?* in the first three months (during the great postal strike); we published our report on Schools Broadcasting which sparked off a considerable 'row' and greatly embarrassed both the BBC and ITV, and, of course, there was Dr Martin Cole, not to mention *The Little Red School Book*.

Martin Cole's Sex Education film *Growing Up*, with its copulation scene and the shots of the young man and the young woman teacher masturbating was, in our view, a thoroughly depraved piece of work. I attended the film's preview in London, along with a variety of politicians, teachers, and health education specialists. As one would expect, it immediately aroused tremendous criticism and controversy and we were very much at the heart of it all. Day after day the newspapers were on to us for comment. I debated with Cole on television and radio. *Growing Up* was the subject of a debate in the House of Lords. The woman teacher concerned was suspended from her job amid blazing headlines. And Mrs Margaret Thatcher, then Secretary of State for Education, said she was 'very perturbed' at the possibility of the film being shown in schools. We were determined to do everything we could to ensure that the film was *not* shown in schools and we expended much time and energy to that end.

Part of our strategy was the issuing of a challenge to the then Archbishop of Canterbury, Dr Michael Ramsey. We asked if he would see the film himself and issue a statement about it both 'to encourage anxious parents and to ensure that the church was *seen* to be caring' about the matter. We knew this was a 'tricky' one because the Archbishop had kept very quiet and had seemed, over the years, unwilling to grapple publicly with the challenge of the 'new morality'. 'But surely this is something on which he *should* give a lead,' I thought.

When my letter arrived at Lambeth Palace I was phoned by a member of the staff of Church House, Westminster and was told that they 'were fully aware that I had put the Archbishop on the spot' and had deliberately chosen this occasion to do so. 'Gracious me,' I thought. Could I assure them 'that this was a foolproof occasion' and that by speaking out the Archbishop 'would not be making a mistake'.

'Heaven help us!' I said to myself after I put the phone down. 'If the Head of the Anglican Church isn't willing to risk a mistake in the face of this threat to the children not only of his own church but of the whole country, what a terrible state we're in.'

Anyway, bless him, although he was on holiday at the time, Dr Ramsey *did* make a statement about the film. 'It diverged from Christian ideas of education and was unsuitable for use in schools,' said the Archbishop.

All was not going well for the 'sex liberators'. About the same time as Dr Ramsey spoke out, *Growing Up* was shown on Dutch TV with the result that the Dutch Government announced that it would withdraw its grant of £4,000 to the Dutch equivalent of Martin Cole's set-up in Birmingham. And the British Attorney General asked the Director of Public Prosecutions to consider whether the film was actionable, having regard to the fact that it was meant for school children.

The battle to ensure that the children were never shown Cole's film was a very public one and a successful one with practically everyone on the same side, not least because the media left people in no doubt what the fuss was all about.

The fight against *The Little Red School Book* was of an entirely different nature. Very few people actually knew what it contained and although there were references to it in some of the 'quality' papers there was nothing like the media support for this campaign that there had been for the last one.

The book followed the now all-too-familiar blueprint for 'revolution', and Richard Handyside, its publisher in Britain, admitted that what he called 'this frank and rather endearing little book' was designed for 11 year-olds and upwards. They were to be well and truly indoctrinated.

- Infiltration – through school magazine, school council and discussion in the playground.
- Create a climate of unrest: Make sure there are a lot

of other pupils who are dissatisfied with the same
things as you
- Openly rebel against standard rules and principles.
- Get leaflets printed to explain what you want.
- Try making your own wall newspaper.
- Intimidation: Collect evidence against the teachers.
  This will have to do with injustices, punishments and
  anything else which enhances the cause.
- Attack the main Authority: To do this you must
  recruit helpers and gain the good will of parents,
  press, television and radio and trade unions.

We had been aware of the *LRSB* for some time. It had been
published by various revolutionary groups in Europe and our
colleagues there, particularly in Denmark, had alerted us to
its contents. So we knew it was obscene as well as subversive.
This meant that we were ready for action when in March
1971 we discovered that it was about to be published in
Britain. We immediately alerted the Director of Public Prosecutions. Five days before publication one of our friends
managed to get hold of two copies. The person from whom
he obtained them said to him, 'Mrs Whitehouse is taking
legal action over this', not knowing of course who his cus-
tomer was, or that my friend was taking one of the copies
straight round to the DPP's office for me. I sent a covering
note to the DPP referring specifically to the offending passages, and asking him to grant me an injunction to prevent
publication of the book.

The following morning Ross McWhirter rang to talk at
length about our action which was widely reported in the
press. He said he thought we 'stood a very good chance with
this one' and offered all the help he could give. But within
minutes I learnt that an individual cannot apply for such an
injunction – it was the Attorney General's prerogative. Time
of course was all important. With publication day drawing
nearer by the hour, every minute counted. I spent the next
half hour being passed from one person to another in the
Law Officers Department, finally speaking to the Attorney
General's Permanent Secretary.

Only a short time afterwards the Vice Squad at New

Scotland Yard, having been instructed by the Attorney General, rang to ask me if I would go to the Yard the following day, which I did. There I met Chief Inspector Fenwick who was then Head of the Vice Squad. He told me that he and his colleagues were 'frankly appalled' by the book and said they were going to raid Stage 1, the publishers. Indeed the warrant came through while I was in Fenwick's office.

It makes me feel quite peculiar now when I realize that beneath the friendly exterior lay the man whom the judge in the 'porn squad' corruption trial of 1976 was to describe as the 'arch villain' of them all. I have often thought since what unknowing 'mugs' we were. For years, until his arrest, I responded to Fenwick's request that I would let him have any information I might have about pornography and the activities of its publishers. No wonder so little action was taken. No wonder that time and again we were put off with smiles and assurances which never seemed to come to anything. But who was *I* to doubt that it must be for reasons beyond my comprehension – as indeed it was.

A couple of days later a publisher friend rang to tell me that at a London publishers' conference the previous day, one of them had brought a sackful of *LRSB*s and distributed them to all the delegates. He told them that the police were taking the case against Stage 1 because it was such a small company and suggested that *all* the publishers present should themselves print the book as quickly as possible. The police would then have to prosecute *all* the London publishers, which would be an impossible task and that would let Stage 1 off the hook. I leaked this story to the press. That will force the pro-*LRSB* lobby to play their cards in the open, I thought.

When he saw the story in the papers Ross McWhirter rang the Chairman of one of the big publishing companies who'd been represented at the meeting and asked him if he knew he would be breaking the law if he produced a reprint. Quite apart from whether or not the book was obscene, such action could lay them open to prosecution on the grounds that they attempted to impede the course of justice. Other publishers got the point too and none of them printed. That was marvellous. But two million copies of the book in English were ready to be imported into Britain from Denmark if the case failed.

Later, Fenwick, who had already taken a statement from me with a view to calling me as a witness, told me that he'd decided against it. 'Get you in the witness box and they'll show you no mercy.' That was very kind, I told him, but if my evidence was of value, I was quite prepared to give it. I said I wasn't afraid of John Mortimer QC.

No day passed without some development to do with the case. Like the time when a young evangelist who constantly travels to the continent rang me up out of the blue to tell me that a young Dane, one of the three responsible for the Danish *LRSB*, had since become a Christian. The evangelist had an affidavit sworn by this young man stating that Mao money had financed the publication of the book in Denmark.

Chief Inspector Fenwick, when I told him this, said he was most anxious to contact the young Dane and that he would send someone to Denmark to persuade him to come to London to give evidence. I put him in touch with the evangelist, who had everything arranged, when he received a phone-call from the Director of Public Prosecutions' office. He was told that the young man's evidence would be 'irrelevant' and that he would be advised to give up his efforts. I know what we all thought about *that*. We've had some peculiar experiences with the DPP's office over the years and this was certainly one of them.

The turmoil of these days was very intense. They held not only the battle against the *LRSB* but also the continuing battle against the sex education film *Growing Up*, and all the preparations for the launching of the Festival of Light which took place in Trafalgar Square on 25 September that year. I became increasingly exhausted as the weeks passed and I realized that I was relying on my *own* strength which, I have found over the years, always leads to trouble!

'If it is true, as has been said to me,' I wrote in my diary, 'though I find it hard to accept that I am "a woman raised up by God for this day and generation," then I am not only inadequate, I am ill-prepared. I do not wait upon the Lord. I depend far too much upon my conviction that because he has given me a job to do he will give me the necessary strength and I leave it at that. My Bible reading and prayer life are nothing like adequate for such a time – I have been losing the senses of his Spirit and the joy and trust which I should have as a true believer in Jesus Christ.'

One way and another it seemed as though eventually all the stress and strain of the previous years, the price that had to be paid for the ridicule and the misrepresentation which had become an integral part of my daily life, had come to a head. My 'tummy', which was always the clearest indicator of stress, ached endlessly and I really did wonder whether I could go on.

It was in the middle of all this that one day, as I walked up Fleet Street on my way to meet a journalist, I experienced one of those rare flashes of insight which last too short a time to measure but which stay with one for ever. I suddenly saw, so simply yet so clearly, that if I continued to carry the burden, if I allowed the personal attacks to pierce my being, they would destroy me. Since, however inadequately, I was doing what I believed God wanted me to do, when the attacks came I must deflect them upwards for him to absorb. *He* would carry the burden, not me. Jesus had taken all the suffering for *us*.

It was an experience which absolutely transformed me. It gave me a peace. It meant that I now looked out, rather than in. It is the source of the vitality and strength which in the years since have given me the energy that many people seem to find amazing for a woman of my age.

The choice of witnesses at trials of this kind tell their own story – not least about the witnesses themselves. We were not surprised that the humanist Dr James Hemming gave evidence in support of the *LRSB*. Not that it did his cause much good, for my diary recalls that Mr Corkery, Prosecuting Counsel 'made mincemeat of him'. Neither was I surprised when the Rev. Paul Oestreicher appeared as a defence witness. But I was sickened by his cold, calculated support for such material and quite amazed at the way he walked across the court to shake hands with me afterwards.

And, as so often happens, the humanist press tells its own

story as, for instance, in the very revealing report on the trial in *The Freethinker*, 10 July 1971:

The occasion had for 'freethinkers' a familiar and – if it were not so disastrous for a struggling young publisher and his fourth title – almost convivial atmosphere. Apart from John Mortimer QC, senior counsel for the Defence, there were a number of radicals in and at the trial. One of the principal defence witnesses was the humanist psychologist, Dr James Hemming, who was advised to take the oath and mumbled 'I swear by Almight Od'. Then came Caspar Brook, director of the Family Planning Association and Dr Anthony Ryle, director of the University of Sussex Health Service, who asked to be allowed to affirm (at which the magistrate promptly intervened, 'You have no religious belief, very well, you may affirm'). This assumption was presumably correct, but a little later another defence witness, the Reverend Paul Oestreicher, vicar of the Church of the Ascension, Blackheath, and director of training in the Diocese of Southwark, asked to affirm on the grounds that the oath was contrary to his religious belief. Among humanists in court throughout the proceedings were Barbara Smoker and Edwina Palmer of the South Place Ethical Society, and Grace Berger, Chairman of the National Council for Civil Liberties. During an intermission at the Old Bailey her son, one of the contributors to the *School Kids OZ*, and Richard Neville, one of the editors and defendants, came along to express solidarity with Richard Handyside.

Shortly after the trial finished someone rang to invite me to meet Richard Handyside, members of a schools' Action Group and a journalist from *New Society*. All things considered, I didn't think I would.

One of the difficulties for those who were – and are – fighting this type of material is that the public as a whole has no idea just how bad the material in question is, not least because of course the press cannot publish it. At the same time the propaganda of the far left, of the Council for Civil

Liberties *et al*, combines to persuade the man-in-the-street that evil lies only in the eye of the beholder (most of all in mine, of course).

The situation is not helped by those in the media who appear totally hostile to any kind of control of the printed word, however foul, or however hostile to, in this case, the true interests of children. They persuade themselves, and try to persuade everyone else, that Magna Carta, Habeas Corpus and the rest are about to be torn up.

Sometimes people wonder how one stands up to the personal attacks, especially in the media, which inevitably seem to follow any successful initiative to control corruption. Part of the answer to that lies in the personal expressions of support which invariably come our way. Take, for instance, this letter written to me the day after *The Little Red School Book* verdict:

> I once counted myself amongst your opponents. I used to seize with glee upon every satirical attack upon you and joyfully talk about you using a highly uncomplimentary corruption of your surname. In short you were an Aunt Sally for the intellectual brickbats of myself and of most of my friends. But I have since married and now have two baby sons whom I love more than I could ever have thought possible. And after reading about your contribution to the successful prosecution concerning the infamous 'Red Book' I look at my sons sleeping peacefully in their beds and I am deeply grateful to you. It depresses me beyond description to think that adults, any adults, could condone children 'getting ideas'[1] from pornography. To think that the issue is so much in doubt that a bitter struggle in the courts was necessary at all is an extremely sad reflection on the times we live in.
>
> When my children reach the age of puberty I hope with all my heart that the pressures and influences will be more wholesome than at the present moment. I love my children and I want to defend them against attacks

---

[1] The *LRSB* said that children might get some 'good ideas' from pornography.

of all kinds. You now appear to be as my ally. I apologise for thinking so ill of you as a younger, less experienced, man.

Chapter 10

Inciting to violence?

But within nation states, or at least within our nation state which is what matters to me, we have chosen the path of reason, to establish that civilized order which is liberty under law, and government by consent.

Of late, that civilized order has been increasingly threatened by unreason and lawlessness, violence and terrorism. Television may well have been, if not the cause, a contributing influence. By reflecting, television may have inflamed. By depicting, television may have magnified. By projecting, television may have incited. By accentuating, television may have encouraged.

Robin Day, *Day by Day*[1]

Here we had one of the most respected – indeed a knighted – television journalist saying in those last few sentences precisely what we had been saying for years!

It is not infrequently claimed that we in National VALA have been more concerned about sex than about violence. But the truth is that our statements about the treatment of sex on television and elsewhere always make headlines. Sex sells newspapers as well as other commodities whereas violence, unless associated with the famous or the notorious, does not, to anything like the same degree.

Wherever, whenever I have spoken in public, televised violence and its effect upon our lives has always been one of the – often *the* – main plank of my argument. This is well illustrated in the following extracts from an address I gave at the Royal College of Nursing Annual Conference in 1970:

[1] William Kimber & Co Ltd, 1975.

When the movement which I represent was founded in 1963, we said quite simply that the constant presentation of violence on our television screens would significantly promote and help to create a violent society. We were ridiculed for our pains, called cranks and accused of being squeamish. We believed then, and have continued to believe, that the screening of violence, horror, shock and obscenity into the home, where the viewer sits comfortably, detached, in his easy chair, where he can switch off mentally or physically whenever he wishes, can have nothing but a destructive effect upon our sensitivities and our society.

The other side of the same coin is the fact that exposure to the violent content of television news programmes can, and indeed has, created in many people a revulsion against violence in all its forces and the political consequence of this is very great. There are those who say it is impossible to believe both these things. But I do! And the key to the apparent contradiction is that the one is an emotional reaction, the other an intellectual one. As I said on the same occasion in 1970:

> We would indeed be totally dehumanized if we did not react with horror and sickness against the sight of mutilation and suffering to the degree shown on our TV screens during, for instance, the Vietnam war. But the process of desensitization is taking place at the same time, especially if the victims are not our own kith and kin.
>
> Are we becoming less physically and emotionally affected by the sufferings of others, especially if those others are a different colour or far enough away not to disturb our equanimity? Do we react with consistent and continuing compassion towards the victims of natural disasters – as in Guatemala – a day's headline, wiped from our mind by the next sensation? So that immeasurable sufferings of countless people get a couple of minutes along with the football results and the weather, just before the 'western'. The appetite for

sensation is insatiable and creates its own insensitivity to what feeds that appetite.

Viewer ratings are the key to many things. Pictures, it would seem, have to be exciting, stimulating, constantly breaking new ground, if they are to hold the attention of a visually satiated public. Therefore, the effect upon so-called entertainment programmes of the violence in news coverage has been profound. In order to attract viewers, techniques of violence in drama and documentary have to step up their impact. Explicitness, the follow-through camera work, the close-up shot, is the product, not of sadistic minds, but of the need to create controversy, to satisfy an apparently insatiable demand for realism.

That's what I thought in 1970. There's nothing, except perhaps the specific references to Guatemala – long, long forgotten – and Vietnam, now nothing much more than an embarrassment for the Americans, that I would change. All that is different is the names of those two countries which can now be replaced with El Salvador and the *degree* of frustration and sadness that one feels. This has increased rather than decreased in the years that have lain between. The price that we have all had to pay, though some more than others, for the media's preoccupation with violence is beyond measure. (The exploitation of man's inhumanity to man has been more obscene than the inhumanity itself.) It has been made the more contemptible by the hypocrisy which has so often characterized the Broadcasting Authorities' attitude to violence on the television screen.

I sometimes think that we have been attacked as we have, not because the perpetrators of TV violence really believed we were the 'cranks' they called us, but because they knew we were touching on the truth.

There have now been over 600 reports emanating from universities, Government bodies, and professional research, all of which support what we have been saying over the years about the link between televised and social violence.

President Johnson's Commission on the Causes and Prevention of Violence, 1969, concluded that: 'Violence on television encourages violent forms of behaviour and fosters moral and social values about violence in family life which are unacceptable in a civilised society.' Two years later the US Surgeon General's Report decisively confirmed that view and the strength of the evidence presented in the Report forced all three major US television networks to concede that their previous insistence that the case against television violence had *not* been proven 'was no longer tenable'.

Still in the States: '50 studies involving 10,000 children and adolescents from every conceivable background, all showed that violence viewing produces increased aggressive behaviour in the young and that immediate remedial action in terms of television programming is warranted.'[1]

A year later the Royal Commission on Violence in Ottawa 1976 reported that it had concluded that: 'We believe that, while increased exploitation and depiction of violence in the media is only one of the many social factors contributing to crime, it is the largest single variable most amenable to rectification.'

The Report 'Television Violence and the Adolescent Boy',[2] the result of six years' research by Dr William Belson of the London School of Economics, found that: 'Serious violence is increased by long term exposure to: plays or films in which close personal relationships are a major theme and which feature verbal or physical violence; programmes in which violence seems just thrown in for its own sake or is not necessary to the plot; programmes featuring fictional violence of a realistic kind; programmes in which the violence is presented as being in a good cause: Westerns of the violent kind.'

It wasn't only the researchers. Lord Swann, then Sir Michael Swann, Chairman of the BBC, had this to say:

> But if pharmaceutical drugs should be carefully
> controlled, because they can on occasion lead to
> deformities (as I'm sure they should) by what logic can
> films and television be exempt if they too produce
> undesirable effects, even if only in a few cases? . . . all
> drugs have now to pass the most immensely stringent

[1] *The Journal of the American Medical Association*, 1975.   [2] 1977.

tests to show that they do not harm even the tiniest proportion of takers. Is violence on the screen so very different? I think not, may it not rather be up to us to show that what we screen does not have ill effects (like a pharmaceutical firm) than up to others to prove that it does?

And, of course, there are the Broadcasting Authorities' own codes on the treatment of violence: 'There is no alternative to a continuing assumption that the portrayal of violence may have harmful effects. . . It is dangerous to assume that depiction of the use of violence for legitimate ends is less harmful than depiction of violence for evil ends' (The IBA). 'Any attempt to make violence an essential characteristic of manliness, for example, should be avoided. . . Violence might not be presented in ways which might glorify it or portray it as a proper solution to interpersonal conflicts' (The BBC).

I realize very well that to document the kind of violence we have been shown on the television screen could well be counter-productive and lay me open to the charge that I am indulging in it myself! On the other hand, I have to make my case and hope to do so with the following brief quotes from some of our monitoring, all of which was carried out *after* the publication of the Annan Report into the Future of Broadcasting (1976), which had concluded that: 'People are right to object to the glorification of violence when its depiction may possibly, even probably, do positive harm, especially to the most vulnerable with the fewest defences.'[1]

The series *Gangsters* (BBC1, 1978) was characterized by violence for violence's sake, eg 'vicious hand-to-hand fighting in a heap of dung – man lying face down in a river trampled upon – victim caught up in a net then cut to pieces by farm machinery'.

I, Claudius (BBC2, 1976 and 1977), a series which was excellent in many ways, was repeated without cuts in spite of public and press criticism of explicit and sadistic violence. Patrick Hutber (*The Sunday Telegraph*, 4 December 1977) referred to the 'quite sickening bloodshed and violence. In the

---

[1] 8 September 1973.

worst of these, which caused some protests at the time, Caligula is shown hoisting up his pregnant sister Drusilla, ripping her clothes off, advancing on her with a knife, and then emerging with bloodied mouth having, we are given to understand, munched the foetus. What is remarkable about this episode is that it does not occur in Graves' book. His words – and I check them as I write – are "Drusilla died. I am certain in my own mind that Caligula killed her, but I have no proof".' So if ever there was violence for violence's sake, this was it.'

Hazell (ITV, 6 February 1978): 'The "hero" pins a villain to the top of a night club bar with corkscrew through his hand; another character had his head smashed repeatedly on the floor as blood gushed out; bottle smashed in a face; man flung hard against wall.'

An Investigation of Murder[1] (BBC1, 1 September 1980): 'The violence is frightful, a homosexual psychopath shoots the passengers in a bus, close-ups are given of the victims and their wounds dwelt upon. Later, in a morgue, the process is repeated. The police are shown shooting up (unnecessarily of course) a tenement where innocent people are shot, policemen killed and a woman falls to her death.'

Marathon Man (ITV, 1 September 1980): according to 'Movies on TV' this play 'suffered from constant doses of gratuitous violence – whether it's plain, old-fashioned stabbings or Lawrence Olivier playing a former dentist who puts his past calling to professional use by torturing Dustin Hoffman, drilling on the most sensitive nerves in captive Hoffman's mouth'.

As well as the physical violence many of the programmes we monitored were characterized by verbal violence of the most extreme and quite unquotable-kind and often by sexual violence too.

In addition to monitoring violence as such we had been studying for some time the treatment of the police, particularly in television drama – the BBC series *Target* (1978) and ITV's *The Sweeney* which had been shown first in the autumn of 1978 and repeated later. And we did, in fact, submit our

[1] See also page 85.

findings on this to the Scarman Inquiry which looked at the causes of the race riots in Brixton and elsewhere. We particularly drew Lord Scarman's attention to the fact that:

> The obscene and blasphemous language used in these two programmes came as much from the police as from the criminals; the often sadistic violence was practised as much by the police as by the criminals; promiscuity was, in fact, much more a characteristic of the police than the criminals. In other words, there was little, if anything, to chose between them.
>
> Time and again *The Sweeney* and *Target* showed, as though it were normal police practice, the kind of violence which, in actuality, occurs in a very small number of cases and with a minute number of criminals and police officers.
>
> In everyday life police officers do not normally carry weapons. We understand from senior police officers that robberies which involve armed violence are the only ones in which guns are issued. Yet the gun is used in these programmes with far greater frequency than authenticity would demand.
>
> When apprehending criminals Det. Supt. Hackett (*Target*) and Det. Insp. Regan (*The Sweeny*) use violence – and of the crudest kind – as a matter of course, as for instance in:
>
> *Target* (first shown 1.12.79) – Chief Supt. Hackett involved in fight with criminal. Feet used brutally by both parties. Hackett ends up with a knife at the criminal's throat. He is pulled away by colleague. Kicks criminal into the sea after having had his foot on his throat. Hackett declares, 'I'll find him, even if I have to live up his backside for a month'.
>
> *The Sweeney* (first shown 12.12.78) – Police officer chases criminal downstairs, traps him at bottom and delivers vicious punch after vicious punch at the bleeding face and head of a now helpless man. Had to be pulled away by colleague.

The BBC1 so-called documentary series *Law and Order*

(March 1978), produced by Tony Garnett who is known for his commitment to 'the left', caused considerable controversy and drew criticism from many sides not least in the columns of the TV critics.

The *Daily Telegraph* wrote: 'How far this picture of the Law represents a true bill and how far it's a diabolical fit-up is something I am glad not to have to evaluate.'

The *London Evening Standard* said: 'Garnett's film was done in an entirely realistic way and for the detective, corruption and brutality were shown to be all part of the day's work. . . To show corruption as the norm is to insult the police and undermine the public trust in them without which their work would be made almost insuperably difficult.'

Some television films have been equally bad and the fact that they often show American rather than British policemen doesn't really make any difference. Take, for example, BBC1's *Serpico* (16 August 1980; see also page 84):

> The police of New York are pictured as corrupt, mean, dishonest, interested only in how many people they can arrest in one day and led by weak seniors who turn a blind eye to the rottenness that is present in the force.
>
> There is little to recommend in this film. The violence is brutal and at an unacceptable level, the picture of dishonesty and corruption in the police overdone, the language banal and vulgar.

As anyone who has written to either Broadcasting Authority will know, the classic defence for almost anything shown on the TV screen is that it 'reflects reality'. But there is an enormous gap, it seems to me, between the easy justification for showing violence because it is 'reality' and the challenging responsibility carried by both Broadcasting Authorities not to transmit material which could 'incite to crime and disorder'. The political and social violence which we had always felt was uncharacteristic of the British way of life, no matter what happened in other countries, was suddenly breaking out in our streets. Yet still we were being fed with violence as entertainment.

As an indication of the intransigence of, in this case, the

IBA to violence on the screen and its unwillingness to take research findings into account, I quote from one of Lord Thomson's letters to me[1] on this subject:

> As you may know the question of the effect on viewers' behaviour of televised violence is a matter on which there has been a great deal of research which the Authority follows closely and which we do not believe sustains the objections of your members to this type of programme.[2] We do, however, watch closely the ways in which our guidelines on violence are observed. *The Sweeney* conforms to these guidelines and is widely regarded as a very well-made series which meets a public taste for police series in a schedule which seeks to avoid the bunching of such adventure/action series and contains other ingredients such as *Coronation Street*, recently *Plays for Pleasure*, and regular documentaries. The Authority does not see why these varying tastes should not be catered for.

In a letter to a viewer[3] Sir Brian Young, Director General of the IBA said:

> We were particularly pleased to notice that, over the last five or six years, fewer and fewer people have thought our programmes violent – indeed, the level of complaint is now only about a third of what it was.

One is bound to ask: Why is Sir Brian so pleased that ITV programmes are perceived as being violent by fewer people? Unless the Authority can show that specific incidents of violence have decreased in comparison with the amount shown several years ago – and this is patently not so – they should be *worried* about the decrease in complaints. This

[1] 22 April 1981.
[2] See *The Sweeney*, above.
[3] 20 March 1981.

indicates the increasing desensitivity on the part of the Authority which is so disturbing.

What is more, in its Annual Report 1981 the IBA claimed that the total number of complaints it had received, on all topics, was only 2,515, of which only 2 per cent related to violence. We later checked with the Authority to find out whether this total included complaints received by the ITV Companies and discovered that it did not do so! One feels that the IBA were less than frank and one wonders what report, if any, the individual ITV companies publish on this matter. We have not come across any.

It was because there appeared to be so little possibility of getting behind the defences of the IBA that we decided to write to the Chairman of each of the companies advertising during the screening of *The Gambler*.[1]

We enclosed a copy of our Monitoring Report on the obscenities and gross violence in the programme, one incident of which showed a man being threatened with flick knife at his throat and then having his face slit open with it in close up. In our letter we said:

> We realise, of course, that you have no immediate control over the placing of your advertisements but hope you will feel that some expression of concern by you would persuade the IBA and indeed the public that, as a company, you regret that you should have been in any way associated with such obscenities.
>
> We should be grateful for any comments you care to make.

The response to our letter was on the whole most encouraging. For instance Mr A. M. Detsiny, Marketing Director of Cadbury Schweppes, wrote in the following terms:

> Whilst we have never sought to control programme content, I must say I am not entirely happy about the fact that our products were advertised during the screening of the film *The Gambler*. The Monitoring

[1] 26 September 1981.

Report you enclose with your letter clearly gives some cause for concern, and I will be drawing the attention of both the IBA and our Advertising Agencies to the points you make.

Thank you for writing to us.

I must say that the reply we received from the Managing Director of Sterling Roncraft, manufacturers of DIY products surprised us somewhat. He took me to task for enclosing the Monitoring Report: 'I must point out to you that the recirculation by your own Association of a selected purple passage round the offices of my organization has succeeded only in causing additional offence to members of my staff. Please do not send any more.'

I thought it odd that while he had such an understandable concern over what came to the eyes of his office staff, he did not seem much concerned that the same material should be heard and seen on television – almost certainly by children.

But suddenly and unexpectedly the whole question of television violence and in particular the coverage of violence in news programmes came to a head.

I nearly fell off my chair! There we were, sitting having tea and watching, as usual, the early evening news when suddenly a picture of me appeared on the TV screen as Richard Baker announced that I'd sent a telegram to both Broadcasting Authorities in which I asked if they would 'Please consider whether the current massive television coverage of acts of vandalism and violence is contributing to the spread of the riots' (in Toxteth and Brixton).

Early that morning[1] I'd said to Ernest, 'You know, those shots on the news last night should *never* have been shown!' I was referring to pictures of young black teenagers taking calculated – and cheerful – running kicks at plate-glass shop windows, coolly helping themselves to the goods inside, shirts, shoes or whatever they could lay their hands on. 'We really should do *something*,' I said. But what? Weren't there already enough people involved, from the Home Secretary down? Anything we might do would be bound to be lost in

[1] 11 July 1981.

the turmoil. 'And of course it's Saturday; there'll be no one at the BBC and ITN but duty officers and no one's interested in anything but sport today.' So I put it out of my mind and got on with my work.

Then half-way through the morning the thought came like a flash – 'send a telegram!' I've learnt over the years not to ignore such powerful, unexpected 'instructions' and although I don't really like taking unilateral action (none of my close colleagues answered my phone-calls) I decided to *send* a telegram. But I was so convinced no one of influence at Broadcasting House or at the IBA was likely to see it that I didn't even add 'President, National Viewers' and Liste- ners' Association' to my name as sender. 'It will cost too much', I thought, 'and they know full well who I am anyway.' But I was very sorry I hadn't when I saw the telegram reproduced on ITN. It looked like a personal rather than an official initiative. However, there it was, right in the middle of the main news story of the day. To the best of my memory this was the very first time the BBC, at any rate, had ever given publicity on television news to anything we had said about television. No wonder I nearly fell of my chair!

Both BBC and ITN had obviously put their heads to- gether, or so it seemed to me, since in their response to my challenge they used almost identical words. Admitting that while there might be 'some copycat' effect of the TV coverage of the rioting, both the BBC and ITN went on to interpret my telegram as a call for a news 'blackout', which it most certainly was not. But that wasn't the end of the matter by any means.

In an official press statement issued within the next few days, Mr Dick Francis, Head of News and Current Affairs at the BBC asked whether they were 'to deny the vast ma- jority of the public information they had a right to know, a picture they had a right to see, for fear of stimulating law breakers on the fringe?'

Well, as I said in a letter published by *The Daily Telegraph* a few days later, 'We've seen an awful lot of law breakers on a pretty broad fringe' and the 'shots of which we complained were absolutely classic teaching experience! Take a running kick, jump back as the glass falls, spring smartly forward over the debris and take your pick. No one will interfere, there's no danger of hurting yourself, there's loot in abundance, and it's fun into the bargain.'

Mr Francis fell back on the hoary old claim that there 'is no conclusive evidence' that television does have the effect that we claimed. Actually we hadn't *claimed* anything. We'd asked the news editors 'Please to consider. . .'

Still, whatever may have been the temptation to 'face save', and one well understands it, the fact remains that the TV treatment of the riots was very different in the following days. There were 'stills' rather than action, long-shots rather than close-ups. And everyone I'm sure felt the better for it.

Of course Mr Francis was in something of a cleft stick. If the broadcasters once admitted that television *news* had the power to affect human behaviour then that principle would also apply to the rest of their out-put, and that would indeed put the fat in the fire. So this particular line had to be held against all-comers, in public at any rate.

However that may be, one top TV man said to me during the course of the following week: 'Mary, not in all your years of campaigning have you achieved so much in so short a space of time as you did with that telegram.' That was an interesting 'inside' view, but I kept feeling there was more to all this than met the eye.

I was still amazed that both Authorities should have responded as they had to my telegram which could so easily have been ignored. I had a strong feeling that through their response to what I had done they were in fact indirectly replying to criticism from *another* source, a source to which they could not respond in so forthright a manner. 'Perhaps the Prime Minister?' I thought to myself.

A few days later (13 July 1981) *The Times* reported that during the Parliamentary Lobby Correspondents' Centenary celebrations in the House of Commons the previous week Mrs Thatcher had expressed similar anxieties. The BBC and ITN, whose lobby correspondents would have heard what she said, could not reply directly as she had not voiced her concern publicly. Did they do so indirectly through the publicity they gave to our telegram and their reaction to it?

Later that same week Mr Dick Francis told the Royal Television Society[1] that he didn't doubt that a lot of people would agree with me, but, of course, I was wrong. So presumably were 'a lot of people', among them the leader writer of *The Times*[2]: 'First we should ask ourselves: can anyone seriously doubt there was a strong copy-cat element in the riots? . . . that many youths wore balaclavas or plastic bags over their heads? that there was a rash of fires in dustbins? or that so many milk floats were commandeered? How else do you explain the spread of this behaviour? Was it by word of mouth from Toxteth to Wood Green? Was it over the telephone? Scarcely a medium of mass communication!'

Late – very late – next day I had a call from the features editor of *The Daily Mail* who was 'very interested indeed in the point we were making and would I write about 1,000 words for the leader page?'

'By when?' I asked.

'By tomorrow teatime,' he replied.

'Heavens – I'm having my hair done in the morning and I'm presenting prizes at a school nearby in the afternoon. I don't see how on earth I can get it done by then,' I protested. But he is a very persuasive, gentle sort of man, over the phone at any rate.

'Well, you think about it and I'll ring at midday tomorrow.'

I went to bed thinking I could not possibly do it. Apart from anything else I'd never produced an article at that speed before – and I had a bad headache. But the phone-call had set my mind working and throughout the night I kept half waking up to lean over and scribble down ideas, in the dark, on a bit of paper which was on the floor at the side of my bed. When I woke soon after 5.30 I found that all my bits of inspiration had been written on top of newsprint so that I couldn't read a single word! But it didn't really matter. Apart from my quick trip to the hairdresser's I worked right through till midday and had just finished when the editor rang.

'What are you thinking this morning?' he asked.

[1] 14 July 1981.
[2] 10 August 1981.

'I've thought,' I replied. 'And I've no idea whether it'll do or not. But now I've got to get my lunch and go off to the prizegiving!' Would I dictate it on to copy as soon as I got back? That's what I did and it appeared in next morning's *Daily Mail* exactly as I'd scribbled it down. What a wonder! To me, anyway.

Apparently the Editor received a number of requests for the syndication rights of the article and as a result I was invited to do a live radio broadcast the following Sunday which was transmitted across Australia at peak listening time. This all confirmed my belief in how vital it is not to miss the 'whispers' or fail to act upon them, however difficult or strange or inappropriate they may seem at the time.

However – and this will surely surprise no one who knows how the media work – in next to no time the British Film Institute's Broadcasting Research Unit leaked[1] the information that it was about to publish research which would show that television had *not* influenced the riots at all; research incidentally which was funded by both the BBC and the IBA. 'That didn't take very long,' I thought, cynically I'm afraid. I thought of the six *years* that had gone into Dr William Belson's research[2] into the effect of television on 1,500 adolescent boys. The Institute's researchers had apparently talked to 50. According to them fewer than 10 per cent of teenagers apparently watch any kind of television news at all.

It's difficult for lay people to challenge that kind of statement, though we may feel in our bones that it's not far short of claptrap. So there was much encouragement in a letter[3] from Dr Marilyn Aitkenhead who in questioning the validity of the Institute's findings referred to long-established research which indicated that the riots could have been 'fuelled by opinion leaders' – in this case perhaps by teenagers who were especially interested in the riots, who watched their progress on television and who reported what they saw to their friends. I don't doubt the debate will go on and on and so I fear will

---

[1] 6 January 1982.
[2] *'Television Violence and the Adolescent Boy'*, 1977.
[3] *The Guardian*, 13 January 1982.

the violence – in spite of the very enlightened codes to govern its treatment which both the BBC and IBA have produced.[1]

There is something very depressing and frustrating about the almost Pavlovian response of the Broadcasting Authorities to a challenge of this kind. One feels in one's bones that whatever research they fund will somehow serve to defend the *status quo*. I'm not in any way impugning the professionalism of the researchers involved, but it is extraordinary that, no matter what other research initiatives may conclude that carried out for the BBC and IBA in this field as in others seems invariably to find for them. It could be, of course, that those involved in this research were hampered by lack of cash. We were given to understand by 'spokesmen' that the BBC's contribution was 'a small amount' while the IBA were more forthcoming and mentioned £1,000. Hardly enough to launch much more than a piece of investigative journalism.

[1] See above.

Chapter 11

Linda Lovelace

My hairdresser's strong fingers were working up a fine lather on my head when a voice whispered in my ear, 'There's a man on the phone who says he's from the Home Office, Mrs Whitehouse. He wants to speak to you urgently.' So, head wrapped in towel, I walked into the shop, smiled somewhat apologetically at waiting customers and picked up the phone. In reply to my cautious 'Hello', a very superior-sounding gentleman at the other end said: 'Mrs Whitehouse, I have just realized that there is a case on in London that Dr Court,[1] whom we understand arrives in London on Sunday morning, could assist us with. We will have an officer at Heathrow to meet him off the plane and he will take him to see the material which is on trial and take a statement from him. We shall then require his attendance at the Court on Monday morning at 10.30.'

In the silence that followed he, no doubt, took a breath. So did I, a very deep one.

'I am not at all sure that I can agree to that,' I said, as the soap began to trickle down my face. It struck me then, as it has struck me many times since, how very funny those two shots juxtaposed would look on television – on one side the top civil servant (*Yes, Minister* and all that) with the telephone to his mouth; on the other Mary's wet towelled head backed by displays of hairnets, hairgrips, hair spray and lacquer!

The reason why I couldn't 'agree to that' lay in the events of the previous weeks.

[1] Associate Professor of Psychology at Flinders University of South Australia.

The *Inside Linda Lovelace*[1] obscenity trial had just finished with a 'Not Guilty' verdict. 'Anything goes now' screamed the headlines and indeed what had become known as 'Mortimer's travelling circus of "expert" witnesses' had pulled it off again.

This particular book, written by the 26 year-old 'star' of the blue movie *Deep Throat*, catalogued the 'hero's' sexual repertoire and dealt at length with what was termed Linda Lovelace's 'speciality' – oral sex. Judge Rigg, in his summing up, emphasized to the jury the importance of the decision they would make, telling them that their verdict would be regarded as a guide as to where the line should be drawn in future. After nearly five hours of deliberation they brought in a 'Not Guilty' verdict. And, of course, it *did* push back the bounds of acceptability a great deal further.

The *Lovelace* case was only one of a string of cases in which pornographic publications had been deemed not obscene in the meaning of the law since the passing of Roy Jenkins' obscenity laws of 1959 and 1964. On the morning after this particular trial *The Times*[2] asked how such acquittals had been achieved and went on to answer its own question:

> There are a number of factors. The defence often uses its right to challenge the jury in order to try to get a number of sympathetic looking jurors, perhaps young men of radical appearance and to remove unsympathetic jurors such as women. Mr John Mortimer QC has a particular gift for amusing irrelevance, which makes the prosecution appear absurd, combined with a passionate devotion to defence of the freedom of pornography. The defence calls their dozen experts like Dr Richards; the prosecution hardly ever calls expert witnesses in rebuttal. In general a detailed and zealous defence faces an inadequate and unconsidered prosecution.

Yes, indeed, the defence did have Dr Richards. As a defence

[1] 28 January 1976.
[2] 30 January 1976.

witness in the Bens Books trials (1975) he gave these answers
when Counsel showed him several pictures in the magazine
concerned:

> *Counsel:* 'This is a picture of a female in chains, tied up
> and a naked man pointing a sword at the woman's
> genitals. . .'
> *Dr Richards:* 'This is for the public good because it
> produces a masturbatory situation. I would certainly
> prescribe this for a patient.'
> *Counsel:* 'Picture of a naked man with a cat of ninetails
> striking a woman on genitals.'
> *Dr Richards:* 'This can stimulate a man. It has great
> therapeutic value.'
> *Counsel:* 'Girl, with distress in her face, arms manacled,
> and has cuts. She is tied up. A man with bayonet is
> inflicting cuts.'
> *Dr Richards:* 'I have know patients who could benefit by
> masturbating on this.'

The Times leader really hit the nail on the head. It had become
increasingly clear, as a series of legal initiatives brought by
the Police against the pornographers were lost one after another because of the inefficiency of the law, that a 'Denmark'
situation was being created here in Britain. What was more,
the police were given no encouragement in their attempts to
combat the flood of pornography by the then Director of
Public Prosecutions, Sir Norman Skelhorn. In fact quite the
reverse, as the *Lovelace* case illustrated perfectly.

We already knew that the police were very concerned
about the likely outcome of this particular trial. They believed
that if this case and the Jacobs pornography trial due to
follow it at Snaresbrook Magistrates Court were lost, there
would be no point in bringing further prosecutions. So clearly
something had to be done.

The first step was to launch a broadside at the Home
Secretary, Mr Roy Jenkins. We made a statement to the
effect that his Government was, by default, condoning the
activities of the pornographers. We said that while it was
putting every other industry under the closest scrutiny it was

allowing the multi-million pound pornography industry, based on human degradation, virtually unlimited freedom. We said that Mr Sam Silkin, the Attorney General, was letting down the police by refusing to call on sound international evidence linking pornography with serious sex crime and by failing to bring into court witnesses capable of refuting the evidence of the so-called 'sex experts' called by the defence.

Having got that off our chest we thought next about John Court in Adelaide, South Australia, arguably the one person capable of destroying the defence's strategy.

I rang the Director of Public Prosecution's office. Would he be prepared to bring Dr Court over? I asked. 'No,' I was told, 'it would cost too much.'

So then I rang John, himself a Londoner by birth. If we found ways of paying his expenses would he come over? 'Yes,' he said without hesitation. 'I'll drop everything.' 'So,' I thought to myself as I put down the phone, 'if we do get John over and the DPP won't use him, we'll call a press conference and give him the opportunity to say what he has to say there.'

When one of the police officers involved in the *Lovelace* case told me he thought the DPP would not use anyone 'associated with a pressure group', I almost exploded. 'What the dickens does he think John Mortimer is? Why, he's a pressure group in himself!' I was also told that the DPP was thoroughly 'embarrassed' and would like to wash his hands not only of this case but of the 'whole business' of obscenity trials. And certainly he showed an increasing reluctance to get involved (not that his successor, Sir Thomas Hetherington, has been particularly eager).

However that may be, we delivered to the DPP's office a copy of John Court's academic research along with a copy of some important American research and a note to the effect that Dr Court was prepared to come to Britain as a prosecution witness at the forthcoming Jacobs obscenity trial at Snaresbrook where we understood defence would be claiming that bestiality was 'for the public good'.

It was at this point that, to our dismay and amazement, we learnt that the DPP did not intend bringing *any* prosecution witnesses at all in the Jacobs case, which if lost would mean that even bestiality would be effectively legal in Britain. What an extraordinary business. Here we were, fighting not only the pornographers but also the apathy and apparent disinterestedness of the DPP's office. So then I wrote a formal letter offering John Court's services to the DPP and waited. On 28 January 1977 the publisher of *Inside Linda Lovelace* was found 'Not Guilty'. On 29 January I rang John Court in Adelaide – got him just as he was going to bed. 'Would he come?' 'Yes.' He'd check flights and ring me back in the morning. So now the deed was done. I had no idea at all where the money was coming from. 'But we must trust,' I thought, not for the first time.

In the meantime *The Times* carried a first leader of forty column inches on the *Lovelace* trial. It concluded: 'The pornographers are sick minded commercial men who sell images of hatred, and particularly hatred of women, for vast profit. We need both a law and law enforcement which will stop them.' A group of Tory MPs went to see Mr Sam Silkin, the Attorney General, telling him they were wholly disgusted with the DPP, that they wished for a full enquiry and that the Tories were now going to launch a campaign to strengthen the obscenity laws. (I wish I knew what's happened to that campaign!) Questions were asked in Parliament; the press had a field day, and in all fairness it has to be said that the great majority of the comment showed dismay with the outcome of the *Lovelace* trial.

Once we knew the time of John Court's arrival we got straight down to the business of arranging his itinerary. We had plenty of plans. 'But first,' I thought, 'it's only courteous to give the DPP and the Attorney General a chance to meet him should they wish to do so, especially as the Jacobs case was already going very badly for the Crown.' So I dropped the DPP a note to tell him of John's arrival. The next morning I went to the hairdressers!

I was cross with what I felt was the DPP's arrogance and lack of care, not least for the fact that John Court was bound to be very tired following what turned out to be a thirty-six-hour flight. I also felt the DPP had had plenty of chances to arrange to bring John over himself. But now that we'd brought him at our expense. . .

When I got home from the hairdresser I felt I needed someone wiser and more experienced, so I rang my old friend Bill Deedes, Editor of *The Daily Telegraph*. His reaction was immediate. 'Be a statesman, Mary, and get your priorities right. And number one is that the Jacobs case is won. Say to the DPP – I will put your needs first and put nothing in the way of you calling Dr Court's evidence if that's what you decide to do. That is the most important thing for us all, Mary, and in the long term the most important thing for you and your campaign.' Of course, he was right. I rang the DPP's office to say John would be arriving on Monday but that we would meet him, bring him home for a rest after his long flight. Then his officer could be the first person to meet and talk to him. And that is how it was.

John was in the witness box for three hours – cross-examined in a very demanding fashion, but he was marvellous, using all his professional experience and research. 'Guilty' was the unanimous verdict with a sentence of twelve months' imprisonment – only the fourth 'guilty' verdict in all the major obscenity cases which had followed the *Lady Chatterley's Lover* trial in 1960.

And John? Apart from his appearance in the witness-box he attended a press conference; met Bill Deedes and William Rees-Mogg, then Editor of *The Times*; appeared on radio and television; had lunch with the Board of W. H. Smith; met a Permanent Under Secretary at the Home Office; had lunch in the House of Lords and went in to the Chamber to watch the introduction of a new Peer. He also met with MPs and heard that two questions were being put down for answer by the Government: 'Why was Dr John Court not called in the *Linda Lovelace* case?' and 'Was the DPP paying Dr Court's fare?' He went to Scotland Yard to meet members of the Obscene Publications Squad and one of the Deputy Commissioners who thanked John on behalf of Sir Robert Mark who was abroad at the time. And he did a broadcast to Australia. He then went to spend the weekend with his parents in Bristol before flying back home. And the money for his fare and other expenses all came in.

I wrote in my diary at the end of that week:

How greatly God has honoured the step we took in faith when I had the whisper personally to invite John when the DPP refused to do so. God has made the visit mean far more than I could ever have imagined. Wonderful to look back on the last three weeks and see how, step by step, the strategy has built up with everyone playing their part. Ernest not least of all, lifting every responsibility off my shoulders so that I could be free to think of nothing but the battle.

Nothing has changed my gratitude for the results of John Court's visit, but I have to say, five years later, that nothing has happened since to lessen my concern about the role of the Home Office and that of the DPP in allowing an almost free hand to the pornographers.

The very latest of a stream of incidents in which the DPP has refused to take action involved a record on sale in shops around the country. The words are foul, the action they so crudely and violently describe involves bestiality, sex with schoolgirls and obscene practices involving human excrement. The DPP refused to take action against the anarchist group involved under Section 2 of the Obscene Publications Act declaring in a letter to me (26 February 1982) that he 'was extremely doubtful whether there was a reasonable prospect of obtaining a conviction'. However, he went on, 'in view of the obvious market for this record among young people I was more than willing to institute Section 2 proceedings if I could be persuaded by Counsel experienced in this type of prosecution that there was a reasonable prospect of success'. But far from seeking to persuade the DPP to prosecute it appears that Counsel 'unhesitatingly' advised that he was indeed correct in his conclusion and that the appropriate action was to advise the police to seize copies of the record, which they did.

Consistently, as a reason for 'no action' under Section 2, the DPP has claimed that a court case would give publicity to an otherwise, in this case, unknown group. That is, of course, a valid point, but in the end where has this policy got us – not to mention the children who buy such records? To a position where, effectively, we have no obscenity law.

It seems to me that at least the producers of the record could have been interviewed and personally warned by the police but even that did not happen. It is, of course, no use blaming the police, for their policies in this area are decided by the DPP.

Chapter 12

Mr Thorsen departs

'Not if we can help it!' we said when we heard in the early summer of the same year that Jens Jorgen Thorsen was coming to Britain to make an 'obscene film about the sex life of Jesus Christ'. The world's press first carried that story in 1973 but it fell out of the headlines and nothing more was heard until early 1976. According to Thorsen the script had already been written and he was ready, so he said, to make the film in Denmark. But the cry of anguish and anger, from the Muslim as well as the Christian world, was so powerful that the Danish Government refused to allow it to be made. So Mr Thorsen took himself and his film script off to Sweden and several months later it was reported that he had obtained financial backing from the Swedish Film Institute.

Once again international concern made itself felt in no uncertain way and, what was more to the point, the Swedish Church according to one Swedish pastor, 'came to life for the first time in decades,' expressing strong and continuous opposition to the project. The Swedish Government, because of its policy of 'no censorship' found itself in considerable difficulties. But so great was the pressure from all sides that new legislation was quickly passed which made it well-nigh impossible for Thorsen to make his film in Sweden. It was at this point that we heard rumours that he intended to come to Britain to make it.

We immediately got in touch with the Swedish Embassy to get all the information we could – which wasn't very much, but we were given the name of Mr Evander, Pastor of the Swedish Church in London. He was extremely concerned and helpful and I was very pleased when he invited me to meet him and the Archbishop of Stockholm's Chaplain, who was coming to London the following week. The Chaplain brought with him a copy of the Swedish Government's latest statement that no monies would be made available for Thorsen's film either from the Swedish Film Institute or the Swedish Broadcasting Corporation which meant, in effect, that the possibilities of making the film in Sweden had disappeared. But that was by no means the end of the story, for less than three weeks later Mr Evander rang to say that Thorsen had raised the money privately and was all set to come to Britain to make the film.

Obviously something had to be done and done quickly. So we wrote[1] at once to Mr Roy Jenkins, then the Home Secretary, to ask if he would declare Thorsen 'an undesirable alien' making special reference to the possibility of public disorder were a film such as he had in mind to be made here. To be honest I wasn't very hopeful. Mr Jenkins' permissive stance was well known and indeed it was as I expected. The Home Secretary replied in an unequivocal fashion that he was not prepared to issue a banning order against Thorsen.

So we then wrote to Mr Callaghan in the hope that he, as Prime Minister, would override the Home Secretary's decision. In the meantime public pressure against the film was building up all over the country. Church leaders in particular were receiving an enormous number of letters asking them to 'do something to stop it' and it was in response to this that Cardinal Hume wrote a letter to *The Times* in which he appealed to Equity to discourage members from taking part in the film. But Peter Plouviez, Chairman of Equity, refused on the grounds that 'artistes should be given complete freedom of expression'. How many times have we heard that over the years?

The Cardinal's letter apparently greatly amused and even flattered the Danish film-maker who said on hearing of it, 'We will certainly invite the Archbishop to watch the film.' He predicted that it would have its preview in Britain on Christmas Eve the following year. 'I think Jesus has been

[1] 25 June 1976.

waiting 2,000 years to get a decent hearing,' he said, and his film would give him one.

A few days later the then Archbishop of Canterbury, Dr Donald Coggan, said at a press conference that he would oppose the making of the film 'with every power in my being'. He went on, 'There is a law of blasphemy still on the Statute Book,' and although the Archbishop said he had not made up his mind whether to invoke that law he was quite sure that 'once the thing came to the point of being shown Thorsen would have to face the blasphemy law and I think he would have to face the wrath of the vast majority of the British people too'. The Free Church Federal Council and the Salvation Army joined in the protests.

The Cambridge Union got in on the act too. Some months previously I had agreed to debate at the Union and to propose the motion 'Pornography is decadence exploited'. However, with all that was happening it had slipped out of my mind until a journalist whom I knew had gone to Sweden to try to find Thorsen caught up with me in London. He told me that he had tracked Thorsen down, spoken to him and been told by him that he was coming to Britain to debate with me at Cambridge!

'So what do you say to that, Mrs Whitehouse?'

'Simple,' I replied. 'If they've got Thorsen they haven't got me!'

It was after I got home that day that I had a phone-call from No. 10 Downing Street. I wrote in my diary that night: 'Very apologetic. PM having a very busy time in Manchester. Has the papers (my letter, etc.) with him, but not yet decided what to say. My own bet is that he's on the horns of a dilemma. His instinct would be with us, but he's afraid of his own left wing and all the accusations of 'censorship' which would be flung at him from all the trendy lefties in and out of the Government. No. 10 will ring again tomorrow'.

Next day Peter Fudakowski, the President of the Cambridge Union phoned me. He'd seen in the morning papers that I would not debate with Thorsen and was very upset.

'But this is a wonderful opportunity for you to change his mind, Mrs Whitehouse,' he pleaded.

'You must be joking,' I said. 'It's a wonderful opportunity for him to get into the country, all expenses paid.'

'Well, if you won't debate with him, who would you like to debate with?' he asked.

'Try Roy Jenkins,' I said.

The President rang again next day to say that he'd cancelled the invitation to Thorsen, not because, as he told *The Times*, 'of any outside pressure, or because of the danger of public disorder, but because, having studied various things Thorsen had said, the quality of his debating would not be up to that expected at Cambridge.' With a brain like, I thought, no wonder he was President of the Cambridge Union.

All this time Parliamentary and public opinion as well as media interest was building up in a fantastic way and Thorsen's projected film made Jesus Christ headline news in Britain day after day as both Christian people and many others were moved to get involved and speak out in a quite unprecedented fashion. But there were manifestations of anger too, which included threats to 'harass' Thorsen if he ever set foot in Britain, to make his life intolerable and even 'do him a physical injury'.

Sir Bernard Braine, MP for SE Essex, who has always been very helpful in such matters, had also written to the Prime Minister and it was to him, as a matter of Parliamentary courtesy, that Mr Callaghan first replied. In his letter the Prime Minister declared that Mr Thorsen 'would be a most unwelcome and undesirable visitor to these shores' and he made it clear that the Home Secretary *did* have the power to stop Common Market nationals entering Britain on grounds which included public order. He said pointedly, 'There is no doubt that to make a film such as the one I have read about would cause deep offence to the great majority of the people in this country among whom I number myself.'

Then Her Majesty the Queen entered the lists! Michael Hastings, a West Indian and a member of our Executive Committee, who was only 18 at the time, was one of the many people who had written to the Queen and she graciously gave permission for her reply to be published. In it she expressed her concern at the possibility of such an 'obnoxious' film being made in Britain and her uncompromising response ensured it pride of place in all the news bulletins. Michael was mightily surprised and delighted to find his photograph transmitted alongside one of the Queen in the first item of television news on that night.

Shortly after this Mr Jenkins became Chancellor of the Exchequer and the new Home Secretary Mr Merlyn Rees, very soon after his appointment, made a statement to the effect that he could do nothing to stop Thorsen unless he broke the law. So it was stalemate. It was at this point that we decided to try to get hold of a copy of the script of the play so that we could get it translated and place it before those who had the power to *do* something. Within a few days one of our friends in Copenhagen, Johannes Facius, sent us exactly what we needed except that it was, of course, printed in Danish. However, on the very day it arrived – and this was just one more miracle among so many that were happening one after another at this time – we found a professional translator living not far away from us and she turned out to be not only Danish but very critical and ashamed of Thorsen's activities. She said she was prepared to drop everything and start translating the play, at a greatly reduced fee, the following morning.

It really was a week to remember. Mrs Johannson and Jane, my secretary, sat for four days with that foul script. The description of the homosexual love scenes between Jesus and John at the last Supper were really revolting beyond description. None of us had ever read anything like it before and I was immensely grateful to them for staying with it to the end, helped not a little by the lovely bouquet of flowers which arrived from one who was in the know. They were sent 'with God's blessing' and I put them on the table by Jane and Mrs Johannson so that every time they felt overcome with the foulness of the words they were translating, they could drink in the sweetness of the flowers. We prayed together every morning that our minds would not be corrupted by the material with which we were dealing.

The news of our activities was widely reported and no sooner had we finished on the Friday morning than we received a call from Mr Whitelaw's personal assistant.

'The Shadow Home Secretary is very anxious to get hold

of a copy of the script today so that he can study it over the weekend and be in a position to make a statement about it at the Tory Party Conference next week.'

So Ernest drove immediately to London and delivered it at Mr Whitelaw's office in the Commons. We were assured that it would not be 'leaked' before the press conference we were holding the following Monday immediately after presenting the translation to the Home Secretary at the Home Office. The media interest in all this was tremendous not only in Britain but abroad. The Canadian and Australian Broadcasting Corporations both sent journalists to interview me over the weekend and, of course, the story as it unfolded was widely covered by both ITV and BBC.

The Times man met us before we went into the press conference. Mr William Rees-Mogg, we were told, was very anxious to have a copy of the script as he was considering printing it in his paper. My jaw dropped in amazement. 'He never will – not when he sees what it's really like,' I said. And indeed he did not. But next morning *The Times* at the end of its news story said, 'A copy of the book has come into the possession of *The Times*: the script is as bad as Mrs Whitehouse suggested, indeed worse.'

At the very crowded press conference we released the text of the letter which we had just delivered, along with the script, to the Home Secretary. In it I said, 'The monstrously obscene homosexual intercourse between Jesus and St John at the Last Supper and the pornographic nature of the explicit sex scene which represents Christ's resurrection amount to the ultimate in spiritual vandalism and corruption.' I drew the Home Secretary's attention to 'the way in which the constant use in the script of quotations from the New Testament, for example the Sermon on the Mount, give a pseudo-authenticity to the character of Jesus'.

In one act the character Jesus speaks of love in the sublime language of the Fourth Gospel but this is immediately followed by his preaching of violent revolution. Love is identified throughout with lust and promiscuity is presented as the pre-requisite of a problem free society.

Pornographic orgies, armed robberies, church desecration, mass sex hysteria: all these are presented as the way to the happiness, joy and peace which Jesus came to proclaim. In the course of the play, Jesus is seen to gaze upon such 'profane' scenes with 'deep satisfaction'.

Jesus' call to 'Follow me' results in Jesus, 'the drunk and the lecher' leading his followers, not to the Kingdom of Heaven but to a brothel where Jesus is physically seduced as whores hail him as 'The Messiah, Son of God'.

The New Testament story of the anointing of Jesus' feet by Mary Magdalene with her precious ointment is presented in this play as an incident of the utmost sexual depravity.

Jesus and his disciples obtain funds for their revolutionary purposes by arming themselves with machine-guns and raiding banks. They are joined by 'the Salvation Army' and by a nun carrying a gun.

The police are identified with Pilate and Herod and are shown on the one hand to be lazy and on the other sadistically to enjoy shooting and killing even kind old ladies. The symbols of Mohammedanism and Buddhism, the Star of David, and Jewish feasts also figure in the play.

That this play is grossly blasphemous and pornographic in language and action there can be no doubt. It is riddled with sedition and infused with hatred while the subliminal techniques employed in the stage directions are geared to poison the mind and soak it with doubt and despair.

Thorsen's aim is clear. It is to give an aura of virtue to social, political and sexual anarchy by identifying them with the virtues of Jesus and so to destroy any faith in Christianity with all that that could mean for the quality of life in our time.

Finally I asked, once again, that Thorsen should be banned from Britain.

The dilemma in which all this placed the Home Secretary

was very real and there is no doubt that the general public was not in the mood to consider the niceties of the law.

The Home Office insisted that there were no regulations which would allow a Government to refuse entrance to an EEC national on the grounds that his presence would deeply offend the prevailing moral climate, although Michael Allison, then Shadow Minister of State at the Home Office, told me that there was no shortage of power to exclude Thorsen if the political will to do so existed. That, of course, was the heart of the matter.

We were given to understand that only if the immigration authorities believed that Thorsen represented a threat to public order could the Home Secretary be recommended to ban such a person. So in theory we were in the anomalous position of having to take the law into our own hands, as it were, in order legally to achieve our object. After petrol bombs were thrown at the Danish Ambassador's residence in Rome, Thorsen was forced to abandon his plan for making the film in Italy. In France, too, he was banned 'as a threat to public order'. So what would happen in Britain? Would the Home Secretary move before or after disorder had broken out, for there were indeed quite a few signs that it might do so, and the longer the Home Secretary prevaricated the more the possibility of violence grew.

But was violence – which we ourselves would never have used – the only weapon left? Of course not. Only a few days after we delivered the script and letter to the Home Secretary I received a letter from Felicity Faulkner, a teacher from Enfield. I had met her briefly for the first time a few evenings previously and had spoken to her of my conviction that there should be a prayer vigil outside the Home Office. 'But,' I told her, 'the trouble is that I really can't organize it because of my other commitments. Someone else will have to.' She wrote to say that she and her clergyman husband Kenneth had been praying and talking about our conversation ever since. And that day, as she had walked the two miles to and from school pondering on *who* could organize such a vigil, she suddenly thought, as she told me afterwards, 'Why somebody else? Why not you? In three week's time you start your half term holiday!'

She was just the person to do it, lively and full of initiative. I think the story should be told in her words as they were published in her local paper the *Enfield Gazette* and *The Catholic Times* the following week:

'You should be round by the back door. That's where the Home Secretary goes in. I know. I clean his windows,' said a window cleaner at the Home Office.

'Sex life? Jesus Christ didn't have one!' exclaimed an outraged American.

All the world certainly converges on London. That was obvious during our week in Whitehall: Americans, Canadians, Australians, New Zealanders, Germans, Austrians, French, Dutch, Danes, Hungarians, Greeks, Israelis, Egyptians, Algerians, South Africans, Pakistanis – all stopped to express their views in support of the Britain they love to visit.

'Jens Thorsen. We are sorry we have him in our country to trouble you,' a Dane apologized.

'I'm an atheist, but this goes too far.'

The quiet vigil on Monday and Tuesday became, on the last three days, a massive 'signing up' at the request of passers-by and in just three days over 2,700 signatures were collected.

'Nobody wants him here, so why didn't the Government say "No" straight away?'

'There shouldn't be any need for you to stand here day after day. . .'

'Well done! Keep it up,' said an employee of the Ministry of Defence; and from one of the Home Office staff. 'Wish I could sign but I work for the man.'

'It isn't Governments which change attitudes, it's always individuals, like Shaftesbury and Wilberforce. . .'

What was frightening and disturbing were the remarks: 'If the Government doesn't take action within the law, we shall be forced to act outside it'; 'Lynch him!' 'Shoot him. No, I'm serious. And if you give me the gun, I'll be glad to do it.'

There was the little crippled lady who could hardly hold the pen but was determined to sign; the elderly man who offered 10p to help with expenses and apologized that it couldn't be more; the painter with his pot of white paint who said, 'Just let him try to come here and I'll paint him white all over'; the youngster who exclaimed, 'That dirty film? No! We don't want that. Disgusting!'

There was the Parliamentary candidate who walked with us from Victoria Station at 7.30 a.m. on Monday; and the Muslim who supported the vigil all that day. There was the 89 year-old who came day after day to stand silently holding a banner; the MP who ran over from the House of Commons to tell us that we had many friends there; the postman who drew up on his bicycle to sign; the bishops who spared time from their central synod meetings to give support and to pray; the nuns who quietly said their rosaries. . .

It must be admitted that, on Thursday, when the rain poured down and pens wouldn't write on the sodden paper, we felt like saying, with St Theresa of Avila, 'Lord, if this is how you treat your friends, no wonder you have so few.' But then, the witness was all the greater in the rain. . .

For the first-time 'campaigner', it was an exhilarating experience. What will stay with me? The kindness and friendliness of the London policemen; the selflessness of those who joined the vigil, the frankness of the Home Secretary, Mr Merlyn Rees, when he came, unbidden, out of the Home Office to speak to us; the overwhelmingly positive and vocal response of the young folk, which in a way was a surprise. The week's experience showed, beyond all doubt, how decent, honest, sincere and solid is the average Britisher, who wants to be proud of his country, bitterly deplores its falling standards and longs for it to stand up, fearlessly, for what it knows to be right.

The 'frankness' of the Home Secretary to which Felicity referred can be filled out a little by my own notes of what she told me occurred. Merlyn Rees she said 'was most kind and encouraging'. He told her that he was a Christian too and that he had given instructions that Thorsen must be stopped if he attempted to come into the country.

'So I can go home now?' she said delightedly and the Home Secretary replied, 'Certainly you have achieved what you set out to do . . . but you are most welcome to stay!'

At one point a man came up to her and told her that he had come from Thorsen – did she have a message for him? 'Tell him the British people won't have him here!' And, as everyone knows, he never came – at least, no closer than Heathrow.

Thorsen, insensitive and determined as ever, arrived in Britain on 9 February the following year carrying a copy of a film script he proposed to make. He was refused entry into Britain by Mr Merlyn Rees who according to the press 'was loudly cheered by both Government and Opposition MPs when he interrupted a speech he was making to announce the banning of the producer'.

The Home Secretary said that Mr Thorsen's exclusion was considered 'conducive to the public good'. The decision to exclude Thorsen was widely believed at the time to have been made personally by Mr Rees. Felicity Faulkner must have felt a very personal interest and warm glow of appreciation when she read that.

It is apparently extremely rare for one Common Market country to ban entry to the citizen of another and it happened only after five hours of questioning – during which time the Home Secretary was kept constantly in touch. Thorsen claimed that the film script he had in his possession was not *Life of Jesus Christ* but another one called *Jesus Returns*. At the end of the questioning by immigration officials a senior officer read the following statement to the squat, bearded Dane:

> You have asked for leave to enter the United Kingdom to attend publicity reviews of the film *The Dream of 13* but you are carrying with you the script of a film of the sex life of Jesus.
>
> I consider that your presence in the United Kingdom would be likely to result in public demonstrations and might occasion breaches of the peace, and I therefore refuse you leave to enter on the

grounds that your exclusion is conducive to the public good.

Before leaving Britain Thorsen said he had been deported because he had with him the script for the second film on the sex life of Jesus – called *Jesus Returns*. He was then put on a Copenhagen-bound plane.

Chapter 13

Kiddie porn

'We are not dealing with little old grandparents who want to photograph the newborn grandchild bare on bearskin rugs. We are dealing with organized crime – the same people who filled this country with narcotics,' Dr Judianne Densen-Gerber told the United States House of Representatives Sub-Committee on Crime in 1977. She went on to demand the introduction of legislation to protect 'children who are being prostituted and "sexualised" by the child pornographers. . . Many such,' she said, 'are now on computers which enable them to be moved from city to city depending on the special desires of the children-hawks and others. . . The fact that the children used in sexual snuff films[1] are purchased from Mexico is well known. Less well known is the fact that many of our children have been sold for this purpose abroad.'

She then referred to the work of Robin Lloyd, author of *Boy Prostitution in America* and said that together they had 'counted 264 different magazines produced each month that use male children. The people who support and buy this kind of material are strengthening their paedophiliac fantasies. Now, when fantasies are stimulated people go home and act out. For example, there is no doubt that incest is on the rise. Indeed, Dr Henry Giarretto, the leading worker in incest in the country had 50 cases reported to him the first year, 350 cases the second year and we will have over 800 cases this year.' She then gave the Committee details of the contents of a magazine *Little Girls* which I could not repeat here, and

---

[1] 'Snuff films': the name given to films in which both children and adults actually die in the carrying out of sexual perversions before the cameras.

went on to claim that: 'A magazine produced in the United States, purchased in Philadelphia, February, called *Pre-Teen Sexuality* tells the reader how to penetrate a pre-pubescent girl who is not yet able because of her smallness to be penetrated in a standard missionary position. . . Work in Australia by Dr Malcolm Copplestone, a gynaecologist and Odyssey Board Member, has shown that children who have pre-pubescent intercourse have the highest incidence of cervical carcinoma of all women in the 20s and 30s age groups. Therefore, we are talking about damage physically as well as emotionally and other psychological ways. Girls at nine were not designed by nature to satisfy the perverted needs of adult males. Also published are primers to tell people how to pick up children in a park, molest them and not be arrested.'

Later Dr Gerber was asked by the Chairman of the Committee, 'How many young people do you think are being affected by abuse and pornography?'

'I have personally counted 400 different children. In a recent arrest in Cleveland, one photographer had 300 children in his employ. But if we include prostitution and the advertising of children for purposes of prostitution then we have close to 1 million children sexually and commercially exploited. . . The Los Angeles Police Department says there are 30,000 children in L.A. alone who are being used sexually. The FBI reports 1 million runaways. The majority are being supported sexually. How else can these children support themselves? Funding for runaways programs is almost non-existent, and so far our Government has not wanted to examine it.'

'In other words,' the Chairman said, 'this problem goes farther than the abuse of children in filming and movies?'

Not only were we in National VALA aware of what was happening in the States; we were also aware of what was happening in Europe. Our colleagues in Germany, Denmark and Sweden had sent us evidence of the proliferation of 'kiddie porn' in their countries. So far as we knew there was very little yet in Britain. But we were determined to be ready for it when it came.

Very shortly after we received a copy of the Densen-

Gerber material from the States, I was approached by a man whom I was to know only by a pseudonym for many months. He told me he had 'inside' information about child pornography in Britain and later gave me details about how to track down one of the main sources of it in the country (this only a few days after the end of the *Gay News* trial – see chapters 14,15). Could I 'seek the seas at His behest and brave another cruise'? Well, there was really only one answer to that.

I was pretty sure that the only way to get legislation onto the statute book to outlaw child pornography was through a Private Member's Bill. All our experience taught us that there was no hope of the Labour Government then in power introducing such a measure. There was no time to waste. Somehow Parliament and the country had to be alerted to just how bad this material was. I thought about Mrs Thatcher, then Leader of the Opposition. 'She's a *woman*, she'll care,' I said to myself. And I was right. I managed to get through to her on the phone the following morning and we talked for about twenty minutes. I noted in my diary that night: 'She shares totally our concern about "kiddie porn" and wants to be involved personally with the fight against it. I told her that I believed the Home Office Committee[1] was a 'loaded' one set up by the Labour Government as an alibi for action. And in any case it was not expected to report for two years. She told me she had to go to the US tomorrow but would meet me as soon as she returns next week.'

It was at this point that I saw some examples of hardcore child pornography for the first time and I could not sleep that night. I lay and thought to myself, 'How can a society which even begins to countenance such things deserve to survive?' And I remembered some words which had been quoted to me in a different context: 'There is a hole in the heart of the world which can be filled only by Almighty God.' 'There is indeed a hole in the heart of the world,' I thought, 'and if we are not careful it's going to be filled with the discarded bodies of little children broken to satisfy human lust for money and for sex.'

---

[1] Home Office Committee on Obscenity and Film Censorship under the Chairmanship of Professor Bernard Williams.

The anger that the photographs aroused in me cleared my mind of any hesitancy and next morning I rang the Home Secretary's Private Office and spoke to Mr Merlyn Rees's personal assistant. I asked if it was possible for me to come and see the Minister and told him why. I said, I 'may as well be honest — I am not prepared to come to the Home Office to be fobbed off with some junior official in the foyer'. I also told him that I would shortly be seeing Mrs Thatcher, the Opposition Leader, but that I felt it only proper and fair that I should present my evidence to the Home Secretary first.

Thus began my tussle with the Home Office civil servants which later gave me so much appreciation of the BBC TV series *Yes, Minister!* Two days later I had a call to say that Mr Rees was 'on holiday' (it was, after all, early September). He was therefore unable to see me personally but he had suggested that I should see Mr Moriarty, Permanent Under Secretary at the Home Office. 'That is not at all what we wanted,' I declared – I hope courteously.

When I look back I am amazed at my own temerity. There was I standing on my high horse and wondering whether or not I'd accept the Home Secretary's suggestion that I should meet one of his staff. But the photographs of those children still burned in my mind and I felt that the Home Secretary and only the Home Secretary would do. But I was very much an amateur in the political field, so I sought the advice of a person whom I knew would guide me wisely. Did he think my hunch was not to accept an invitation to meet a Permanent Under Secretary was right?

'Absolutely,' he said but suggested that I write at once to Mr Rees to explain why I felt it essential that I should see him. I should make the point that he, as an MP, was an elected representative of the people and in a position to demand the immediate attention of the House and ensure that the necessary legislation be put on the statute book. A civil servant, no matter how senior, did not have this power. So that was what I did.

Incidentally I heard later that the civil servant who had first written to say that the Home Secretary could not see me had done so off his own bat and had never mentioned the matter to the Minister at all. But no doubt that's what personal assistants are for!

However, in the meantime I'd been to the House of Commons to meet Mrs Thatcher. She'd come in specially, holidays or no holidays, to give me whatever time was necessary. We had a long talk and then she sat down at her desk and wrote a letter to the Home Secretary and after discussing it with the Shadow Home Secretary, Mr Whitelaw, she sent it round by a messenger to the Home Office. 'Run as fast as your legs will take you!' she told him. She allowed five minutes for him to get there and then we went out to meet the press.

A *Times* leader had this to say next morning: '. . . the case against child pornography was put succinctly in a letter to the Home Secretary by Mrs Thatcher. She has given her firm support to Mrs Whitehouse's campaign for a change in the law. Above all our children must be protected from those who would use them in this way. They cannot protect themselves and we have a duty to see that they are protected by law. . . Mrs Thatcher and Mrs Whitehouse . are absolutely right to demand early legislation in this field. There is no reason why the Home Secretary should not promise to bring in a Bill as soon as the Parliamentary timetable permits.'

All the press coverage of these events had their own spin-off and their lighter side. The following morning my phone rang at 7.30. An obviously very illiterate man said he'd found some pornographic magazines in a waste bin outside a primary school.

'Well,' I said, 'why not take them to the police station?'

'I can't do *that*,' he said. 'They'd put me inside.' Perhaps he'd been rummaging in the bin for his morning's breakfast, poor chap.

But in all the correspondence which passed between the Minister's Private Secretary, Mr P. J. Honour, and myself it remained clear that Mr Rees was personally determined to by-pass our anxieties if he could.

On the general issues of obscenity and film censorship the Home Secretary has appointed a Committee of

Inquiry[1] . . . the responsibility for the investigation of alleged criminal offences rests with the Chief Officer of the police concerned advised as appropriate by the Director of Public Prosecutions (2 September 1977).

I pointed out to the Home Secretary (9 September 1977) that the whole point of the exercise was to introduce *new* legislation. That was the role of Parliament and not the role of the police or the DPP. They could only operate such laws as already existed. Not, of course, that he didn't already know that.

A few days later Mr James Callaghan, then the Prime Minister, made a major speech (12 September) in which he said that oil was 'God's gift to Britain'. So it may be, I said in a letter to him:

But how much more are the children? You challenge us not to waste our resources. How, then, can you be so silent in the face of the greatest exploitation of all – namely the use of children's bodies to gratify the lusts of men?

It is a source of constant amazement and dismay to many of us that your Government and party, rooted as it was in the Methodist revival, now seems so reluctant to speak out on moral issues.

All I got in reply to *that* was a suggestion that the Williams Committee would 'be very glad to receive any evidence' that we could put to them and a renewed hope that I would meet with, by this time my old friend, Mr Moriarty.

This letter from the Prime Minister was followed by a letter from Mr Moriarty himself asking me to deliver our evidence to him or arrange for him to collect it so that he could draw the attention of the police to it. In my reply I said that the police had already seen the material in question and that it was in the hands of the Obscene Publications Department of the Metropolitan Police and of senior police officers in Liverpool and Birmingham. But I told him, too

[1] The Williams Committee on Obscenity and Film Censorship.

(again!) that: 'It remains a matter of regret to me that the Home Secretary or his Minister of State[1] has not seen fit to express his personal view more directly.'

But the Home Secretary was not moved. He was 'advised', he told Parliament (November 1977), that in the field of child pornography 'offences which might not be caught by existing legislation rarely occur'. I wrote to *The Times* (23 November) to say that I was surprised by the Home Secretary's statement:

Take first what is now the considerable import of such material from the Continent by means of the 'roll-on, roll-off' container lorries. All law enforcement bodies are aware of this and of course it presents a difficult problem. We are currently endeavouring to raise this matter through the good offices of sympathisers in Europe and in Britain with the Council of Europe. But why us? Why has not the Government itself dealt with this matter by demanding that the European Governments concerned ensure that British Customs and Excise legislation is not deliberately infringed in this way?

Take next the freely available magazines which contain titillating, though not obscene, photographs, particularly of young boys. These are not covered by any law. Our information is that the police are aware of studios in our big cities where young boys, and sometimes young girls, are photographed in the nude for such magazines and are not infrequently sexually assaulted. Even in these circumstances there are difficulties in bringing action.

The Home Secretary should also look at that flourishing section of the pornography industry, largely left unprosecuted, which publishes – in many so-called 'girlie' magazines – obscene and indecent photographs of young female models dressed as children. Such material surely amounts to incitement to commit

[1] The Rt Hon. Brynmor John.

offences against children? This vogue has inevitably led
to the use of real children.

The truth is that in the whole area of public decency
there has existed in the Home Office, the office of the
Director of Public Prosecutions and the office of the
Attorney General a consistent unwillingness to take
effective action. It is this attitude which has finally put
the Home Secretary at such a disadvantage now that
he, the Government and the Country are face to face
with a form of exploitation which deeply shocks us all.

Ronald Butt writing in *The Times* urged that Parliament
should not let Merlyn Rees wait 'timorously' for the Williams
Report because the 'abominable evil' of child pornography
destroyed children in two ways. 'Directly, it murders emotionally those whom it uses to make its marketable products.
Indirectly, it damages more children by stimulating and encouraging deviance of those whose own sexual drive is dangerous to them. If our society concludes that this doesn't
matter, then it concludes that nothing does.'

But barely a week later the whole argument moved into
a different dimension. Mr Cyril Townsend, Conservative MP
for Bexley Heath announced at his constituency meeting that
he proposed to use the opportunity provided by his success
in the draw for Private Members' Bills to introduce legislation
to control child pornography.

In the meantime I had a phone-call from Cardinal
Hume's press officer. The Cardinal was meeting with the
Archbishop of Canterbury, the Chief Rabbi, the Moderator
of the Free Church Council, and he intended to raise the
matter of child pornography with them. The Cardinal himself
needs no persuading, I was told, but does find himself at a
disadvantage in his approach to the other church leaders, as
he has not *seen* any. Could I send him some? 'Heavens,' I
said. 'I'd be run in.' Imagine the headlines: 'Mrs Whitehouse
charged with sending obscene material through the post to
His Eminence the Cardinal.' The mind boggled! However,
I did put a catalogue advertising child pornography and
some of the 'boy magazines' into an envelope and posted it

to the press officer without giving any indication of who had sent it.

As the early weeks and months of 1978 passed it became evident that the Labour Government did not intend to support Cyril Townsend's Bill – in spite of the fact that our ABUSE[1] petition carried 1,600,000 names, i.e. 99.9 per cent of those who'd had the opportunity to sign it – and the fear that it might be 'talked out' by someone on the Government benches was very real. What else, we asked ourselves, could still be done to arouse public and parliamentary opinion so that the Government would *have* to change its attitude? It was at this point that I thought again of Dr Judianne Densen-Gerber. Could we persuade her to come over to Britain?

On 9 January 1978 I rang Dr Densen-Gerber's secretary at the Odyssey Institute in New York. We'd had a quick look at National VALA's bank account and decided that we could just manage the cost of her return flight (tourist). We could keep down expenses by arranging accommodation for her in the home of one of our friends rather than in an hotel.

A call came from New York on the 12th – Dr Densen-Gerber had been making enquiries about us and was apparently quite satisfied with what she heard. She would be happy to come to Britain, 'but there were problems – because of a certain physical ailment it would be necessary for her to travel first class'. More than a little taken aback I said I'd talk it over and ring back. When we discovered that the round first class fare would be £1,000 instead of the £300 for which we were budgeting we were even more taken aback. However we felt that we should go ahead with her visit, and trust that the money would come.

In the middle of all this I contracted the cough which was to play such havoc with me later, and it was while I was spending a couple of days in bed that I was told that the Home Office – in other words the Home Secretary – had called off the team of eight police officers allocated to child pornography in one of the London boroughs 'even though

[1] Action to Ban Sexual Exploitation of Children.

they had uncovered enough crime connected with it to keep them busy for three years. The police have uncovered a racket in children which extends across the country but the Home Office is not prepared to take the matter any further'.

Later the same week we finalized Dr Densen-Gerber's visit over the phone with New York and in the process were told that because her health made it inadvisable that she travel alone she would be bringing with her Dr Stepan Hutchson, an Attorney and Executive Director of the Institute of Law and Medicine. He was, we were told, 'the world expert on child pornography law having advised thirty-four States on behalf of the Federal Government'. However, he would be prepared to travel tourist – which was just as well!

Hardly had I recovered from that when I got a call from Judianne Densen-Gerber herself. It was the first time we'd spoken to one another; she sounded a most warm and friendly person. She'd rung to say that her great friend 'whose husband owns the biggest off-shore oil well in the world' would be flying out to London at the same time ('Heavens, not another fare!' I thought desperately) so that they could do some theatres together. Did I think she, too, could stay with the young American couple who were giving her hospitality (these were the same friends that gave me much support in the court during the blasphemy case several months before).

By now I felt rather as though the whole project had taken off into outer space with me inside! And that feeling wasn't dispelled when, shortly after, I had a call from a friend of Judianne's in London. She'd apparently been with her in New York when I first rang.

'She is huge,' she said. 'She weighs about 20 stone though she is slimming – but she's beautiful – has a mind like a rapier which cuts through the slightest sign of humbug or prevarication.'

'What's she like on television?' I asked weakly.

'Magnificent,' she said.

By now I felt completely overwhelmed – and worried. I wondered how much the whole visit was going to embarrass Cyril Townsend, let alone everyone else. I talked over my anxieties with my friends in the office.

'Well,' said one of them, 'it's all in the hands of the Lord.'

Somewhat testily I replied, 'You can hardly expect him to knock off half a dozen stones in little more than a week!'

About a quarter of an hour later the phone rang again – it was the same woman.

'I'm so sorry. I should have said that Judi weighed 200 pounds, not 20 stone.' That was precisely what he had done! So not for the first time in this extraordinary experience I lifted a thankful heart.

The next day I shall never forget. London Weekend – who were doing a programme about me for their *Credo* series – came at 10 a.m. and we worked through till 3 p.m. I should have done this interview several weeks previously but had been unable to do so because of my cough. I had no time whatever to prepare for that night's debate at Cambridge University and on the way there I felt so ill and was so sick at the side of the road that I said to Ernest, who was driving me there, 'What on earth am I doing driving along on this dark, rainy night in the middle of winter when I should be in bed at home. I must be *mad*.' We felt very tempted to turn round and go home but, of course, we didn't. Even so, I felt it was make or break – I have *never* felt so ill and exhausted before a meeting. LWE who were filming the whole debate for the *Credo* programme were already there when we arrived. I wrote in my diary next morning:

When it came to it, not only did I manage it, voice non-existent and all, but I felt more abandoned and free than I have ever done before. The students gave me – and the Union was packed to capacity and beyond – a tremendous reception. The applause went on and on! Mind you, we lost the motion by 150 votes. But that I think was because the motion 'That the press was abusing its freedom' was turned by the Opposition into a debate about the freedom of the press, which is quite a different thing. Ernest, who'd been up in the gallery, gave me the most tremendous hug in front of everyone when he came into the retiring room afterwards. Sandy Gaul of ITN and 'William Hickey' with whom I'd been debating were very kind too!

Then back to the Densen-Gerber visit.

My letter enquiring whether the Home Secretary would like to meet her had not been answered, so I rang the Minister's Office. The letter had been drafted. The Minister was grateful for the suggestion but he was too busy to spare the time. A journalist whom I knew well told me later that the reason being given privately by the Home Office was my refusal to see Mr Moriarty last summer. As I entered this in my diary at the time, I went on: 'I'd wondered about that myself but dismissed the idea as too absurd. But isn't it incredible that a powerful Ministry like the Home Office – or any other Ministry for that matter – should so demean itself as to put the welfare of the nation's children at risk because someone's peeved!'

But the same day we heard that at least the Government would not oppose Cyril Townsend's Bill and indeed with the signatures pouring in on the Abuse petition – 1,600,000 in little more than three months – it would have been very foolhardy to have done so.

Judi Densen-Gerber's week in Britain was certainly memorable for us and I think for her too. She heard that the President of the United States had signed what was to all intents and purposes *her* Bill to make 'kiddie porn' illegal on the very day that she arrived in Britain to help get similar legislation on the statute book here by the end of that week.

Media interviews with her followed one after another. She visited New Scotland Yard then went to the House of Commons to meet the Shadow Home Secretary, William Whitelaw, and the Shadow Attorney General, Sir Michael Havers. I wrote in my diary that night that both men had seen the child pornography which the DPP had in his possession but some of Judi's material involving very little children was so shattering that Mr Whitelaw dropped his head into his hands, he was so distressed by it.

We went from there to meet Baroness Elles who was very anxious to ensure that the Bill got safely and quickly through the Lords, and Judianne addressed a meeting of MPs in the House of Commons. But still the Home Secretary was not prepared to meet her.

In the middle of this very busy week, while I was in

London for the day, a man who said he was speaking on behalf of the International Socialists rang home to say that I was going to be killed. Whoever it was gave poor Ernest the impression that they had already got hold of me. He rang through to friends in London to see if I was there and was told that I had gone to catch a train considerably earlier than the one I actually caught. He went to meet it and, of course, I wasn't there – though I turned up safely several hours later. Then next day there was a threat to burn the house down. I thought then, as I've thought many times, that it's often a great deal easier to be at the centre of the action than to sit on the sidelines, as Ernest was doing that week.

On the Friday of that week[1] the Protection of the Child Bill had its second reading. Judi and I sat together in the House of Commons gallery from 10.45 a.m. to 3.55 p.m. The demand for the Speaker's eye during the debate was intense. Almost every Member seemed to jump up when one sat down. The Home Office in the shape of Mr Brynmor John had considerably changed its position – denied any lagging behind. The reference by Mrs Jill Knight, Conservative MP for Edgbaston, to the fact that the Home Secretary had been unwilling to see me or Dr Densen-Gerber caused one of the few rows of the day.

Clearly all the meetings and especially the time Judi had had with William Whitelaw and Sir Michael Havers had paid off marvellously, for she was referred to time and again during the debate. At one point she asked me – in the gallery where one is not supposed to utter a word – if I would send a telegram to the Home Secretary asking if he would see her before she left for home on Sunday.

'No good sending a telegram because he's sitting down below,' I whispered. 'But I'll go down and write a note to that effect, so it can be passed in to him.' This I did, telling the Home Secretary that Dr Densen-Gerber was in the gallery and would be very happy to meet him at any time. When I got back to my seat I asked if Mr Rees had been given the note. She nodded.

'What did he do?' I whispered again.

[1] 10 February 1978.

'Tore it up,' she said.

However, she didn't let that spoil what had been a wonderful week. The US Congress had passed unanimously what was virtually her Bill at the beginning of it and at the end she had seen a similar Bill given its second reading in the UK Parliament without a dissenting voice. The sound of the roar of that unanimous 'Aye' and the dead silence when the Speaker called for the 'No's' – I shall never forget. Neither shall I forget what happened when I went down into the Central Lobby to write the note to the Home Secretary. A parliamentary official came up to me and asked if I would speak to a clown who was amongst those demonstrating outside in favour of the Bill. They brought him into the Central Lobby and it turned out to be none other than Pierre Coco's successor – a rather splendid young man dressed in his full regalia. He gave me his telephone number and asked me to call him any time I felt he could help, which was lovely.

This was the day on which the coach-load of 'gays' came to demonstrate outside our house. It was also the day on which I retired to bed with pneumonia. This eventually led to me having to rest my voice completely for several months later that year – that was when the idea that I was retiring got around!

The Child Protection Bill, which Cyril Townsend had so skilfully piloted through Parliament, finally became law in July 1978. This despite Mr Ian Mikardo's attempt to talk it out and the opposition to it in the Lords from the humanist peer Lord Houghton.

Chapter 14

'Scurrilous profanity'

I wonder if any prayer uttered in recent years has been given such notoriety as the one which I and several of my friends offered up in the corridors of the Old Bailey on 12 July 1977? Or for that matter has been so misrepresented?

It all happened because the journalist from *The Guardian* covering the *Gay News* blasphemy case reported that my friends and I had 'prayed' together while waiting for the verdict. Before we knew where we were, not only had we gone down on our knees in the middle of the milling crowds outside Court, but we were praying, so Lord Willis the humanist peer said when he introduced his Bill to repeal the blasphemy law (23 February 1978), 'to Jesus Christ to influence a verdict which could send a man to prison'. He found this 'not only repulsive but a blasphemy of the worst kind' which 'seared itself upon his consciousness'.

'Did the gentle Jesus in whom Christians so devoutly believe applaud when he heard those prayers ascending from the Old Bailey?' Lord Willis wondered. 'If he exists,' he went on, 'I prefer to think that he watered heaven with his tears, weeping for the foolishness and prejudice of mankind.'

Poor Lord Willis. If he had taken the trouble to ask us what actually happened while we waited for hour after hour for the verdict I could certainly have saved him a lot of pain. The truth of the matter was very different. Perhaps I should go back to the beginning of the story.

I first saw a copy of the poem 'The love that dares to speak its name' on 1 November 1976, just as our campaign against the Thorsen film ended. It came in the morning's post, without any indication of where it had been published, and as I read it through the initial shock was very great. Coming so quickly after the Thorsen saga it was almost overwhelming as its immediate impact. There seemed no end to the vilification of Christ.

I felt quite simply deeply ashamed that Christ should be treated in this way. It seemed to me like a kind of re-crucifixion, only this time with twentieth-century weapons. And I experienced a great longing to try to make some kind of reparation out of love for him. It seemed to me that if I did nothing I would be like that priest and Levite in Jesus' story of the Good Samaritan, who 'passed by on the other side'.

Despite all that came and went in the months and indeed years that followed – and much did – nothing changed that initial reaction or altered my motivation.

Both Graham Ross-Cornes, my solicitor, and John Smyth QC are committed Christians and I knew I could trust their judgement. In the event they were both quite convinced that the poem, which spoke of the homosexual relationships Jesus was purported to have had with his disciples and about the violation of his dead body as it hung on the cross, transgressed the law of blasphemous libel. The fact there had been no blasphemy action for fifty-two years seemed to them quite irrelevant. The blasphemy law had been restated throughout the intervening years and indeed as recently as 1975, so there was no question of us – as so many of my opponents have said – turning to the use of 'outdated' legislation.

A private prosecution in my name was launched against *Gay News* and at no time did the Attorney General take over the case, though it was frequently claimed that he did. As a matter of fact, at just about the same time but unknown to us, the Earl of Lauderdale did send a copy of the poem to the Director of Public Prosecutions, then Sir Norman Skelhorn who, in his reply, said that he was about to discuss the matter with the police when he saw the report in *The Times* that I was initiating legal action. The Director stated that he would 'consider taking over the case in the public interest' were I to request him to do so. But I felt that we had a very special commitment to this case and that we neither could nor should pass it over to someone else.

We learnt many things the hard way in the months that

lay ahead. We had decided to approach church leaders in
case expert witnesses would be called but it became clear
before very long that there existed considerable reluctance
within the church to get involved. Considering the recent
uproar over the Thorsen project and not least Dr Coggan's
statement that he himself might use the blasphemy law to
stop Thorsen, this seemed to us to be quite extraordinary
and I wrote to the Archbishops of Canterbury and York in
the following terms:

> I understand that there is some anxiety lest the church
> is seen to be associated with a case which is lost on a
> technical point. But the judge who gave leave to us to
> bring the prosecution looked most carefully into every
> aspect of the case and satisfied himself that there was
> no such possibility. But may I please say that if the case
> were lost on such a point, at least the world will see
> that the church leaders were ready to defend their Lord,
> and only the *case* would be lost. If there is no voice from
> the church and the case is lost because John Mortimer,
> who is defending (and does so always in pornography
> cases on the grounds of how silly it is to make a fuss
> about such a triviality) will be able to say 'Dear me,
> what is all the fuss about. Evidently this is not really
> blasphemous or surely the leaders of the church would
> have something to say!' The case could be lost on far
> more serious grounds than a technical point, and could
> well be the last blasphemy case which ever could be
> brought.
>
> You may well ask whether it was wise to bring the
> case in the first place. But *Gay News* is not a little back-
> street publication – it is sold in some branches of W. H.
> Smith, it is found in all public libraries, and goes into
> many schools, and into all colleges and universities. The
> poem was not written by some lonely pathetic
> homosexual, but by an Englishman who holds the Chair
> of Poetry at an American University and has done
> similar work in a number of European Universities.
>
> One has seen how, in the whole field of
> pornography, the effectiveness of the law has been

destroyed by the failure of prosecuting authorities to
take action. If this poem had been allowed to pass then
what would have happened next?

I trust that you will forgive me if I say that the
developments over the last week have left me
dumbfounded. In no way could I ever have imagined
that this poem could have done anything but rouse the
church to action. Now I find myself alone – that is
irrelevant in terms of what happens to me, but for the
idea that the Lord was homosexual, and for the
perverted practices on his dead body not to be seen to
be blasphemous if the case is lost – about that I am lost
for words!

Dr Coggan replied by saying that he was 'puzzled' by my
letter. 'Cardinal Basil Hume and I refused to come forward
as witnesses in the *Gay News* trial only after most careful
thought, and Mr Ross-Cornes assured my Registrar, Mr
David Carey, that he fully understood our reasons. We are
not suggesting that (to use a phrase in your letter) there
should be "no voice from the church" or that you would
"find yourself alone". What we are suggesting is that a jury
of twelve persons who may in the main, or perhaps all, be
non-believers is far more likely to be influenced by an ordinary person who testifies that the poem satisfies the definition
of blasphemy (i.e. is "ribald, indecent and offensive") than
by "professional" church leaders like ourselves put up as
witnesses.' That indeed is understandable, but it has been
suggested many times since that the real reason why the
church leaders did not wish to become involved lay in the
topic of the poem, namely homosexuality. And certainly a
massive media campaign was launched to make it appear
that my motivation was not love of Christ but hatred of
homosexuals. Nothing could have been further from the
truth.

I still feel, looking back, that this was a sad business for
the church and certainly as events developed and I was seen
to be, publicly at least, alone, it looked increasingly as though
the church had been very clever in the ways of the world.

It was at our first legal conference that we discovered that

James Kirkup, who wrote the poem, was in fact Professor of Poetry at Massachusetts University with about six column inches to his name in *Who's Who*. Not that that really made any difference except that one could see what John Mortimer, defending counsel on this, as on so many other obscenity trials, would make of it. I could hear the cries of 'Philistine', 'Censorship' echoing through the land.

The 'opposition' was not slow to mobilize. *The Guardian* (13 December) announced that a 'fighting fund' was to be launched for *Gay News* because it 'cannot possibly compete with Mary Whitehouse and her backers'. It was a strange expression to use. As I wrote in my diary, 'If by my backer they mean God Almighty, well that is true, but if they are referring to a human backer, he doesn't exist!' As far as finance was concerned I had to trust – and I did and do – that God would provide.

A couple of days later *The Guardian* carried a letter from Nicolas Walter of the Rationalist Press saying that the *Gay News* poem would be sent to anyone sending a stamped addressed envelope. So often I have been accused of bringing the poem to the attention of people who would not otherwise have seen it, but I was not responsible for the activities of the Gay/humanist lobby which continued after the verdict and the appeal, when clearly the distribution itself was illegal.

Then there was the incredible 'United Order of Blasphemers' – formed in 1844 so one was given to understand, 'to assist publishers and booksellers persecuted for distributing blasphemous literature' and now reformed by opponents of the blasphemy law 'to publish works which have resulted in blasphemous prosecutions'. They marked the first anniversary of the *Gay News* trial by sending – so they said – copies of James Kirkup's poem to Judge King-Hamilton and the Director of Public Prosecutions. (They don't seem to have celebrated an anniversary since!)

A bad business, but at least people could see what the trouble was all about and could be challenged in their own consciences. As a matter of fact quite a number of homosexuals wrote to me to say that they were very unhappy that the poem should have been printed at all.

The *Gay News* trial was held at the Central Criminal

Court in London 4–12 July 1977 presided over by Judge King-Hamilton. *Gay News* was defended by Geoffrey Robertson and Denis Lemon by John Mortimer QC. The events of those days were extensively written about, not only in Britain but in many countries abroad. They were reproduced on television in the BBC1 *Everyman* series and the preparation for that programme began well before the trial actually started. Incidentally, one of the many letters I received about that programme said that 'The trial came over as a classical example of British justice. Counsel on both sides were brilliant and equally matched. The Judge's summing up was masterly and the jury took their time.'

One of my most vivid memories of the trial was the sight and sound of Geoffrey Robertson, who is a 'protestant sceptic', speaking with such intimate knowledge – and indeed perception – of the New Testament and its teachings. I was told that he had 'rarely been seen without a copy in his hands for the last six months' and I would like to think that the effect of his study of it will not have ended with the trial.

At the end of the first day I told my diary:

Mortimer, usually so confident and full of joking assumption that, of course, the prosecution's case is a lot of silly nonsense and no one could really take it seriously, seemed much less so today. The whole of the morning was spent trying to persuade the jury that the case should not have been brought to court at all, that there was no justification for a blasphemy law since Britain was no longer Christian, that it was an insult to other religions for Christians alone to be protected, and that if the poem had to come before the court at all it should be under the Obscene Publications Act. All these contentions were firmly dismissed by Judge King-Hamilton, who also turned down *Gay News'* request that they should be allowed to tape-record the proceedings. 'Can you give me a good reason why the normal procedure of the Court should be waived Mr Mortimer?'

John Mortimer also wanted John Smyth to make his opening address *before* the jury had seen a copy of the

poem, because, he said, this is normal practice in
obscenity cases. 'But this is not an obscenity case, Mr
Mortimer' said the Judge. He was overruled and it was
at this point that the jury – 14 objections to its
composition had been made by the defence – were given
the poem to read for the first time. What a pregnant
and total silence descended on the Court and I felt for
those very ordinary people who cannot have read
anything like it before. I just prayed, and I knew that
friends dotted about amongst the crowd of Gay-libbers
in the corridors outside the Court were praying too, that
the Holy Spirit would move in their hearts. John
Smyth's address to them was splendid – very simple
and illuminated by his own Christian faith as he went
through the poem, line by line.

The following day – in fact every day of the trial – was
equally dramatic. The poor jury was inside the Court for
only about three minutes and they spent a glorious summer
day cooped up in an anteroom waiting to be re-called. Much
of the argument was around the defence's request that it
should be allowed to call 'expert witnesses'. I wrote in my
diary that night: 'Mortimer and Robertson tried hard to
persuade the judge that experts should be called because,
they said, the tenets of the Christian faith have changed –
Christ was a man – capable of sin – the jury with their lack
of knowledge of modern theology could not know this. So my
hunch was correct – before this case is out, if they have their
way, Christ will be a homosexual too! The rest of the day
was like something out of a fantasy – Mortimer would not
concede that the man in the dock *was* Denis Lemon or that
the copy of *Gay News* which the judge held up in his hand
was a copy of *Gay News* or, for that matter, that the paper
existed.'
    I shall never forget the dreadful sense of despair which
overwhelmed me after hearing Geoffrey Robertson sum up
for the defence seven days later. It was a truly remarkable
performance. His manner was gentle and persuasive. In the
silence that fell upon the court Robertson talked about God's
love for sinners, and for homosexuals who, like everyone else,

must have the hope of salvation and redemption – how I agreed. He spoke about the imagery which characterized the Christian faith.

Then he picked up *The Book of Common Prayer* and drew the attention of the jury to the words of the communion service: 'This is my Body – *eat* this. This is my Blood – *drink* this.' But, as I wrote that night: 'in some strange unbelievable way there has been more of the Gospel preached in this Court this week – in spite of the motivation of those who preached it – than surely ever before in its history. God *must* have spoken through Robertson's words, whatever his intent. All the Gays, secularists, and others who packed that Court must have glimpsed something of the wonder and beauty of the Christian faith and God must surely have spoken in many hearts. A wonderful example of the way he can and does use all things to his purpose.' Even so, as one legal expert said to me as I left the Court that day, referring to Geoffrey Robertson's address to the jury, 'After that, the phrase "The Devil's Advocate" takes on a whole new meaning.' It did indeed.

I left the Court quite overwhelmed by a feeling that, after listening to Robertson, the jury would be bound to return a verdict of 'Not Guilty'. If that was so, by bringing the case to Court I could well have opened the floodgates not only to the obscene but to the utterly and unbelievably blasphemous. As I travelled home I felt utterly desolate. The burden of what I felt I had done was insupportable. And the whole of that weekend I was utterly exhausted both phsycially and mentally. I just lay in the garden, lovingly cared for by my family.

Late on Sunday night one of the friends who had been in Court all day with me the previous Friday rang me up. 'Turn to 2 Chronicles Chapter 20 verses 15–18,' he said and rang off. I reached for my Bible and this is what I read:

Thus saith the Lord unto you, be not afraid nor
dismayed by reason of this great multitude; for the
battle is not yours, but God's. Tomorrow go ye down
. . . ye shall not need to fight in this battle: set
yourselves, stand ye still, and see the salvation of the

Lord. . . Fear not, nor be dismayed . . . for the Lord will
be with you.

'*Tomorrow go ye down.*' How amazing. Those words brought
peace and I fell asleep to wake rested in the morning.

It was a day carved for ever on my memory. I wrote in
my diary that evening:

> In his summing up Judge King-Hamilton stripped all
> the nonsense off Geoffrey Robertson's "symbolism". He
> praised him for the eloquence of his speech which,
> however, he said was totally irrelevant. He dealt firmly
> with John Mortimer's references to "a private
> individual" who according to him had brought the case
> "out of malice", and as good as told the jury that the
> threat of "the dark prison cell" to which Mortimer had
> told the jury they would condemn Lemon if they found
> him guilty, was to be put out of their minds. He
> instructed them to cast their minds back to the moment
> when they had first read the poem – that was what
> mattered, he said. Was it possible to conceive anything
> more obscene and blasphemous than, particularly, the
> fourth verse of the poem?

The jury went out at 12.30 p.m. and the tension outside the
Court as press and public waited for the jury to return was
intense.

The prayer we knew was going up all over the country
was a great support. It was just before 5.30 p.m. when Mary
Davey, the young American girl who came every day to the
trial and whom I had never met before that week, stopped
as we walked together along the corridor. She said, 'I have
such a strong feeling that we should stand still and pray *now*
that God's will – not ours or anyone else's – shall be done in
that jury room.' That is exactly what we did. Less than ten
minutes later the jury returned.

As the BBC producer responsible for the *Everyman* programme said to me later: 'the emotional feeling in that Court
was overwhelming'. And, indeed, as the judge rose to leave
after accepting the 'Guilty' verdict there was a hush more

reminiscent of a church than a Court. Not a sound broke the silence.

By this time the Gays who had stood outside throughout the case had for some reason rolled up their banners and gone home, and after the press had asked me for a comment we walked quietly out unnoticed. There was no jubilation only gratitude, not least for the courage and integrity of the jury who had been exposed to the most brilliant and experienced advocacy in order to persuade them to bring in a 'Not Guilty' verdict.

In passing sentence[1] the following morning Judge King-Hamilton said that the publication of the poem revealed 'an astonishing and lamentable bad taste and error of judgement . . . a reckless disregard for the feelings of Christians, whether practising or non-practising, and for millions of non-Christians who sympathize with the doctrine of Christianity.' Referring to the jury's verdict he told Lemon:

Despite the fact that the company and yourself exercized your undoubted right to challenge the maximum possible number of jurors, which meant that a total of 14 potential jurors were challenged off the jury to try this case, it availed you nothing because 10 of the remaining had the moral courage to reach the verdict they did in accordance with their conscience and what I venture to think is good common sense.

It is perhaps being a little too optimistic in this era of obscenity, but it is possible to hope that by this verdict the pendulum of public opinion is beginning to swing back to a more healthy climate.

Although I sometimes read poetry and as a rule like what I read, I do not profess to be a judge of it and therefore would not presume to express an opinion as to whether this particular poem is a good one, a bad one or an indifferent one.

But I have no doubt whatever, and apparently 10 of the jury agree with me, that this poem is quite

[1] By a majority verdict of 10 to 2 Denis Lemon was found guilty of publishing a blasphemous libel. He was sentenced to nine months' imprisonment, suspended for eighteen months and fined £500. *Gay News* was fined £1,000.

appalling and it contains the most scurrilous profanity
and I hope never to see the like of it again.

But life's funny. Not long after this I was walking in the lane
when a car passed, drew up and backed. A cheery hand was
waving – it was Geoffrey Robertson. We chatted for a minute
or two and then he and his girlfriend came in for a cup of
tea. We all got on very well.

Chapter 15

No unexceptional offence

The end of the *Gay News* trial was by no manner of means the end of the matter. But sometimes wonderful things happen to lighten the pressure. One of these, coming just a few days after the *Gay News* verdict, and in the full flow of public debate which followed, lifted my spirit immensely.

I was invited as a guest of The Honourable Society of the Middle Temple to Dinner in Middle Temple Hall on its Grand Day. I treasure the unique memory of that night as a great privilege and a real tonic. The Lord Chancellor, The Rt Hon. Elwyn Jones, and the Lord Chief Justice, Lord Widgery, were there and I was escorted into dinner by John Sparrow, then Warden of All Souls College, Oxford. The passing of the great silver loving-cup, the rose petals in the water on the huge silver platters in which the gentlemen dipped their napkins and wiped their brows, were something from another world.

The Lord Chancellor was very friendly, coming over to introduce himself to me and, with a twinkle in his eye, raising his glass to me from time to time during dinner. As we at the top table left to retire to the 'Parliament House', there was hissing from some of the lower tables, immediately followed by a burst of clapping. John Swallow turned to me and said, 'You know who that's for? You. That's the answer to the hissing.'

I found myself seated as the Guest of Honour as everyone enjoyed the dessert, ginger, snuff, port and cigars and, of course, the talk. It was a glorious evening. Later we went out into the beautiful Temple Gardens. The borders of red geraniums, white petunias and blue lobelia and the new herb

garden to commemorate the Queen's Jubilee were immacu-
lately kept. They lay quiet under an intense blue sky across
which rolled silver clouds illuminated by the lights of London.
The Union Jack high on a nearby building curled in shining
solitude against the sky. Memorable indeed.

I was very glad that Denis Lemon did not go to prison.
As I said in reply to a question in the *Everyman* programme
on the trial (18 September 1978): 'If you are asking me if I
have any bitterness, or hatred, or resentment against Denis
Lemon for publishing his poem, I don't have those feelings
towards him. This is something he must settle with his own
conscience.'

The programme itself, made under great difficulties not
least because the case had already gone to appeal, was in the
words of one TV journalist 'the fairest treatment the BBC
have ever given you'. The programme used again the TV
news film of the crowd of Gays walking through the streets
of London holding banners with the slogan 'Whitehouse kills'
and pictures of me alongside pictures of Hitler. I remember
how strange those newsreel pictures had seemed to me as I
sat in my home watching them when they were first transmitted. It was all so unreal. 'That can't be *me* they're marching against,' I thought. 'Not me and *Hitler*!'

But as Mike Tracey and Dave Morrison[1] were to write
later:

> With the conviction, however, came the storm, and one
> of such proportions that it even surprised and hurt
> Whitehouse, who was no newcomer to controversy and
> vilification. Neither was it just the crank threats which
> hurt her, though there were threats on her life and those
> of her family. Rather what hurt her was the sense of
> isolation. Not isolation in total terms, since she received
> an enormous number of letters, mainly from ordinary
> Church people, attesting their support and praising her
> efforts. What hurt her though was the sense of public
> isolation: 'The three weeks that followed the verdict –
> well, I hardly know how to describe them. I lost a stone

[1] Tracey and Morrison, *Whitehouse*, MacMillan 1978.

in those three weeks'; and again she referred back to the difference between the response to the Thorsen situation and the response to the poem and once more, 'the silence of the Church'. And there is no doubt that it was a very loud and self-conscious silence. She felt, as she put it, 'dreadfully isolated' despite the volume of support from the public.

'You see, the thing is I cared very much about the Church. I knew that what people were saying was "where's the Church?" and that was what was so dreadful. Here in the first place we'd had Jesus Christ treated like that and in the second place His Church wasn't even prepared to come out. . . It was the amazement at what was happening that shook me so profoundly. I couldn't believe it that all of a sudden what I had done was being so widely misinterpreted and that the Church allowed itself to be so overwhelmed with what you might call the general gay lobby.'

There *was* an enormous outcry over the trial and there can be no doubt that it was to a great degree orchestrated by the Gay/humanist lobby. In view of the fact that an appeal was pending, the extent of it was somewhat surprising – or perhaps I should say it *would* have been surprising in circumstances dealing with any issue other than homosexuality. I put some of my feelings in a letter to *The Times* (29 July 1977):

I have been reminded, many times, on reading your correspondence on the recent blasphemy case, of a game we used to play as children. Called 'Pass it on' it began with one person whispering a message to the next, and so on, the last one shouting out loud what he had heard. That this bore no relation to the original, that it was often as it passed round the circle deliberately embellished and distorted was all part of the fun. Only it hasn't been so funny this time.

The sight of the homosexual/intellectual/humanist lobby at bay has been at times an intimidating

spectacle, but may I, before some of the wilder flights of
its imagination become the established mythology of the
case, put the record straight as far as I am free to do
so? May I also say, in passing, that I have been amazed
at the degree of licence offered by your columns in a
matter which is still, with an appeal evidently pending,
sub judice?

I do not 'pore over', or for that matter ever buy *Gay
News*. I rarely see it and carry out no vendetta against
it, though I have expressed concern, and will continue
to do so, at the proselytising of the immature adolescent
by the so-called 'Gay liberation' movement.

Now I find myself falling into the same trap as so
many of your correspondents. The blasphemy trial was
not about homosexuality. It was about the right of
Christians and sympathisers with the Christian faith not
to be offended in the matter of their religious feelings.
But this right has been almost completely submerged in
an argument about the right of homosexuals not to have
their feelings offended!

I accept no responsibility whatever for the
distribution of this poem during and since the trial. If
certain people decide to challenge the law that is their
business, not mine. Neither do I regret the fact that
millions now know something of the nature of the poem.
If the publicity given to this case has profoundly
shocked a public and a Church, not to mention a
Government, which has been unwilling by and large to
face the degree of corruption within our culture, then
that is a good thing, not a bad one. The shame of the
publication of that poem lies on us all, not simply on
those who maybe felt they had good reason for believing
they could get away with it in these days of pseudo-
freedom.

On 11 February 1978 a demonstration organized by the *Gay
News* Defence Committee, of about 5,000 Gays met in
Trafalgar Square. Contingents from all over Britain carried
banners decorated – if that's the word – with what could
only be described as grotesque cartoons of me and chanted

'Whitehouse – kill, kill, kill.' Again there were photographs of me side by side with ones of Hitler.

Time and time again, in this and in many other ways, I was accused of being motivated by a hatred of homosexuals. So perhaps I may quote here what I said in my book *Whatever Happened To Sex?*:

> When I say what is true – that I am not against homosexuals as people, but believe homosexual practices to be wrong, I am very conscious of the inadequacy of what probably sounds a very negative declaration. Homosexuals have as much right to be fully understood, to be treated with compassionate love as the rest of us. And as people they should be 'judged' no more no less, than are those of us whose problems are perhaps less obvious but equally undesirable. Compassion without patronage, but without compromise – how to achieve it?
>
> The natural repugnance which most people feel when homosexuality and lesbianism is mentioned can result in a harshness of attitude and thinking which is, at least, unhelpful and certainly as unChristian as the perverse practices which are condemned. But to go to the other extreme and elevate people suffering from such abnormalities into a norm for society not only threatens society but is dangerous to the individuals themselves, since it excludes them from the consideration of help and treatment. Society, to its shame, once hurled that word at the homosexual. In our crazy 'value-free' society the 'shame' is now attached only to those who dare say that homosexuality is less than 'gay'.
>
> Such an attitude is as dogmatic, doctrinal and restrictive in its own way as was the fearful silence or sniggering scorn of earlier decades.

But whatever I may say about my actions and motivation the Gays were clearly bitterly angry with me, with an anger that persisted for a long time and surfaced not least in my visits to universities. The amount of opposition varied from

the occasional heckle and loaded question to more dramatic
happenings of the kind I experienced at Birmingham University early in October 1977. Once again I refer to my diary:

> Very lively and interesting debate at Birmingham
> University tonight. Had to close the Union half an hour
> before it began and indeed it was packed far beyond
> capacity. I debated with Arthur Butterworth, warden of
> one of the Colleges. The motion was 'That this House
> would find no place for commercial pornography' and
> when I had proposed the motion I was given
> tremendous applause which went on and on. Then
> Butterworth, as seems always to be the case, used the
> occasion for bitter personal attack – terribly bitter –
> called me 'evil and dangerous', linked me with the
> National Front and Nazism – with the persecution of
> homosexuals – with repression and oppression – what
> lay behind my 'charm and persuasiveness' was repulsive
> indeed. I go still inside when I hear these things and let
> them go over me – I have to.
> During the contributions from the floor a young man
> took the microphone – but couldn't hold it as he was
> shaking so much and crying. 'I am a homosexual' he
> cried, turning and pointing his finger at me as he tried
> to speak. 'I go in fear and trembling of my life because
> of *you* – I am anathema to you' he shouted and then
> dropping the microphone he walked slowly out of the
> hall in tears shouting and gesticulating at me as he
> went. Terribly pathetic. Everyone clapped, including me
> – I felt I wanted to do something to make him feel less
> isolated. When I came to sum up I said how sorry I
> was that he had gone 'because I would like him to
> know that he was not anathema to me, that I did not
> hate him.'
> We lost the motion by 30 votes although over 100
> abstained but, as the President said to me afterwards
> 'many of those really wanted to vote for you but lacked
> the courage', and that I can believe. When the
> President thanked me for coming I got a tremendous
> standing ovation, which was quite moving – unknown

in the Union, I was told, and the crowd 'the biggest in living memory!' Well I hope perhaps I gave them something worthwhile to think about – that is the real value of such an occasion.

Afterwards as I left the hall and walked down the steps into the main lobby I saw the young man standing there with a number of his friends, and I went to him with my hand stretched out.

'I'm sorry you did not hear what I said after you left,' I said to him.

'But I did, Mrs Whitehouse,' he replied, 'I was standing outside the hall listening – and I'm sorry I said the things I did about you.' Then he hastily added, 'But I am so afraid!'

I gently put my hand on his shoulder. 'I'm sorry – but does it surprise you to know that I suffer from misunderstanding too?' and I asked him to try to understand and accept that because people like me believe homosexual practices to be wrong that does not at all mean that we hate and despise homosexuals as people.

It was at this point that a tall, much bigger, older man pushed himself to the centre of the group. He said in a loud and ingratiating voice that he was my 'brother in Christ', that he was a practising homosexual who 'counselled' his homosexual friends. After calling me his 'dear sister in Christ' he claimed that I had 'not experienced the Sword of the Spirit' and was not really a Christian. 'These, not you, are my brothers and sisters in Christ.' All this no doubt was intended to attract as many of the moving crowds as possible!

There have not been many occasions when I have seen through a person with such immediate clarity. He was clearly aiming to dominate and control these 'dear brothers' with the power of his own personality and I spoke to him as I've never spoken to anyone else before or since.

'Just go away,' I said. 'You're a hypocrite. You're not my brother in Christ and I doubt if you're theirs. Just go away,' I said again. 'I can talk to these young people and we understand one another – but you . . .' and I turned my back upon him and carried on talking to the student homosexuals for quite a while.

That incident most vividly illustrated to me the way in which vulnerable young homosexuals are sometimes – perhaps often – controlled and manipulated by others more powerful who are often, as no doubt this interloper was, ideologically motivated. I've never forgotten that first young man who wept. I hope all is well with him now.

Just before Christmas that same year (1977) a reporter from the *East Anglian Daily Times* rang about five o'clock one evening to ask if I had heard that a crowd of the Gay-lib. people were coming to sing obscene carols outside our house that night. No, I hadn't.

'Will you be at home?'

'What's that got to do with you?' I laughingly asked.

'Well, if you are I shall lose my night off and if you aren't, I shan't,' he replied.

I still told him he'd 'have to wait and see' and certainly wasn't going to tell him that we were having a party that evening! This meant that the 'Gays' probably wouldn't be able to get anywhere near the house for the cars, which was precisely what happened. The only intimation we had that they were there at all was the occasional flash bulb going off outside the windows – we didn't even have to tell our friends what was going on and eventually the 'Gays' departed no doubt very disconsolate after a 100-mile return trip which turned out to be a very damp squib indeed. The fact that we live way out in the country meant that no one else saw them either!

It was extraordinary that the night they chose turned out to be the one on which we were having our first big party since we'd moved into the house two years previously. It most certainly would have been a very different story if we'd been on our own.

According to the press our visitors were the 'Defence Committee of the *Gay News* Blasphemy case'. They had evidently informed the national dailies in advance that they were coming. Several of the papers rang late in the evening to see what had happened. We told them that we'd heard nothing, took the phone off the hook and enjoyed our fun.

Some of the Gays' other activities were not so funny – death, bomb and arson threats to me and to our family and our home. These were taken seriously by the police and for some time we were under regular surveillance. Even so we didn't altogether lose our sense of humour. I made this entry in my diary for 6 March 1978:

> Two more threatening calls. John[1] took them both, and we had our moneysworth of fun out of them! An Irish voice said, 'If the appeal is lost we still intend to get her'. 'Get her what?' asked John innocently! Later the same day came another call which we managed to record on the machine set up by the Police. A very different 'class' of voice from the one we'd heard earlier – cooler, more educated and younger. 'This is to let you know the assassination is still on.' 'Pardon?' said John. 'The assassination is still on.' 'Oh, thank you very much,' said John, taken aback. End of exchange. How we laughed! As we said, 'Well, we knew John was *polite!*'

Then there was the picket. Once again their timing was very bad. They chose the day (10 February 1978) on which Cyril Townsend's Protection of the Child Bill, making child pornography illegal, was to have its second reading in the Commons. We had been tipped off by the police – though I don't know who tipped *them* off – that a coach load of Gay students and sympathizers from Essex University were coming to picket our house during the day.

I had left the house very early to go to London, the venetian blinds on the side of the house visible from the road were pulled down, no one inside went out. And apart from a visit to the door by one of them accompanied by a policeman to hand in a letter, nothing was seen of them at all and they certainly saw nothing of us. It also happened to be the first really cold day of the winter and some of them, I gathered later, came in T-shirts. They were evidently kept moving by the police and stayed in the lane for only about half an hour before walking through the village and disappearing. Our house is only one of two – the other stands far back –

---

[1] John Beyer, Organizing Secretary, National VALA.

in a lane which is well outside the village. So there was no satisfaction to be gained from passers-by or interested neighbours either.

The following day there was a call to tell us that 5,000 Gays were demonstrating in London against me and against Judge King-Hamilton. They were marching down Charing Cross Road when this friend rang. But there wasn't a single word in the press or television, possibly because any such coverage could amount to contempt of Court as the case had gone to appeal. So that fell rather flat too!

The *Gay News* Appeal which was heard early in 1978 was dismissed. The appeal judge found, contrary to the claims made by *Gay News* and Denis Lemon, that Judge King-Hamilton was correct in directing that: 1. it was sufficient if the jury took the view that the publication complained of vilified Christ in his life and crucifixion; and 2. it was not necessary for the Crown to establish any further intention on the part of the appellants beyond an intention to publish that which in the jury's view was a blasphemous libel.

Later, *Gay News* made an appeal to the House of Lords and that, too, was dismissed.

It was made perfectly clear throughout by Judge King-Hamilton, the appeal judges and by the law lords that criticisms and attacks on the Christian faith, as long as they are made in 'sober and temperate style', would not offend against the law of blasphemous libel. The fact that there had been no blasphemous libel case for fifty-five years does not mean that people care less, simply that nothing so blasphemous – apart from the Thorsen *Jesus* film – had been published in the interim.

It is worth remembering that it was unanimously agreed by all nine judges concerned with the trial and appeal that the *Gay News* poem describing 'in explicit detail acts of sodomy and fellatio with the body of Christ immediately after the moment of his death' (Judge Roskill) was 'quite appallingly shocking and outrageous' (Lord Russell of Killowen). It was during that hearing in the House of Lords that Lord Justice Scarman voiced these memorable words:

I do not subscribe to the view that the common law

offence of blasphemous libel serves no useful purpose in the modern law. On the contrary, I think there is a case for legislation extending it to protect the religious beliefs and feelings of non-Christians. The offence belongs to a group of criminal offences designed to safeguard the internal tranquility of the kingdom. In an increasingly plural society, such as that of modern Britain, it is necessary not only to respect the differing religious beliefs, feelings and practices of all but also to protect them from scurrility, vilification, ridicule, and contempt. . .

I will not lend my voice to a view of the law relating to blasphemous libel which would render it a dead letter, or diminish its efficacy to protect religious feeling from outrage and insult. My criticism of the common law offence of blasphemy is not that it exists but that it is not sufficiently comprehensive.

So the conviction stood. It could well be that the determination of Lord Willis, the National Secular Society and others to remove the law relating to blasphemy from the statute book was reflected in the Law Commission's suggestion (April 1981) that the crime of blasphemy should no longer exist. This was in spite of the fact that the United Nations Declaration on Human Rights has identified religion, along with race and class, as areas in which men and women should not be given offence.

I was very glad to see that *The Times'* first leader (30 April) came out strongly against any such claim and concluded:

There is much to be said for leaving the law as it is, for all its uncertainty, limitation and anomalies. There is no evidence that it will be inappropriately or oppressively used. The success of Mrs Whitehouse has not provoked a rash of blasphemy prosecutions. If the law falls into another lengthy period of inaction, no harm will be done by that. To ask Parliament now to pass an Act abolishing blasphemy altogether, would seem to imply that society had come to regard blasphemy as an unexceptionable offence. That cannot yet be the case.

Looking back now I am still amazed at the difference in the attitude of the church – and indeed not only the church – to those two publications, Thorsen's *Life of Christ* play and the *Gay News* poem.

I have read both, and I say without reservation that there was, in essence, little to choose between the two, though the play, of course, was much longer than the poem and therefore there was more scope to extend and develop the blasphemy. In the event there is no doubt that the cleverly organized counter-attack by the humanist/Gay/left-wing lobby in defence of the poem was highly successful in the short term. In the end, of course, it gained them nothing and lost the church a great deal. But it did establish the blasphemy law as relevant to and effective in our day. Let's hope, to turn to the last words of *The Times* leader, that the day when society regards blasphemy as an unexceptional offence will never come. But in this matter, as in so much else, 'eternal vigilance is the price of freedom' and perhaps of faith too.

There is no doubt whatsoever in my mind that, had the appeal against the verdict been allowed, those who have been so busy illegally distributing the poem to all and sundry since the original verdict would then have published – if that is possible! – even more blasphemous material, since their campaigning is born out of a bitter hatred of Christ and of the Christian religion.

It is of no mean significance that those who would willingly, indeed gladly, expose 'the feelings of Christians and Christian sympathizers' to the grossest offence are often the very people who shout loudest about 'human rights' in other fields. Not to be given offence in one's cherished religious beliefs is a basic human right. The fact that those feelings are more at risk in the world in which we live, is all the more reason to maintain the blasphemy law. The religious feelings of those who worship in other faiths have an equal right to protection. I would only add that the blasphemy case, as far as I am concerned, had much more to do with love of the Lord than with protecting my own feelings.

Chapter 16

Custard pies 'down under'

Fascinating and immensely worthwhile as was my first trip to Australia it really paled beside the drama of my next one in September 1978. Had I but known it, the 'red alert' at Heathrow on the day that I left set the mood of the trip!

The sight of the Opera House lifted my heart as we circled over Sydney Harbour bridge at 7.30 in the morning. I felt rather as though I was coming home again – so many friends to meet.

News of the *Gay News* blasphemy trial and all that followed had already reached Australia. At dinner that first evening in the home of Lance Shilton, Dean of Sydney, I heard of the organized resistance to my visit. A meeting of lesbians, trotskyites and Gays had been held in Sydney three weeks previously, solely to work out a strategy to disrupt our meetings and frighten people away from them. But I was not told until nearly the end of the tour about a leaflet which was produced at the meeting for distribution in all the towns I visited. It carried a drawing of me with a meat cleaver plunged into my back and the caption 'Let the blood flow'. The police had been tipped off and had infiltrated the meeting and picked up one of the leaflets. As a result I had heavy police protection wherever I went throughout Australia. I was instructed always 'to register under a pseudonym' and 'don't ever go out on your own' – not even to buy paper hankies from across the road, I discovered. No matter where I wanted to go in Sydney I had to ring Syd and Fred, who accompanied me everywhere I went – as did their counterparts elsewhere.

Peter Duncan, the 33 year-old Marxist Attorney General

of South Australia, 'youngest and brashest' of the Premier's advisors (*Sydney Sun-Herald*, September 1978) received a deputation of Gays who were obviously determined to make the maximum capital out of my visit. At a press conference afterwards he described me as 'an agent of darkness' and as 'that notorious Pom'. He even claimed that Ernest was the Chairman of the National Front in Britain! All this made banner headlines in the press. When I was asked to comment, I challenged Mr Duncan to say these things face to face with me on television. I said that 'I was amazed that someone holding the dignity of his office should so lower himself to make accusations of that kind without checking his facts'. Within an hour this was being reported on radio and TV stations right across the continent, as was the statement put out by the Dean of Sydney to the effect that Mr Duncan's statement was 'untrue and unworthy of a person in his position'. What a start to my visit.

The following day Mr Duncan attacked me again, this time on radio and tried to justify his refusal to meet me on TV by saying he 'did not wish to give legitimacy' to my tour – whatever that may have meant.

In the meantime I had started my first full days 'work'. A young woman reporter from *The Sydney Herald* arrived in my hotel room at 7.15 a.m. The TV team from Channel 2 who were following me around all day – as she was – arrived half an hour later and stayed with me till 7 p.m. I did eleven radio and TV interviews that day, moving from one to the other at such speed that at times I hardly knew where I was! Time and again the Attorney General's remarks cropped up and then, in the middle of make-up for the *Mike Walsh Show*, ABC's nationwide *PM* programme rang to say that he had agreed after all to debate with me. They would link me in Sydney with him in Adelaide between 6.05 and 6.15 that evening.

We had an absolutely hair-raising struggle in the pouring rain to get to the ABC studio in time – driving the wrong way down at least one 'one way' street – only to be told when I dashed in at the last minute and sat down in front of the microphone, that the Attorney General had cancelled! Owing, his aide said, to 'a previous appointment'. What an anti-climax. But the interview went ahead just with me and I learnt later that a Cabinet Meeting had been held in Adelaide that afternoon during which Duncan had been instructed to withdraw from the broadcast. The next day, *en route* via Melbourne to Hobart, Tasmania, I was called to the phone at the airport to be told by the press that the Attorney General had put out a statement. He acknowledged that I had a right to speak and admitted that he was speaking solely for himself and in no way for the Government of South Australia – a statement which, we were later told, was made on the express instruction of the Premier, Mr Dunstan.

After the first few hectic days Tasmania was a rest cure. I was the Guest of Honour at a luncheon for about 300 people, at which Tasmania's Attorney General sat on my right, 'absolutely disgusted' at what he called 'Duncan's antics'. On my left was a Federal Senator and at the same table the Lord Mayor and Mayoress of Hobart and a leading judge. As a TV commentator put it in the first item of news nationwide that evening, 'If Mrs Whitehouse is an agent of darkness then an awful lot of Tasmania's top people are agents of darkness too.'

At a dinner the following night given by the Adelaide National Council of Women I met the Shadow Attorney General of South Australia and a number of MPs and we talked about Peter Duncan's attacks on me. I was told that these had greatly embarrassed the Government and could well have done permanent damage to the political career of the Attorney General himself. Indeed the following day we heard that the Premier, Mr Dunstan – also a declared Marxist – had ordered him to 'take a holiday. I don't care where you go but keep out of sight until that woman has left the country!'

This controversy gave the campaign an enormous boost and all sorts of people who would perhaps not otherwise have done so turned out to support us. At the end of one of the meetings a young man who said he was a homosexual came up to me and gave me a tam-o-shanter he'd crocheted for me during the meeting. Someone else brought me a copy of the *Evening News* poster for the day I arrived – 'She's here! Caped Crusader flies in!' I brought that home and stuck it on the wall of the office. I brought the cap home too and still have it.

There was no doubt that the situation in South Australia as far as pornography was concerned was very bad indeed. For example, officially labelled for 'unrestricted' sale were 'boy' magazines of the most explicit kind, as well as much hard-core pornography. And the people themselves seemed quite bemused. When I had been there in 1973 South Australia was still the church-going, non-permissive kind of community which had given the State such a good reputation. Since then laws had been passed which allowed pornography free passage and publication. No one seemed to know quite what had hit them, or how to get the situation reversed. Hence the tremendous interest in my tour.

The enthusiasm of some Australians at least was illustrated by the advertisement for one of the Adelaide meetings. When I saw the banner headline 'Come and hear the woman who changed the course of British history,' I thought, 'I'll go to that, perhaps I'll get a chance to meet her.' Honestly!

There were lots of marvellous moments with people as I travelled around, most of whom seemed to recognize me because of all the TV coverage. 'Hi-yer gal! Keep it up!' shouted the man from the other side of the road. There was the lady who invited us in to see her garden in the valley – it really was very beautiful – and picked me a huge bunch of magnolia flowers which I took back to my room and floated on a big silver tray. And there was the wedding party in one of Adelaide's parks. We, that is Sid and Geoff, my body-guards, and myself were invited to join the wedding breakfast and be photographed with the bride and groom!

Throughout the tour the Gays never weakened in their attempts to disrupt our meetings but this did have its positive side. Wherever we went we had tremendous media coverage and great audiences in every sense of the word.

Following our three hectic but immensely enjoyable days in Adelaide we went on to Perth and then to Melbourne. At the customary meeting with the police on arrival, they told me that the Gays were likely to be more in evidence here than anywhere else so far, and that they had had planning meetings in the University, etc. There was talk of 300 protestors at the public meeting and the police officer told me that in the State of Victoria the police work on the principle of over-manning rather than under-manning (one to every five demonstrators). 'That way,' he said, 'we remain in control. Anything less and there's trouble.' I told him that I was determined to go in by the front door, 'no back doors for me.' 'Good,' he said.

But in between meetings there was a little light relief. I had an appointment with 'Edna Everage' at the theatre where 'she' was appearing. 'One really does have to hand it to Barry Humphries,' I wrote in my diary afterwards, 'he really is brilliant – almost impossible to realize one's talking to a man!' Anyway it was all great fun and he gave me a huge Koala Bear. From Melbourne I went to speak at Geelong Grammar School where Prince Charles was educated for a time.

In Darwin protestors and TV cameras were out in full force for the Town Hall meeting. It was very obvious to me as I sat on the platform that the first three rows were taken by the 'opposition', mostly hard-faced women but with several men among them.

All went well, and 'the opposition' gave the impression of being intensely interested, till suddenly at a given signal those at the end of the row immediately in front of me jumped up and rushed the platform shouting and screaming and aiming 'pies' straight at me. They were about ten inches across and filled with the most revolting mess. I learnt afterwards that it was shaving-cream and red dye! One hit me in the chest and covered my brand-new pink blouse with great lumps of the stuff. Another landed on my stomach covering my skirt with the same mess. Some broke on the floor. Another hit the lectern and covered my papers. The demonstrators, still shouting at the tops of their voices, ran out – straight into the arms of the police. (Six were later charged with causing an affray.)

The men on the platform rushed over to help. But my immediate reaction was to stay put – they must not succeed in silencing me. Scraping handfuls of the concoction off myself and flinging it on the floor, I shouted above the hubbub, 'At least it matches my blouse!' I then carried on with my speech, to great applause from the hall. But when I sat down twenty minutes later I felt thoroughly wet and cold, for the moisture had gone right through my clothes. So I left the platform briefly to go behind the scenes, take off my blouse and put on a cardigan.

There I found two plain clothes police officers waiting for me. They wanted me to make a statement straight away but I told them that I must go back onto the platform for the rest of the meeting. No one was going to have the satisfaction of thinking I had been driven off it! The cardigan solved the problem of my wet blouse but my skirt was a different matter! My stomach was getting colder and colder. As I looked around for a solution, I spotted a pile of quite clean butter muslin on the floor, folded it into a pad and tucked it under my skirt.

A couple of hours later, when all the statements were made, we got up to leave and I was suddenly aware of a huge police officer looking rather oddly at the bottom of my skirt.

'Excuse me, ma'am. Excuse me, ma'am,' he said, his face getting pinker and pinker – I think he thought I was losing my pants! 'Oh,' I said, 'I know what that is,' and I reached down, got hold of the bit of material that was showing and pulled out yard after yard of butter muslin. I don't think he'd seen anything quite like that before. And we finished a fraught evening with a good laugh.

Next day I thought I should ring home to tell them all was well, in case they had heard some garbled account of what had happened the night before. But before I could get a word out: 'How did you enjoy the strawberry pies, Mum?' The story of my adventures the night before had been carried on BBC news that morning!

The following afternoon I was scheduled to put in an appearance at the 'shoppers rally' in Sydney's City Square. The police kept me out of sight behind the TV cameras until it was time to speak. I excused my voice, which by now was very 'croaky', made one or two points, and then the 'fun' started. Shrieking women rushed at me but the police were ready for them. They leapt forward and grabbed the women – and the pies, real ones this time with cream inside, shot in all directions. I managed to carry on speaking for a minute or two but then the police who'd arrested eight people insisted on escorting me back to my hotel. The flying pies and my swirling cape as I swung from side to side in an effort to avoid the 'ammunition' enlivened television news that night. What was more, the item finished with details of the rally the following Sunday. 'Hundreds if not thousands of dollars-worth of free publicity,' we told ourselves afterwards.

The police control and presence at Sydney Town Hall that day was impressive. I was escorted up the steps and into the Hall by a bodyguard of police – the people rising to applaud as I made my way through. There's no doubt that all the TV coverage of the various 'attacks' had done much to warm the hearts of the 'Aussies'.

It was a great meeting and once again representatives of the Prime Minister Mr Fraser, of the Leader of the Opposition, of the Cardinal, the Archbishop, the Council of Churches, and the State Government, came to the microphone to welcome me and to pledge support for the Australian Festival of Light's fight, for the family and against those things which destroy it.

The 'opposition' was there, but the police presence was so well organized that it never really stood a chance. Some stink bombs were thrown and there were occasional shouts, but nothing really disturbed the meeting. Security was tight and bags were searched. No press or TV were allowed in without identification. (I heard afterwards that one man claiming to be a freelance photographer had rotten fruit hidden under his camera in a hold-all!) It was obvious to us on the platform that two of the 'opposition' were in the third row facing me and we wondered what was going to happen but two plain clothes men also spotted them and quietly asked the people on each side of them to move and sat down in their places. I had to smile to myself – here were these two beefy Australians pretending to be anything but coppers, chewing gum and leaning over towards this young man and woman, who sank lower and lower in their seats while the policemen appeared to get bigger and bigger!

At the end of the meeting the Commissioner of Police asked everyone to keep their seats and came to escort me out of the hall. The audience stood and applauded and reached out to shake hands as we walked out and straight down the steps into a waiting car to be driven off at great speed. Then the rest of the audience – about 3,000 – marched from the Town Hall to Australia's Hyde Park in the centre of Sydney.

At the end of all this, and a day in Canberra, I couldn't help but wish I was going straight back to the UK instead of on for a week's meetings in New Zealand and a visit to Utah on my way home.

The Utah visit proved quite an experience. I was invited to attend a meeting of some 6,000 men – the Mormon's Annual Convention – while the women and children, all looking immaculate, all behaving impeccably, picnicked outside in the sunshine. The apparent perfection of it all – no children seemed to cry, no one got cross – seemed too good to be true. But it was wonderful to hear the magnificent Mormon Tabernacle Choir.

After lunch we took a ski-lift 11,000 feet up into the Rockies. It was the beginning of 'the fall' and the turning leaves on the trees as we travelled up were breathtaking in their beauty. Standing at the top, with the dark mountains on either side and the sun-lit city of Utah lying tranquilly on the far horizon I could well understand how the Mormons, fleeing from persecution, saw the shining stillness of the plain as their land of milk and honey. My promised land, a good deal less peaceful but *home*, lay 5,000 miles away, and by this time I was so anxious to get there.

That night I spoke at a public meeting recorded by Public Radio. I was asked to sign an agreement for my speech to be broadcast *in toto* (45 minutes) 'to every State in the USA'. What a finale that was to my five-week tour.

It had been a wonderful, in many ways a quite amazing, trip . But there was one aspect which was *not* so good. About ten days into my five-week tour I contracted a very severe throat infection. Because of all the work which had been put into organizing my visit, and because I stayed in any one place for only a couple of days before I had to move on, there was no way that I could retire to bed without disappointing an awful lot of people. (I did go to bed one afternoon and missed the evening engagement, but that was all.) So by the time I arrived home my throat was like raw meat and I was desperately tired.

Mercifully I came home to a glorious Indian summer and I was able to lie in the garden and rest for the next ten days or so.

But I couldn't go on resting indefinitely, and my first public engagement after my return was a lunch-time speaking engagement at Southampton University on an unbelievably hot day at the end of October. The hall was absolutely packed and the audience quiet and attentive until suddenly from behind me someone shot a spray of cold water down my back, over my head, and on to my papers. I took no notice until eggs – which mercifully missed me – were thrown. Then I turned round and said to the small hostile group behind me 'For goodness sake grow up'. I was heartily supported from the hall and continued speaking until a tennis ball, thrown very hard at me from a few yards away, hit me in the back of my neck.

However a few days later I had a letter from a young Christian student who was present which made it all worthwhile:

> Despite the delay and the trouble it was a real victory for the truth and most of those present, Christian and non-Christian, were very impressed. . .
>
> There were about 850 people at the meeting and about 500 had to be turned away. Support for you amongst the student Christian bodies is now very strong and we will follow this up. The meeting was reported in the *Southampton Echo*, Radio Victory and on the Radio 2 news at nine o'clock on the morning after. Thank you again for coming and every encouragement and our prayers in your difficult work. God bless you.

Even after the holiday which my doctor advised, my voice and throat were still giving me a great deal of trouble and eventually we decided to seek advice. When he first heard me speak the throat specialist felt pretty sure that I would have to have an operation. But no. All that was necessary was complete rest from public speaking as far as possible for the next three or four months.

Although my voice gives me little trouble now, the annual programme of over a hundred major speaking engagements between late September and April, which had characterized my life for the previous fifteen years, was not to happen again. I do still speak at public meetings and am glad to be able to do so. But the pattern of things has changed. I sometimes feel that my throat trouble, far from being a disadvantage, has meant that I can concentrate on writing, on personal meetings, visits to Parliament and the like. I am also far more available at short notice than I was when my diary was packed full months in advance. So, as it so often does, good came out of evil.

Chapter 17

The Williams Report

Give me the liberty to know, to utter, to argue freely according
to conscience above all liberties. . . That which is impious or
evil absolutely, either against faith or manners, no law can
possibly permit that intends not to unlaw itself.

An Addendum to the Parliament of England, from John Milton's
Areopagitica

'Oh, but Mrs Whitehouse! Don't you know that Professor
Williams has the reputation of being the cleverest man in
Britain?' The shock and disbelief in the almost hushed voice
of the journalist who had rung to give me the first details of
the Williams Report[1] was only the first of such intimations
that the quality of the professor's brain was to provide all
the justification necessary for the recommendations of his
Report.

'That may be so,' I replied, 'but that doesn't make him
the wisest.' And that night I wrote in my diary:

If he (the journalist) has got it right, what a dreadful
business! The printed word to be free of all restraint –
unbelievable! Imagine what that will do to broadcasting
which is so dependent on the printed word! He says
they're proposing that practically all hard-core
pornography, including even bestiality be made legal,
excluding only child pornography – which is already
illegal anyway[2] – and pornography which has involved
actual physical harm to the participants, like the 'snuff'

---

[1] Report of the Committee on Obscenity and Film Censorship, November 1979.
[2] Protection of Children Act, 1978.

pornography in the States. But daftest of all apparently
they've defined obscenity as that which 'reasonable
people would find unreasonably offensive'. Can't see
this Tory Government doing anything but chuck it out.
Not even honest – said they'd had difficulty in
establishing any link between pornography and sex
crime! Incredible! Asked for comment by *The Sunday
Times* I said 'that we were moving out of the quicksands
into a quagmire and a very dirty one at that!'

It was an explosion of words which no doubt says as much
about me as about the Williams Report. But now, two years
later, I wouldn't change much of what I said then, though
no doubt I'd phrase my comments more elegantly.

In December 1976 Lord Harris, who was then Minister
of State at the Home Office, announced in the House of
Lords that the Government had decided 'not to change the
present obscenity laws until the whole subject had been
looked at by a committee'.

That, of course, was the well-established method of getting rid of a hot potato. Throw it to a Committee and see if
it can 'cool it'. And it was a *very* hot potato indeed. Public
dismay about the way in which 'girlie books', and worse,
were proliferating in Britain – with the police apparently
powerless to do anything to stop the flood – could no longer
be ignored. It was obvious, though, that the Labour Government then in power, afraid of being accused of 'censorship'
by the media, by its own left-wing Ministers and backbench-
ers, would never introduce more effective obscenity laws.
However, in the face of growing public anxiety it had to do
something and in June 1977 the Home Secretary, Mr Merlyn
Rees, announced that Professor Bernard Williams (Knights-
bridge Professor of Philosophy at Cambridge University) had
been appointed as Chairman of a committee whose terms of
reference were:

to review the laws concerning obscenity, indecency and
violence in publications, displays and entertainments in
England and Wales, except in broadcasting, and to

review film censorship arrangements, and make recommendations.

We weren't the least bit happy at the choice of Professor Williams as Chairman, although we didn't go as far as the all-party group of MPs, led by Mr Michael Allison, then Conservative front-bench spokesman on Home Office affairs, who met with Mr Rees to express its misgivings over the appointment of someone 'whose philosophy of humanism and detachment from religious commitment is very far from being representative of the broad mass of feeling in the country'.

I have to admit that I had some sympathy with Professor Williams when he responded by saying: 'I think it is a great disservice to this issue to think the only people who can take an objective look at it or be concerned about it are Christian believers.' After all, it was no time at all since Lord Annan, himself a humanist, had published his very sensitive and far-sighted Report on the Future of Broadcasting.

When the names[1] of his committee were announced it became clear that Professor Williams' promise that the Home Office would appoint people 'with a wide range of views' had not been realized. So as soon as we received an invitation to give evidence I wrote to ask if I could come and see him before doing so. We were unhappy not only about the composition of his committee but about the fact that broadcasting, once again, was excluded from its terms of reference. We fixed our meeting for the weekend I was going to Cambridge to speak at the Annual Dinner and Dance of the Young Newspapermen's Association. I wrote in my diary:

> I told Bernard Williams that we were specially concerned about the presence on his Committee of Dr Anthony Storr as the only psychiatrist. He would, we felt sure, be permissive in his approach. And of the Bishop of Bristol whom we also felt would be too 'soft'.

[1] B. Hooberman Esq
Richard Matthews Esq, CBE QPM
Ms Sheila Rothwell
Dr Anthony Storr
David Robinson Esq.
The Rt. Reverend John Tinsley
Professor J. G. Weightman
His Honour Judge John Leonard QC
Professor A. W. B. Simpson
Mrs M. J. Taylor
Miss Polly Toynbee
V. A. White Esq, MBE

We could not give evidence to a Committee which we felt was 'weighted' at these very key points. I told him that I already knew what kind of report they would produce. Williams conceded that to have Storr as the only psychiatrist was a mistake but said there was nothing he could do about it. He laughed heartily when I mentioned the Bishop. He told me that the Bishop put forward by the Home Office 'was just about the most radical Bishop in the Church of England – though I'm not going to tell you his name. To have him on the Committee would have destroyed its credibility'. The Home Office, he said, had refused to provide him with another one and had told him 'to find his own' so he turned to Church House, Westminster which recommended Dr Tinsley. What interests me particularly in all this is the attitude of the Home Office – there must be some pretty radical officials there!

I got on with him very well actually and liked him much more than I expected to – his charm is almost as legendary as his brain! He made it very clear that he was very anxious indeed that we should give evidence. But I told him that my book *Whatever Happened to Sex?* which contained everything which we would have said had just been published and that we certainly hadn't got the time to start putting something else together. He suggested that I submit the book as our evidence and said he 'felt sure that whatever other material the Committee read they will all read that'. He also, and very importantly, said in answer to my question about calling John Court from Australia that the Committee *would* be prepared to do so if John's research was questioned.

In the event the bibliography at the end of the Williams Report carried no reference to my book – even though we were asked to provide the Committee with six more copies.

In addition to submitting *Whatever Happened to Sex?* we wrote formally to the Committee in the following terms:

We would particularly draw your attention to the work

of Dr John Court, a graduate of Reading University, now working at Flinders University, Adelaide, Australia. His research is unique, and we trust that the Committee will accept his evidence as vital and be wary of any attempts which may be made to dismiss or discredit it.

We would go so far as to suggest that a personal interview with Dr Court is essential as we have no doubt that attempts will be made to dismiss his work by those who are part of the 'anti-censorship' lobby both here and particularly in Denmark. We would remind the Committee that it was Dr Court's appearance as a prosecution witness – in the box for three hours – which resulted in a 'Guilty' verdict in the important Snaresbrook trial in 1975.[1]

If the Committee finds itself unable to bring him over in person, may we suggest that he be given the opportunity to answer questions on tape?

We also wish to put on record our concern about the exclusion of broadcasting from the terms of reference by which your Committee is working. There is in our view, no rational justification for this.

As far as the actual structure of the law is concerned we would wish to see removed that clause which demands proof of 'a tendency to deprave and corrupt those likely to read' the material under trial. A tendency is improvable, any realistic assessment of those likely to read is impossible since, as the pornographers themselves acknowledge, between 10 and 100 persons read any given piece of published pornography.

We believe the law has to be explicit and must list as illegal the actual or simulated presentation of particular acts.

Later in the life of the Committee we did in fact present a list of precisely those sexual acts which if illustrated should, in our view, be considered obscene, but this proposal was dismissed in the Report with the words 'to base a law on an

[1] See Chapter 11.

explicit statement of what is prohibited required that the statement should also be exhaustive. We found, however, that it was far from easy to be satisfied that any definition covered all the ground that it should'. But as the Earl of Halsbury said in the debate on the Williams Report in the House of Lords:[1] 'Why should it be exhaustive? If it catches 90 per cent of what you want to catch, is that not better than catching nothing at all?' Indeed it is. His words, like ours, fell on very deaf ears. But how interested I was to receive – actually while I was writing this chapter – a report in *Newsweek*[2] the American news magazine headed 'Making it hot for Porn':

He's been called an overzealous prude, but Hinson McAuliffe, 61 years old Solicitor General of Georgia's Fulton County, has done a remarkable thing; in a 12 year, one man crusade, he has largely driven pornography out of Atlanta. The city's last 3 'triple X rated' movie houses closed last month and 19 adult bookstores shut their doors in January. Not a peep show, porn shop or X rated remains. 'It just wasn't worth it, economically or politically, to try to remain open', says Attorney Glenn Zell, who unsuccessfully defended dozens of theatres and book-store owners.

McAuliffe's chief weapon has been a tough state anti-obscenity law patterned after a landmark 1973 US Supreme Court decision. In recent years McAuliffe has prosecuted so many porn brokers that the state courts set aside one week each month to hear the cases.

Unable to locate many of the outlet's hidden owners, McAuliffe went after projectionists, managers and other employees – and even brought 'nuisance' suits against customers, netting several prominent citizens in his raids.

We need to know more about how he's done it, I thought and was fascinated and encouraged to read the material the

[1] 16 January 1980.
[2] 25 May 1981.

Solicitor General sent me in reply to my letter to him, and his offer to help us in any way he could – we asked him to come over and speak!

What was the secret of his success? Why, legislation which specifically listed and identified the nature of the material which was to be classed as obscene – in almost the same words as we had submitted to the Williams Committee.

Before settling down to study the Williams Report in detail I glanced at the Appendix. This contained reports of the situation in other countries as far as obscenity legislation is concerned and because of my great interest – and some experience – in that country, I turned to the section on Australia and made there the first of many discoveries. Each state of that continent was dealt with separately and in some detail but there was no sign of South Australia. All the other states but not that one. Quite frankly I was amazed, though I suspected I knew the reason for the omission.

In 1971 the South Australian Government had passed legislation very similar to that recommended by the Williams Committee. Its effect was to send the figures for serious sex crime soaring in the years that followed. The Report's exclusion of South Australia was symptomatic of other discoveries I made as I spent the next few days closeted with 'Williams'.

I already knew the Committee had sent some of its members to Denmark to meet Dr Berl Kutchinsky, the Danish criminologist. Having met and discussed these matters with him myself I was most anxious to discover how far he was responsible for the Committee's claim that there 'was little evidence of any causal link between pornography and sex crime'.

Kutchinsky's often repeated claim that people became less interested in pornography and less interested, also, in engaging in sexually deviant behaviour as a result of viewing it, has profoundly influenced public – and official – opinion through the Western world.

The fact that Kutchinsky himself admits that the research on which he based this claim was only 'a pilot experiment', an 'exploratory study' and that the people he used in it were 'more experienced with pornography than the average population of Copenhagen' and had 'volunteered' for the experiment surely says something not only about the kind of people they were but about the value of this particular piece of Kutchinsky's work.

'Only the tourists buy porn in Denmark' is another myth for which he is responsible. How did he come to that conclusion? He makes no secret about it. He just 'sampled' thirty of the sixty sex shops in Copenhagen by standing in each one for half an hour. He 'eyeballed' the customers as they came in, not speaking to them, not asking whether in fact they *were* tourists, just making up his own mind whether or not they were. The weakness of his research was known long before the Williams Committee sent its representatives to Denmark to sit at his feet.

Kutchinsky had given evidence to the discredited American Presidential Commission (1971) which had similar terms of reference to the Williams Committee and came to similar conclusions.

When all the research carried out for that Commission – under pressure from two members who were concerned that it had not all been made public – was published it was found that the Commission Report contained a 'great variety of common errors, omissions, drawing of incorrect conclusions from flawed research, a manifest systematic bias in marshalling evidence and reporting it'.

In fact it was found that 90 per cent of this research had been suppressed and not given to the Committee which published the Commission's final report. If this had not been so, the Committee could not have claimed that there was 'little evidence of any causal link between pornography and sex crime'. What sort of research was suppressed? Five Commission studies linking pornography and sexual arousal with aggression; the evidence of 254 psychotherapists who found pornography to be an instigator or contributor to a sex crime; the evidence of 84 per cent of the psychiatrists questioned who found similar effects; the fact that media violence was found to be a model for sado-masochistic and sexually violent behaviour. What is more, it was revealed that some of the statistics concerning Danish and USA sex crimes were reported to the Commission as exactly the opposite to what they actually were.

As Professor Eysenck said, 'the Report slid from scientific research to propaganda', and, in due course, it was thrown out by the American Senate by 61 votes to 5.

It was incredible that history should be allowed to repeat itself; amazing that the Williams Committee, although blandly admitting that Kutchinsky's long-promised updating of his early research had not yet been published, should take that early work as the king pin of its 'no harm' conclusions. Was the Committee totally ignorant of the scandal of the American Presidential Report, even though all the evidence to which I refer has been widely published and debated? Or were there, among the Home Office advisors to the Committee, some who knowing of that discredited Report were nonetheless prepared to 'risk it' in the hope that no one would challenge their interpretation of the submissions made to the Presidential Committee?

I vividly remember the visit John Court and I paid to the Home Office in 1975. We realized, perhaps for the first time, just how far a commitment to permissiveness and libertarianism had penetrated the Civil Service at the Home Office, and how totally resistant it was to any suggestion that it would need to rethink its acceptance of Kutchinsky's research. John and I both felt that the evidence he had to offer went 'like water off a duck's back'. It was as though the collective mind of the Home Office had closed in 1970 when the libertarian lobby took Kutchinsky to its heart. This despite the fact that his research was published only a year after the legalization of pornography in Denmark, and long before any valid conclusions could be drawn about its effect.

In spite of Professor Williams' promise to me that if John Court's evidence 'was questioned' – and questioned is hardly a strong enough word for what they did to it – they would 'call him from Australia', they did not do so. Not only that, they would not even accept his offer to send a tape to clarify any points the Committee wanted to raise with him.

What is more, the Committee gave tremendous weight to the review of pornography presented to it by Mr Maurice Jaffe, who had been an 'expert' *defence* witness in some of the most notorious pornography cases of the early 70s. With one 'Not Guilty' verdict after another, thanks to the evidence of the 'experts', these cases pushed back the limits of what was accepted as legal. Jaffe was hardly the person to approach his brief with impartiality.

But what's so special about John Court? Why should the Committee go to so much trouble to talk to him?

John Court has been invited to present the results of his research into whether the availability of pornography and obscenity is in some way associated with harm – and, if so, at what level and of what kind – at professional conferences all over the world. Since he began his research in 1970 the results have been widely published in academic journals and books in many countries and he has been called as a witness in pornography trials in the States, in Australia, and, of course, at Snaresbrook in London.

There has of course been criticism – much of it quite uninformed – of his work. Study of the effect of pornography on human behaviour has been consistently bedevilled by the activities of the permissive lobby and even more so by those with a vested financial interest in the multi-million-pound pornography industry. Endless words and unlimited cash have been poured into propaganda aimed at destroying what they have termed 'the myth' of a link between pornography and sex crime. But it is incredible that the prestigious Home Office sponsored Committee should fall so wholeheartedly for these tactics.

I am sure the Williams Committee did not deliberately intend to further the cause of the pornographers. But some of its most influential members were committed to the intel-lectual/humanist doctrine, so prevalent in the 70s, that man had now 'come of age' and is therefore mature enough to 'handle' pornography without damage to himself, to other people, or to society as a whole. This meant that the Com-mittee's approach to the question of 'harm' was less than objective.

John Court's claim that the evidence placed before it 'was reviewed selectively, evaluated in a biased fashion and ig-nored when convenient' was all too true. The treatment of his own submission to the Committee is proof of that. He presented over 100 pages of scientific, statistical and anecdotal evidence, much of which illustrated the 'harm' associated with pornography. When the Williams Report was published it became clear that although more space (19 pages) was devoted to Court's submission than to any other, that space was devoted to criticism of only twenty-five lines out of the whole of his submission. Ninety-five per cent of it was virtually ignored. Shades of the American Presidential Report! The Home Office representative who assessed John's work for the Williams Committee (Stephen Brody) was the same man we both met at the Home Office in 1975 and whose mind seemed so totally closed to any suggestion that Kutschinsky's work was outdated.

There is one other, by no means insignificant, aspect of the Williams Report which needs to be mentioned. After all the 'palaver' about pornography and the difficulties of showing that any harm results from it, the Committee turned its attention to films – the future of film censorship being the other half of its terms of reference. They saw some film, and this is what the Report said about it:

> It is not simply the extremity of the violence which concerns us: we found it extremely disturbing that highly explicit depictions of mutilation, savagery, menace and humiliation should be presented for the entertainment of an audience in a way that appeared to emphasize the pleasures of sadism. . . It may be that this very graphically presented sadistic material serves only as a vivid object of fantasy, and does no harm at all. There is certainly no conclusive evidence to the contrary. But . . . in this connection it seems entirely sensible to be cautious. . . We are more impressed by the consideration that the extreme vividness and immediacy of film may make it harder rather than easier for some who are attracted to sadistic material to tell the difference between fantasy and reality.

I could almost have written that myself. (It certainly made me wonder whether the Committee had ever actually seen hard-core pornography or whether it had just worked its way through academic argument.) The Committee clearly experienced the same kind of intuitive reaction to pornographic violence in *films* that many people, including me, experienced in relation to pornography generally. The result of that reaction was the Committee's recommendation of what *The Times* described as 'an apparatus of censorship' for the cinema 'exceeding in severity anything known at present to the laws of England'.

The Williams Committee, the paper went on, should 'leave the field as they found it, effectively contested by those who take a more consistently serious view of the harmful consequences of pornography'.

But, of course, the Committee did no such thing. They left behind them almost insurmountable difficulties for those who had been 'effectively contesting' the need for responsibility and compassion and for legislation which enabled this responsibility and compassion to be effective. Certainly I felt more burdened than I ever remember feeling in all the years of campaigning. How could we possibly answer in any kind of effective manner this seductive, elegantly written publication with its half truths, even untruths, its tactical omissions and selective facts, almost all of which the media had accepted at face value? 'There was no dissenting voice in the Committee' was a phrase we heard many times in succeeding months, not least from William Whitelaw, the Home Secretary, as though that were sufficient proof in itself that the Committee's findings should not be questioned. It never seemed to cross anyone's mind that with key positions held by such persuasive, such apparently expert figures as Professor Williams, Anthony Storr and others the rest of the Committee would find it very difficult to dissent. As I wrote in my diary: 'Bernard Williams says so – it must be so. Heaven help us.' And I meant that quite literally.

It was against the background of the findings of the Williams Report that Count Nicolai Tolstoy at National VALA's 1981 Annual Convention had this to say:

> Germany's Weimar Republic (1919–33) was just the sort of society which most of us are trying to prevent arriving here. A distinguished historian of that period says of the pre-Nazi German Republic: 'Morality came to be divorced from sexual matters and in Berlin all

manner of sexual licence and aberrations could be indulged without shame or restraint. Virginity lost its esteem and contraceptive practices gained official recognition. Nudism, homosexuality, sadism, masochism flaunted themselves with immoderation that shocked visitors from Latin countries. The repulsive licence of republican Germany was a preparation for the callous immorality indoctrinated by the Nazi creed. The ascendance of cruelty had begun. A generation which rejected the authority of moral law accepted as divinely inspired by its own parents could have little cause to abide by code of international conduct or humanitarian ethic laid down by a collection of elderly bourgeois gentlemen at Geneva. But while the events of these years atomised and disintegrated the fabric of the German nation, the framework of the State remained absolutely intact. Its official services continued to function so smoothly that often the most attentive observers overlooked the material of moral anarchy beneath. All classes had been eroded by an insidious disease, and so the nation was ready to surrender to radical political doctrine while the machine of state was ready to hand for the demagogue dictator.'

A far cry from what is happening here in Britain? Perhaps not so far. That the signs are written on the wall no one can doubt and neither can we judge the point of no return.

Chapter 18

Just another statistic?

Dear Mrs Whitehouse,

My husband and I both served and survived in the last war and our joy since then has been in successfully raising our children to become useful and worthy members of society. Our elder son is an Environmental Health Officer and the younger a teacher of Biology; but our life has now become marred by worry and constant care and attention of our 16 year-old daughter who suffers with Anorexia Nervosa. At the moment she weighs 6¾ stones, at her worst she was 4¾ stones, and but for the skill and care of our doctors and the grace of God, she would have died. Her normal weight was, and should be, roughly 8¼ stones; she should have sat her 'O' level examinations but, alas, almost two years have been spent in and out of hospitals.

What, you will be asking, has all this to do with the law on obscenity? It transpired, whilst our daughter was under psychotherapy, that she revealed that boys at school had got hold of some offensive Danish mail-order type of material (believed taken from one of their parents bedrooms!). Thus suitably excited and stimulated, they wanted then to see if the female genitalia did really look like the pictures, and so our daughter was one that had to be pinned and held for exploration. Not quite rape – and yet was it? An experience that made her reject her beautiful female body and life in general. If her weight does not soon become normal and remain stable, she could become

sterile and our daughter will need the help of her
Consultant Psychiatrist for a long time yet.

A thoughtful, pretty and talented girl. We are
encouraged by the medical world to lead as normal a
family life as we can and are venturing on holiday
abroad in three weeks time – a threat we hardly dare
permit outselves, as the illness apart, we are also self-
employed. Our daughter, we know, will go through
mental agony at meal times in the Hotel, and we shall
have excuses to make for lack of appetite, etc.; but we
also hope that the holiday could prove a turning point.

If the flow of obscene material of any kind from
Scandinavian countries could be stemmed, and too, if
some of the 'girlie' or soft porn books removed from the
newsagents, I for one would feel a little happier in the
knowledge that perhaps other girls entering puberty
would not have to go through the same torment.
Perhaps other parents too could be spared the
heartbreak.

After that I didn't hesitate any more! And my determination
to fight the Williams Report was made even stronger by the
news of a case in the north of England in which a man was
sentenced to five years' imprisonment for what he had done
to his six-year-old niece. This little girl took her uncle his
newspaper every Sunday morning, stayed there for a while
and then came home. One day, on her way back she was run
over and killed by a car. At the inquest it was stated that
when the post-mortem was carried out on the child it became
evident that the man had used her tiny body in a way, the
judge said, that 'exactly reflected the sexual perversions
shown in the pornographic material found in the prisoner's
house'.

That little one haunts me still. I think of her, too young
to tell, perhaps too bemused by what had happened to her
even to see the car that killed her. Just another statistic? Or
perhaps not even that, perhaps just the kind of 'anecdotal
evidence' for which the Williams Committee had so little
time. We *had* to expose the fallacies of the Report however
entrenched its advocates might be.

We decided it was essential to try to bring John Court over from Australia. We did so in early July 1980. He was speaking at a Leipzig Convention in the middle of that month and was more than willing to break his journey and come to Britain for the best part of a week. His visit this time proved, if anything, even more hectic than when he came to give evidence in the Snaresbrook trial in 1977.

A fortnight before he came, trying to get everything organized, I tripped up the step from the lawn and went 'a purler' on the concrete terrace as I was running in from the garden to answer the phone. That thoroughly shook me and left me with a *very* stiff and painful leg and a sharp pain in my ribs.

This was the very weekend it was announced that I was included in the Queen's Honours List. I found that overwhelming too, and much more disorientating in a strange kind of way than the endless brickbats. I suppose they'd become almost a way of life for me, but to be made a CBE! It was wonderful, of course, and the day at the Palace with my family several months later and the words the Queen exchanged with me were most memorable and a privilege which I shall always treasure.

As soon as I knew John was coming I wrote to Professor Williams to ask if he would be prepared to meet Dr Court 'publicly'. He rang to ask what I meant by 'publicly'. It was 'a word to cover all possibilities', I replied. He agreed in principle but – quite understandably – said he would *not* be interested in a short TV confrontation. Taking a deep breath I asked if he would be prepared to be interviewed for an 'in-depth' article, along with John by, say, *The Times* – for that was what I most wanted to happen. He said he would, which was marvellous.

The account in my diary of John's three-day visit is full of such things as:

Early phone call from *World at One* – would Dr Court be available if Professor Williams was agreeable to be available too? Most certainly . . . John interviewed by Brian Hayes of London Broadcasting Company – in great form . . . both of us filmed crossing Fleet Street as we went to St Bride's for our very well-attended press conference – had to cross several times because the traffic hid us from the TV cameras. . . Phone-call from *World at One* to say Professor Williams *not* available . . . John did several other radio interviews and a long TV interview before going to the House of Lords to address a group of Peers and MPs after which we had dinner there.

A bit futher on:

All arrangements for Thursday thrown into disarray because ATV invited us both to take part in a current affairs programme to be recorded that morning – with Professor Simpson of the Williams Committee, John Lindsey the sex shop operator and Martin Cole. . . Back to London for a meeting with Head of Obscene Publications Department at New Scotland Yard and several of its officers. Then out – by police car – to a lovely house once owned by Conan Doyle, now a police sports club, where I was due to speak anyway. Back to Fleet Street to meet Peregrine Worsthorne at *The Sunday Telegraph* offices – his piece the following Sunday concluded that "the sooner it (the Williams Report) was forgotten the better" . . . John spoke to a group of doctors at the Royal Society of Medicine. . . Met publisher of his new book at the Royal Commonwealth Club – John fell asleep in the middle of the conversation – not the least bit surprised – he hasn't stopped since he arrived at Heathrow . . . Across to the New Gallery for John's one public meeting – *very* good – David Webb and his 'anti-censorship brigade' were there endeavouring to take over the meeting and shout John down, i.e. censor everyone else's opportunity to speak if they're not saying things you want them to say! James Firman of the British Board of Film Censors was there, so was the President of the National Council of Women and the Police Federation and the Church of England Board of Social Responsibility were represented. . .

Interview for Terry Wogan's programme . . . meeting
with some further colleagues from Edinburgh. . .

Most important of all during that week Mr Whitelaw, the
Home Secretary, agreed that Dr Brian Mawhinney, MP for
Peterborough, should take John to meet him in his room at
the Commons.

Pressure had been building for the Home Secretary to see
John Court personally. Ronald Butt, political columnist of
The Times, devoted the whole of his centre page article (26
June 1980) to the significance of John's visit, telling Mr
Whitelaw that he 'should rise above the Williams Report and
start by seeing Dr Court'. After declaring that the Williams
Report was 'suffused throughout by the formalistic, logic
chopping, low grade philosophising for which the late Professor Joad had achieved a certain fame' (ouch!) Ronald Butt
went on to tell the Home Secretary that he 'should reflect
that the knowledge and instinct of the public in this matter
is more important than the skill of a handful of committee
sitters using their intellectual agility to verbalise a social
problem out of existence'. The Home Secretary said after his
meeting with John and Dr Mawhinney that although this
was a private occasion John was perfectly free to say that
they had met and talked together and that he, Mr Whitelaw,
had found the conversation – which went on considerably
longer than the time allotted for it – 'most useful'.

John had already left Britain when the BBC rang, wanting
to do a phone-in programme with him. But Gerald Priestland
devoted the whole of his Saturday morning *Thought for the
Day* to John's new book *Pornography – a Christian Critique*
(Paternoster Press). And *The Daily Star* rang for John's
address in Leipzig, cross with themselves that they'd missed
him. The meeting between John Court and Professor Williams did take place at *The Times.* It was, I gathered, a very
civilized occasion lasting about an hour and a half. But for
better or worse it was never published. This may have been
because, by the time it was ready for publication, so much
publicity had already been given to John's visit and his views.

By the end of that week I think it would be true to say
that many people had at least a large question mark in their

minds as to the value of the Williams Report. John Court's visit certainly left us in a much stronger position to carry on our fight. Other things were happening too.

One of our earliest moves had been to send a copy of the Williams Report to Denmark. We wanted to get an objective assessment of the real situation in that country. Dr Inge Krogh, who is not only a member of the Danish Parliament but also Chief Psychiatrist at the Mental Hospital in Nyborg, was one of those who read it and this was her assessment:

> From the Bernard Williams Report of the Committee on Obscenity and Film Censorship it appears, that after the legalization of pornography in Denmark in 1969 there was a heavy decline in the interest in pornography. That is not true. There are still a large number of shops with pornography only.
>
> A district in Copenhagen, Vesterbro, has been completely changed into a district with porno-shops, massage clinics and prostitution. The streets are characterized by drug addicts, alcoholic abuse and violence. Formerly it was a residential quarter; now only a few guest workers live there. In a street in this district, Istedgade, there are 30 porno-shops with 'cinemas', showing non-stop films, in a distance of 400 metres. . . In the Copenhagen municipality 60–70 people have the licence to run such 'cinemas'. Except for these shops, where solely pornography is sold, you can see pornographic booklets and cassettes with films and exposures in practically every newsstand all over the country.

And as for the comment in the Williams Report that sex crimes had 'evened out' in the early 70s Dr Krogh, *referring* to the official gazette of statistics, had this to say:

> In 1970, 47 cases of rape and the like were reported in the police districts of greater Copenhagen; during the years 1971 to 1978 inclusive, the number of reported cases was 101, 83, 87, 94, 97, 101, 110 and 257 respectively. I have unofficially been informed that there

was an increase of some 200 additional cases in 1979. Heterosexual infringement of minors was reported in 1970 in 75 cases. For the years 1971 to 1978 inclusive the number of cases was 87, 79, 77, 142, 123, 82, 124 and 112 respectively.

The statistics likewise based on the police districts of greater Copenhagen regarding homosexual immorality involving children under 15 years of age include 69, 60, 33, 34, 55, 103, 56, 269, and 82 reported cases for the years 1970 to 1978 respectively.

She added:

A police inspector in one of our larger towns has informed me that in 90 per cent of all rape cases they find that pornography has been used by the sex criminals. . . One must conclude therefore that liberation of pornography has resulted in a constant flood of pornography in our country and ordinary magazines read by children and young people being strongly influenced thereby.

Clearly there are those who are less than happy about what has been called 'the Danish experiment'. And it is now clear that there are unhappy people in Sweden too. Hans Nestius who twenty-five years ago led the campaign for the repeal of what he termed 'public morality' legislation says[1] that what he wanted to do was ensure that 'everything should be free and open. We wanted light and air in the sexual sense'. But he admits that he now 'bitterly regrets' what he did, for pornography in Sweden now 'plunges from excess to excess' while sexual crimes have continued to rise and prostitution has increased. 'Sex capitalism has taken over' he declares. 'Something like every third man in Sweden' reads a man's magazine in which pornography is mixed with allegedly serious news reports. All this has caused Mr Nestius, now he says an 'older, wiser man', to spearhead a new campaign *against* the pornography moguls and *for* tighter obscenity

[1] *Sweden Today*, Spring 1981.

legislation. Apparently he has already had some minor successes.

Why then does Britain have to tread the same disastrous path before we learn the bitter lesson of Sweden and Denmark? *Why* will we not learn?

What in the long run did all our own efforts amount to? On the positive side, the Danish 'myth' which had established the idea that when obscenity is legalized sex crime diminishes certainly became a great deal more mythical. John Court's deliberately tarnished reputation was much enhanced and he became known to millions as a very articulate, highly intelligent person (no longer some vague name from 'down under') and to Government, MPs and journalists as a responsible and well-informed academic to be taken very seriously indeed. Our own position was greatly strengthened and we had placed in the hands of the Home Office all the ammunition necessary to reject the Williams Report.

But now, looking back, what do we find? As far as the official attitude towards Williams is concerned it would seem we might almost as well not have bothered. The Government, after considerable pressure including from its own back-benchers, did finally debate Williams, but only as the House adjourned for the summer recess in 1981. No vote was taken. So Williams effectively stood.

The failure of the Home Office to reject the Report's recommendation that shops with blank windows should be permitted to sell hard-core pornography to anyone of eighteen years or over resulted in the plague of sex shops which are now causing so much alarm and distress. Its recommendation that the printed word should not be covered by obscene legislation has meant that public libraries up and down the country are now stocking a great many books which would previously have been rejected. Its recommendation that only pornography showing actual bodily harm should be prosecuted has meant that Chief Constables have received 'advice' that this should indeed be their policy.

In one of our meetings with Mr Whitelaw to discuss Williams, the Home Secretary said to me, 'Mrs Whitehouse, I am sure you believe that if I *would*, I *could*. But I cannot.' He was clearly convinced that Parliament would not support firmer legislation on pornography and obscenity. I have never believed that to be true. I am as sure as I can be that, whatever their personal prediliction might be, constituency pressure on individual MPs would be irresistible. Of course, Mr Whitelaw knows Parliament a great deal better than I do, but I honestly believe he has made a serious misjudgement.

In the meantime the lengths to which the pornography industry has gone to persuade the population that sex shops are just what we have all been waiting for, are, to the average person inexperienced in the corruption which lies at the heart of that industry, almost unbelievable.

One small example is the letters signed by one 'Louise London', Secretary of something called 'The Society for the Campaign for Freedom in Publishing,' which she says 'supports the complete legalization of the sale of pornography in "Adult only bookshops" '. These letters have appeared in provincial and local newspapers all over the country. For some years now one of our colleagues has set himself the task of reporting not only to us but, at our request, to the press through an arrangement in which they know neither his name nor the telephone number from which he speaks.

His work has been absolutely invaluable not only to us but also to the police. He had previously 'looked into' an address in Leytonstone given by Louise London and as a result the police raided the premises. These premises were in fact a lock-up garage stocked with 'girlie' magazines and Miss London herself is based at another address—one of the best-known outlets for pornography in Britain, and one of the many shops used by self-styled pornography king David Sullivan.

Sullivan, who lives in a £1 million mansion in the fashionable Essex suburb of Chigwell is best known in the pornography world as the man who launched Mary Millington, the sex queen who committed suicide in 1979 – not very long after she changed her name by deed poll to 'Mary Whitehouse' to launch *Whitehouse* magazine, one of the most pornographic magazines on sale in Britain today.

Interesting too that another colleague of ours who wrote to Louise London for details of her campaign received in reply a leaflet setting out the campaign's aims which carried the same telephone number as Conegate, Junecroft, Centre-wall – all sex shop syndicates.

We knew that firms like Sullivan's were buying up prop-erty in towns all over the country, even before the Williams Committee reported. They must have had a strong suspicion that it would produce a permissive report.

The Government's failure specifically to reject at least certain parts of the Williams Report has effectively given the go-ahead to the pornography. They have taken advantage of the Government inaction and presented it with a *fait accompli* which gets ever more difficult to cope with as day by day more shops open and become established.

In 1981 the Greater London Council produced a Bill which would give it power to licence sex shops. I have always felt that when a Government 'licences' anything whether it be sex shops – or, heaven help us, brothels[1] – it gives an aura of acceptability, even legitimacy, to such establishments.

In the meantime we had asked our legal advisers to pre-pare a Bill to bring the establishment of sex shops under planning control, since it seemed to us, and I think to most other people, that only so could the will of the people living within a community be decisive.

We had suggested such legislation to the Home Office on a number of occasions but without success, so we felt that the only hope lay in a Private Member's Bill. If we were to succeed in finding an MP who would present such a Bill we had to move very quickly when the new Session of Parliament opened in November 1981. We had six copies of our Bill duplicated, I wrote six letters and attached appropriate back-ground material, and set off for the House of Commons to arrive in the Central Lobby on the dot of 12.30 on 12 Novem-ber. The draw for the names of MPs who would be able to present a Private Member's Bill took place at that hour and the Voting Officer in the House had agreed to meet me

[1] On 25 November 1981 Mr Giles Shaw, Under Secretary of State for the Environment, speaking in the House of Commons announced that the Home Secretary's Criminal Law Revision Committee would be shortly issuing a Working Paper to include discussion on whether brothels should be licensed or otherwise permitted in certain areas.

immediately afterwards with the names of the top six MPs. This was, of course, public knowledge once the draw was made. I filled in their names on my letters and the policeman in the Central Lobby delivered them for me. One MP was quoted in *The Guardian* as saying that he received his letter within five minutes of the draw being made!

Little good it all did – in spite of the fact that a very great number of letters went to the various MPs asking them to introduce our Bill. A telegram was even sent from the City of London Rotary Club at whose lunch, at the Cafe Royal, Regent Street, I was speaking the following day.

All the MPs to whom we'd written replied and several of them expressed considerable interest, one in particular. But, in the end, nothing came of it because the Government made it clear, unofficially, that it would not be willing to support such a Bill, and without such support there was no hope that it could reach the statute book.

To say that we were disappointed is an understatement. We reckoned that the GLC Bill could not be law, anyway, before the summer of 1982 at the earliest. The Government would then want to 'assess its practicality' before extending the law to the rest of the country. 'How long does it take to make any real assessments?' we asked ourselves. 'Certainly beyond the lifetime of this Government,' we reckoned. And in the meantime? Well, one thing was certain – Conegate, the major sex shop firm, would have long passed its target of 150 shops.

I often wish I could bring the people who actually suffer in a situation like this face to face with the politicians. Take, for example, the good, clean-living couple who found themselves in receipt of one obscene phone-call after another, asking for the perverted sex practices they were apparently offering. Why? Because, having seen this couple's name and address at the bottom of a letter they had written to the local paper expressing objections to a proposed sex shop in their vicinity, the sex shop entrepreneurs found their telephone number and placed it in a 'contact' magazine.

Whether the licensing of these establishments becomes a legal necessity or not, the fact remains that until effective obscenity laws are passed their managers will be free to sell blatantly pornographic material. The Government admits that the 1959 Obscene Publications Act is 'in ruins', and no wonder. In 1977 the DPP issued confidential 'guide lines' to the police. These advised that legal action should only be taken against pornography involving actual physical harm, such as flagellation, bondage, what is euphemistically described as 'Scandinavian butcher-shop sex', bestiality, buggery and certain perversions connected with bodily excreta. Since then much material which by both dictionary and common definition would have been considered obscene has passed over the counter without legal let or hindrance.

It has seemed to us that in so doing the DPP has interpreted the law in a way which is contrary to the original intention of Parliament and, arguably, usurped the role of Parliament itself. What is more, the existence of such a 'list' as a practical guide really destroys the case of those in the Home Office who, throughout the lifetime of successive Governments, have rejected our proposals for obscenity legislation which would state precisely the type of publication which would be actionable.

In pressing for such action we know that we have the support of those who have to enforce the law. As a Deputy Commissioner at New Scotland Yard said to us[1]: 'The whole subject is complex. All police forces are of the opinion that the present law should be clarified – and simplified – in order that police and public alike are able to distinguish what is or is not prosecutable without recourse to legal arguments and interpretation of sometimes vague words and phrases.'

What is more, in a letter[2] to me the Prime Minister said that she recognized and shared the widespread concern that exists about pornography. She went on: 'The Government's duty is to find solutions which are acceptable to Parliament and the country and which would be lasting and enforceable.' Up to the time of writing, there are no signs of 'lasting and enforceable laws' to control pornography and it is against this background that the licensing of sex shops appears not only as the easy way out but as a denial of what the Govern-

[1] 23 March 1981.
[2] 26 March 1981.

ment itself would wish to do. What is the obstacle? And why is it that when it comes to the crunch the Conservative Government is as unwilling – or unable? – as its predecessors to do anything to tighten these disastrous laws?

All our campaigning in this field has brought us up against the total resistance of the Home Office to any fresh obscenity legislation. Such intransigence can only be explained by the commitment to the liberal/'permissive' establishment which has run deep and far amongst the permanent staff in that Ministry. It is when all our efforts founder on the seemingly impregnable power and prejudice which exists at that level amongst unelected bureaucrats that we begin to understand the breaking-point of democracy.

As far as we could see only one alternative was left to us and that was to raise the matter with the United Nations. But before doing so I wrote to Mr Whitelaw to ask him:

> . . . whether, prior to the Government's decision to licence sex shops, you withdrew your contract as a signatory to the International Convention for the Suppression of the Circulation of and Traffic in Obscene Publications.
>
> You will be aware that, under Article 1 of the Convention, the British Government agreed 'to take all measures to discover, prosecute and punish any person commiting the offence of distributing obscene articles by way of trade'.
>
> We are of the firm belief that, unless such a withdrawal has taken place, the Government is in serious breach of its contract under that Convention on two counts.
>
> First: through its failure to replace with effective legislation the Obscenity Laws of 1959 and 1964, now recognized by you yourself Sir, by Parliament, by the courts, by police and by the public to be 'in ruins'.
>
> Second: by its intention of licensing sex shops in the full knowledge that obscene material will be distributed 'by way of trade' in these establishments.
>
> Public anxiety over the current prevalence of the crime of rape, the suffering inflicted by it, highlights the

established link between pornography and serious sex crime, international evidence of which we have consistently presented to successive Governments, including your own.

The Government's intention of licensing sex shops could well constitute a breach of international law as set out in the Convention mentioned above. Moreover, by failing, at the same time, to introduce effective obscenity law the Government exposes the women of this country to considerable risk and in so doing abdicates its duty to protect the life and liberty of its people.

In his reply the Home Secretary said:

As regards the point you raised about compliance with the International Convention for the suppression of the circulation of and traffic in obscene publications, the Government has no reason for thinking that the introduction of the proposed arrangements would conflict with the requirements of the Convention. The grant of a licence would confer no immunity from the provisions of the Obscene Publications Acts or other relevant legislation which we believe fulfil our obligations under the Convention. The amendments which have been tabled to the Local Government (Miscellaneous Provisions) Bill and which were passed at the Report Stage at the Bill on 3 February made it clear that the proposed licensing arrangements will not render anything lawful which is at present unlawful.

My diary, 22 December 1981:

It was like the slamming of a door at the end of a tunnel. 'I can't believe it!' I told the journalist at the other end of the phone. 'But it's just been announced in the House of Commons!' he replied.

'It' was an announcement by the Government that it intended to bring sex shops *all over the country* under licensing control immediately. I felt shattered. As long as the Government was in a state of waiting to see how the GLC legislation was working, we felt we had *time*. Now, once the shops are licensed, without doubt the heat will go out of the controversy surrounding them, and people will feel that the problem was dealt with. Whatever care may be used in the early days, before long the licensing of sex shops will become routine council business – how can people be expected to carry the burden of vigilance year after year? It is inhuman to expect it, and naive to think it could happen.

And without effective obscenity laws? Inevitably the licensing process will give respectability to what lies beneath – talk about the Victorians and their penchant, so we're told, for covering up table legs! They had nothing on us!

It may indeed be that our next move has to be with the United Nations.

Chapter 19

Signs of hope

First, I am not a critic of the West. I repeat that for nearly all our lives we worshipped it – note the word 'worshipped'. I am not a critic of the West, I am a critic of the weakness of the West. I am a critic of a fact which we can't comprehend: how one can lose one's spiritual strength, one's will-power, and possessing freedom not value it, not be willing to make sacrifices for it. . .

. . . those people who have lived in the most terrible conditions, on the frontier between life and death, be it people from the West or from the East – they all understand that between good and evil there is an irreconcilable contradiction, that good or evil are not one and the same thing, that one cannot build one's life without regard to this distinction.

Alexander Solzhenitsyn, 'Warning to the Western World', *Panorama* interview, 1 March 1976

'Tell us, Mrs Whitehouse' – the faces of the small group of students were smiling but sceptical – 'are all those stories about your early visits to Cambridge *true*?'

'Like the skull?' I asked. They nodded vigorously.

'It's all part of Cambridge mythology – the story is handed down from year to year and we thought it'd probably been much embroidered in the process!'

'There was no need to embroider what happened *that* night,' I told them.

This was during the reception before the debate in the Cambridge Union in November 1981 on the motion that 'A law on obscenity is a necessary protection for the individual and society'. I was proposing and Victor Lownes, the sacked Chairman of the *Playboy* organization in Britain, was opposing. We had met earlier the same year at Oxford, when I had been supported by John Smyth QC (Prosecuting Counsel in the *Gay News* case) and by Tim Sainsbury MP whose Indecent Displays Bill became law later that year.

On that occasion – and well in advance – Victor Lownes had informed the press that he was bringing Christine Keeler and Mandy Rice Davies to support him. Such is their notoriety, even twenty years after the Profumo affair, that the media 'build up' to the event and the coverage of the debate itself was tremendous.

We won that night by fifteen votes, even though the wording of the motion 'A licence for pornography is a denial of freedom' was so confusing that many students who were sympathetic to the idea behind the motion abstained. (The word 'A' was inserted at the last moment to please Victor Lownes.)

When later in the year Giles Kavanagh, President of the Cambridge Union, rang to ask if I would take part in a similar debate there, I very quickly replied, 'Not likely. I'm not going around in a circus with Mr Lownes!'

'Oh, but Mrs Whitehouse, we heard what a marvellous debate it was and we didn't hear it, won't you please. . .' etc, etc. So I agreed.

This time the Rt Rev. Maurice Wood, Lord Bishop of Norwich, who took time out from the Church Assembly to come to Cambridge, spoke for the motion with me – how the students appreciated both him as a person and what he said! As several of them sat having a 'nightcap' with me afterwards and discussing the debate, they all agreed that the Bishop's visit 'had meant much to the University'.

'This place is full of clerics – either too trendy to command our respect or too theological to be able to communicate naturally with us – it was marvellous to see him debating like that on the floor of the Union.'

We won by 161 votes! I was so grateful for that – in the very week in which Mr William Whitelaw, the Home Secretary, had written once again to say that he could not take action to tighten up the obscenity law because there was 'no consensus'. I don't know whether he read *The Times* report next morning, but if he did I hope he took note of the fact that our two greatest universities had voted, in one case resoundingly and directly, in favour of the stand we were taking.

But back to the 'skeleton'. For very different reasons the 1971 debate was as memorable as this latest one. Covered by BBC TV for an open-ended *Aquarius* programme[1] – though in the end that had to be considerably cut because of the obscenities used by Richard Neville of *School Kids OZ* 'fame' – it attracted a huge audience.

When we arrived at the Union we had almost literally to fight our way past a long queue of students angered that they could not get into an already packed hall. The seats and standing-room had apparently been filled an hour before the debate began.

Of course, the line-up of speakers was, to say the least, newsworthy. The motion 'That pornography should never be prohibited' was proposed by John Mortimer QC, supported by Richard Neville. I opposed the motion, as did Lord Longford and several brave students.

It so happpend that I was suffering from one of my 'throats' and my voice was in very poor shape indeed – in fact I had got out of bed for the first time for several days to go to Cambridge. Ernest drove me there on a dark, wet and foggy night. Half-way he stopped the car because I felt so sick and ill and we really did wonder if we should turn back. But we said a little prayer and went on. I asked Arianna Stassinopoulos, President of the Union, and in the Chair, whether she would explain that I had hardly any voice when she introduced me, but she didn't and I stood up wondering just what sort of a sound, if any, was going to come out of my mouth. But, as so often happens on these occasions, I was given the strength I needed – and I needed a lot.

The noise, certainly when Frank Longford and I were speaking, was loud and continuous and there was much laughter at our expense, though most of it was good humoured. I learnt later that one roar of laughter, which bewildered me, was accounted for by the fact that I'd quite unconsciously given the 'V' sign in the obscene way. However, the greatest roar came when some wag let down a skull

[1] 6 November 1971.

from the balcony behind me while I was speaking. I, of course, couldn't see it. I hadn't the faintest idea what the noise was all about or the reason for the cry of 'Alas, poor Yorick' from the floor. That started the laughter all over again. It was only when I watched the TV programme later that I realized what the excitement was all about.

Richard Neville, whose appeal against the *School Kids OZ* verdict was to be heard the following week, was given a hero's welcome by the students many of whom wore the long flowing hair which had been his style before it was cut off when he was kept in custody. He spent most of his time quoting selectively from my then newly-published book, *Who does she think she is?* I said later that I was glad it had been published, as otherwise 'what on earth would he have found to say?' At the end of it all, 400 voted for the motion and 200 against – which really, considering the circumstances both in the Union itself and in the 'hippy' world outside at that time, was not too bad.

I suppose of all my debating experiences the worst ever was at Leicester University in the late 60s, though I don't remember the wording of the motion because we never got round to debating it. I'd been invited to debate with John Trevelyan, then Secretary of the British Board of Film Censors, but when I arrived there was no sign of him. In his place was Edward Bond, the playwright, author of the notorious play *Saved* which had been shown at the Royal Court Theatre several years previously. It was of this play that Penelope Gilliatt wrote in *The Spectator*: 'I spent a lot of the first act·shaking with claustrophobia and thinking I was going to be sick. The scene where a baby is pelted to death is nauseating. The swagger of sex jokes is almost worse. . .'

In a packed-beyond-capacity house Bond opened the proceedings by referring not to the motion but to the obscene descriptions of me he *said* he'd read on the walls of the lavatory he'd just visited. Bond whipped up the audience into what could only be described as a frenzy. He accused me, amongst other things of being 'responsible for the Moors murders'.

When I stood up to speak the obscenities flowed thick and fast, both from the mouths of individuals and as endless chants from students standing up and gesticulating in the gallery, while on the floor others crawled round and round my feet. A madhouse? Indeed it seemed very much like it as I battled on for about forty minutes, unable to make my voice heard, let alone present any argument. The President of the Union found it impossible to control the meeting, though one of Bond's visiting supporters took the microphone and disassociated himself from what was happening.

Whenever I tell this story people say to me 'Why on earth did you stand there all that time?' I wasn't capable of thinking very coherently about it, I just had a gut feeling that as long as I stood in front of them, I was a challenge. I was, after all, more than old enough to be their mother. Would they allow what was happening to me to happen to their own mothers? Afterwards some of the students who'd sat silent through it all came over to apologize shamefacedly not only for what had happened but for their own lack of courage in staying silent. A measure of just how bad it was that night was highlighted by the provincial paper, *The Leicester Mercury*, the following night. It contained a space empty except for the statement that it had been reserved for a report on the debate but that the proceedings had been too obscene to publish.

At the end of it all I was totally exhausted. But, as so often happens, good came out of it. Malcolm Muggeridge rang me a few days later and, hearing the tiredness in my voice, asked what was the matter. After I had explained he said to me, 'Mary, what are we going to *do* for these young people?' How can we 'mobilize the cohorts and demonstrate our faith and belief?' 'We must have a great festival of *light*,' he said. And that was when the idea which blossomed in the great Festival of Light demonstration in Trafalgar Square in 1971 was born.

It was during a debate in the early 70s at an Essex Sixth Form Conference that one of the participants – a member of the BBC Religious Department – called me 'a most dangerous woman', though he has been by no means the only one to regard me as such! But I have always treasured the memory of the courage and kindness of the boy at the back of the hall who, after all the members of the panel had had their 'go' at me, stood up and called out, 'I don't necessarily agree with all that Mrs Whitehouse has been saying, but I can't keep quiet any longer. She spoke about the need to think about the vulnerable people, but it seems to me that she's the most vulnerable person of all, and I feel so ashamed that all of us, staff as well, have sat here without anyone raising a voice in her defence.' There was dead silence when he sat down and I have to confess my eyes filled with tears.

These sorts of experience were in one way and other commonplace for me during the 60s and indeed well into the 70s. But they all had their encouraging sides, too. After Professor Richard Hoggart, during a 'Teach-in on Censorship' – where I'd clearly been set up as, hopefully, the Aunt Sally – made some reference to me being 'abnormal', George Bilainkin, the writer, quietly took the microphone from him and defended me. It was only afterwards that I realized that he had come all the way to Leicester University with eight stitches in his head and against doctor's orders because he said he was convinced that something of this kind would happen and, 'I wanted to make sure that someone stood up for you.' Dear George.

My first appearance at the Oxford Union followed a phone-call from the President.

'Mrs Whitehouse – we are most anxious to have you in the Union, but you never seem prepared to debate the motions we offer you.'

'That's because they're always such silly ones,' I replied.

'Then perhaps you would like to suggest one that you *would* be prepared to debate?' he promptly asked, and then gladly accepted the proposition that 'This House regrets the failure of the Broadcasting Authorities to provide adequate facilities for public participation'.

'By the way – who do you have in mind to oppose the motion?' I asked.

'Mr Charles Curran, Director-General of the BBC,' came the reply.

'You'll be lucky!' I laughed. 'Not at all,' countered the President. 'Mr Curran has already promised he will debate in the Union to defend the BBC.'

I was quite convinced that Mr Curran would not meet *me* in this setting, but, whoever I eventually faced across the floor of the Oxford Union, I felt it would be a very great honour to stand where so many famous men had stood in the past.

But what a disappointment it all was.

Part of the University building was 'occupied' on this particular night and this, no doubt, had its effect on the evening's proceedings. The two students who were 'supporting' my motion did just the reverse, evading any serious discussion, and ridiculing the type of person who wanted to 'clean up' TV. One of them referred contemptuously to the 'plastic flowers which doubtless filled my window pots'. Me, *plastic* flowers! Urged on by my neighbour, and by now thoroughly fed-up with the whole business, I jumped to my feet for a point of 'information'. 'But why is the Honourable Proposer so critical of plastic flowers – is he not himself an enthusiast for this material? I judge by the nature of the jacket he is wearing.' This brought roars of delighted approval from the House, and a welcome bonus to me.

Speaking against the motion was Christi Davis, former President of the Cambridge Union and later a BBC producer, who made the rafters shake in a tirade reminiscent of the 30s, and which left me branded as a 'fascist' and of course a 'reactionary' but did not attempt to reply to the motion.

Personal abuse, misquotation and untruths, came so thick and fast on such occasions that I used to feel almost punch-drunk and quite unable to deal adequately with what one grew to recognize as the anarchistic tactics of the opposition. On that particular occasion I could not help but reflect as I found my own way back to my hotel around midnight, how strange it was that those who yell loudest in the cause of *student* participation fight to the death any idea of *public* participation in a medium which has such a profound effect upon all our lives!'

Things were better at Birmingham, where my proposition that 'There is too much sex and violence on television', at a debate described by the University magazine *Red Brick* as 'the biggest of the year', resulted in an incredible vote of 185 for the motion, 58 against and 133 abstentions.

This debate was the first sign of the change in student attitudes not only to our work but to the permissive society as a whole. Interesting too that some of its protagonists, such as the publisher John Calder and John Mortimer himself, no longer seem anything like as anxious as they used to be to meet me in debate. I don't think I am now saying anything fundamentally different from what I always have, though I may say it with more confidence and from time to time with more humour.

The change is, I think, in the students themselves. Many, many times during the earlier years of my campaigning and when things have been most difficult, I have been comforted by the belief that if one could hold on long enough the time would come when the so-called radical, progressive ideas and personalities of 'the revolutionary sixties' would themselves become the hated 'establishment'. I felt confident, in my heart, that the young then growing up would do what the young have always done to a greater or lesser degree – rebel against it. And now indeed this is happening.

But many of the young people I meet now in the universities are not rebelling in any negative sense, rather they are throwing off the shackles the so-called freedom of the 'permissive years' has cast around them, not least because they are finding the true freedom of spirit and love which is embodied in the Christian experience. At both Oxford and Cambridge I have been told that the Christian Unions and other Christian groups are the strongest and fastest growing societies among student organizations. And to be told, as I was at the Oxford debate with Victor Lownes, that four men students – I met them afterwards – had come all the way from Cambridge to attend the debate and sit praying for me throughout, was wonderful. The care that lay behind that made me feel almost like a child, such security it gave me.

What do I *say* at university debates? These days I rarely speak from a prepared speech, not least because there are always topical issues – such as the Williams Report or the sex shops, social violence – which have to be incorporated. But I did prepare very carefully a speech I gave at Bristol University when I debated with John Calder[1] on the matter

---

[1] Publisher of *Last Exit to Brooklyn*.

of censorship and I think part of that address illustrates that what I'm *actually* saying about censorship is not necessarily what is so often attributed to me.

The censorship of fact, whether political or civil is indefensible, and I would defend everyone's right to put down his ideas and experiences however turbulent or destructive these may be.

The issue of 'control' arises at the point when these creative exercises, whether in the field of TV, literature, the stage, cinema or photography, are offered for public presentation.

I hope that Mr Calder, who sees a censor under every bed, will be able tonight to give you his specific reasons for believing that all forms of censorship should be abolished, instead of simply adopting his usual technique of equating censorship with political views we all deplore.

The move towards total abolition of censorship has come not primarily from the young, but from those who have something to gain from a change of public attitudes and in the law. Motives may be personal – Aldous Huxley confessed, at the end of his life, that the efforts of himself and his friends to normalize perversion were motivated by the desire 'to make all men like themselves'; they may be political, for pornography is an ideological weapon – the soft, the in-turned, the indulgent will not fight on any level, while the corrupted will sell not only themselves but their country; and most obviously, they may be financial.

But behind all the guile and no doubt deliberately-created confusion lies a simple choice. It is between genuine freedom and total licence, between cultural responsibility and cultural anarchy. Public sex is a restriction of our private freedom. Most of us are nauseated by it because it offends the personal privacy which is an essential part of the rights of the individual – we resist when this liberty is curtailed.

The 'new libertarians' are, in fact, the new tyrants. While they try to discredit with a yell of 'fascist' those who defend decency and culture, they themselves launch an assault upon the senses and freedom of the individual which is the essence of the worst kind of dictatorship. The radical left are convinced that sexual permissiveness and moral relaxation are primary conditions to the establishment of the 'alternative society' and those who think that the increasing acceptance of blasphemies and obscenities is simply part of an evolving contemporary society are being dangerously naive. James Michener, author of *Kent State – What Happened and Why?*, says: 'Numerous committed revolutionaries have preached that the debasement of language is one of the most powerful agencies for the destruction of existing society. They argue, "if you destroy the word, you can destroy the system", and they have consciously set out to do both.' So pornography and obscenity are seen not simply as a matter of personal taste but as accepted ideological weapons.

The greatest danger, particularly to the young, is that we may come to accept as normal what is, in fact, exceptional and vile. Speaking in Oxford recently Mr Calder said that he 'refused to believe that art can make people better or worse' and that 'books do not affect behaviour'. Extraordinary! Is Mr Calder claiming that the Bible and *Das Kapital* have never affected behaviour? And there is humbug and hypocrisy of a similar kind in the attitude of many of the anti-censorship brigade to the question of violence – so often the people who rightly castigate the brutality of the Vietnam War are found defending the sadistic in literature, films, stage and television. . .

Alongside the demand for a removal of controls of all kinds from the media, we have often from the same source a denigration, a destruction, and indeed a censorship of the proven values which give us a basis for judgement. Consequently, the basic fight between good and evil which is the essence of drama – and of life – have been largely obliterated from contemporary art. In these respects we are a deprived society. 'Evil be thou my good' is the essence of 'Paradise lost', not only in Milton's day but in our own.

Responsible control on every level is the only answer. That way we shall make progress. The creative growth of a society, as well as its stability, depend upon the willingness of the individual to accept responsibility for his behaviour within that society. Only so can the vitality of the community be released and engage itself with the problems which face it on all levels.

The other path, which Mr Calder advocates, leads us into a new dark age.

I gave that address ten years ago – I have given the substance of it in many forms and in many places, many times since. What I think I can say now, with a fair amount of accuracy, is that whereas such ideas were once, and not so long ago, laughed out of court by the trendies, the libertarians, and those with vested interests in permissiveness, they are listened to now with respect and with a certain hunger for things to be different.

I visited Cambridge University again only a few weeks ago. I was told that every Saturday night around 800 students meet for Bible study. Every *Saturday* night! What joy and hope for the future lies there.

Chapter 20

The Romans
in Britain

Dear Mary,

I have read in the papers that you are against the play *The Romans in Britain* currently running at the National Theatre. I am fifteen years old and I must say that I support you in your campaign to have these people prosecuted. From what I have read and heard this play sounds obscene and filthy and if this sort of 'smut' is all the National Theatre can do with our money then I suggest that they close down. We, the teenagers of today, are labelled troublemakers and hooligans but if that is the sort of example we are being set by our more intelligent elders who are more 'experienced' than us then all I can say is 'God help us!' If this play is to be allowed to continue running then how many more plays and films like it are going to be made? Already the controversial film *Caligula* has been released and to think that 50 years ago a nude love scene would have been considered pornographic. If this sort of thing is stopped before other plays like this can be made, OK, but if it isn't then our future generations will grow up with demented minds like the actors, writers, and producers of these plays.

I have written to the National Theatre to express my disgust but I doubt if my letter would change their minds so I am also writing to you in the hope that this, after you have read it, can be passed on to some higher authority.

I do English Literature at school and there are

many fine plays which they could have chosen. Also I am not the only person who will be writing to you from this area as already three of my friends have. I hope that this letter will give you some support and that you know this expresses the general feeling the youth has about this play. I have spoken to many people before writing this letter and young and old we all express the same feeling so it is not one person's cry for reform.

Please, please, please take heed of this letter. I am willing to help you in any way and don't let the press and that upset you. As my father would say, 'you're doing a grand job lass!' Keep it up.

Yours faithfully,
Alison

My diary provides an account of the case as it happened.

17 October 1980 Press Association rang, just as I was sitting down to my lunch, about the new play at the National Theatre, *The Romans in Britain*. Three Roman soldiers are apparently tearing off all their clothes and raping three young male Britons in full view of the audience! Would I like to comment? I said if they'd ring back at 3 p.m. I might be able to.

In the meantime read the reviews – extremely critical. Then there was the interview on *The World at One* with Felix Barker the theatre critic. He was also extremely critical. Sir Horace Cutler and other members of the GLC have called for the cutting of the National Theatre's grant. Decided to ring New Scotland Yard – spoke to a member of the Obscene Publications Dept. and he said he would draw it to the attention of Chief Inspector Shepherd (one of those I met when I went to the Yard with John Court). He rang me back and said that he had studied what the leader writers had had to say and was going to ask the DPP to look at the play! When Press Association rang I told them what I'd done, though I didn't mention the DPP; that was for the Yard to say. After about half an hour all the papers began to ring. BBC News did an interview with me and ITN rang to ask what I felt:

'This brings Soho pornography on to the National stage and its effect could be profound and very far reaching.'

Hope I've done the right thing, but one really can't let this happen without doing *something*. *We* haven't given it publicity; it already had that.

One journalist told me that Peter Hall had said that the things seen in the play had actually happened and people needed to be shown them explicitly so that they would know. I said, 'That's ridiculous and arrogant. It has been known for 2,000 years how the Romans – some of them – behaved in Britain. We haven't needed to wait all those years for the National Theatre to come and show us what the words homosexual, rape, etc. mean!'

18 October 1980 *The Romans in Britain* gets an atrocious press; not a single paper has a good thing to say for it and all of them carry the story of our asking the police to take action. We all laughed at *The Times* front page headline – WHITEHOUSE TAKES ON THE ROMANS. As though I've taken on everything else and now its the turn of the Romans!

A number of complete strangers rang today to ask what they can do to help, so I suggested letters of support for Horace Cutler and the Obscene Publications Squad at the Yard. It is really very difficult to believe that the Attorney General will not take action. If this is not obscene then nothing could be.

24 October 1980 Saw in today's *Daily Telegraph* that the Attorney General was sending a lawyer to see *The Romans in Britain* tonight. Ernest said, 'Why don't we do the same?' Rang Robert[1] and discussed the matter with him. He felt we should go ahead and that Opinion would probably cost about £200. So I rang Mr Graham

---

[1] Mr Robert Standring, Executive Chairman and Treasurer, National VALA.

Ross-Cornes[1] who entirely concurred with the plan. He rang Mr John Smyth QC, who said that he would get back in time from Southampton to go to the theatre – incidentally, no problem about tickets in spite of all the talk about a 'sell out'.

While all this was going on, BBC 2's *Newsnight* rang to say they were doing a feature tonight on the play and were linking it with tomorrow night's *Lady Chatterley's Lover* trial dramatization – wanted to do vox pop of people coming out of play. Would I be part of a panel to discuss the play? Some panel! Just Harold Hobson the theatre critic and me on the balcony of the National Theatre.

At this point Mr Smyth came out of the theatre and passed his advice to me in the form of a handwritten note. It read, 'having seen the play I have no doubt whatever but that a *prima facie* case exists that a criminal offence has been committed'. He advised that 'the Attorney General should be asked to take action or give permission that action should be taken'. This opinion I read to camera but in the event it was cut out.

Incidentally when I arrived I was hastily hidden in the BBC's outside broadcast van – they didn't want *News at Ten* (who were there) to talk to me and since they had paid for my overnight stay I couldn't very well demur! In the event the TV interview was certainly not worth the effort involved. But Queen's Counsel's visit most certainly was.

25 October 1980 Counsel told me this morning that he would never have believed that what went on on that stage could *ever* have happened – clearly very shaken. Says he will advise that Graham Ross-Cornes writes to the Attorney General – the DPP was informed that Counsel was attending on our instructions by phone before he went – and ask him to take action or, failing that, to give permission for us to take action. By this

[1] National VALA's legal adviser.

time I was wondering what on earth we were letting ourselves in for, not least financially. But Counsel assures me that, since action cannot be taken without the Attorney General's permission, if he grants it this shows that the action is in the public interest and the Crown will bear the cost, or the defendants!

There have been many comments – often critical – on the fact that I have not seen the play. But quite apart from the fact that both our legal adviser and leading Counsel advised against it, what was the point? Because of the enormous press coverage everyone, including me, knew what happened on the stage. The important thing was not what I thought about it but whether it broke the law – only legal minds could decide that. Either way, I knew I was for it! If I had seen it the cry would have been – has it corrupted her? If not, why should she think it would corrupt anyone else? And if it *has* – where does that leave poor Mrs Whitehouse?

25 November 1980 Phone call from Graham – he's been told by the Attorney General's office that a letter had been sent to him which said that the AG is not going to give us permission to take action against *The Romans in Britain*. So now what do we do? What do we say? Wondered if something could be done in Parliament in view of the Solicitor General's statement, at the time of the passing of the Theatres Act, to the effect that the clause which stated that the AG's permission had to be sought before any individual can take action must not be used to inhibit action by serious and responsible people – it was only intended to prevent frivolous actions being brought!

26 November 1980 Conference at John Smyth's chambers. The Attorney General's letter had still not arrived. Graham's assistant solicitor Helen Corbett went round to his office to pick up a photostat – what a tatty, unsatisfactory thing it was – not from AG himself, a word crossed out, no reason given why he would not prosecute, no indication that he'd actually read John

Smyth's weighty submission to him, no apology for the
fact that two pages of that document had been
destroyed 'by accident', no indication either that the
Attorney General, the Solicitor General, the Director of
Public Prosecutions or anyone acting on their behalf
had seen the play. The whole thing thoroughly
discourteous – almost contemptuous.

27 November 1980 I gather that the Attorney General
was quite cross yesterday when tackled by an MP on
why he would not bring a prosecution. He said he did
not believe there was any chance of a successful
prosecution. The MP replied that that was no reason
for not having one. If the law was really so bad then
'let's have a case and let it be lost so that the public can
see what a disaster it is and then something can be
done about it!' He told the Attorney General that there
was an enormous ground-swell of concern about these
matters in the country and it would not do for him or
the Home Secretary to 'sit in the middle and
compromise'. 'Well, there's Williams[1] you know – it's
very difficult.' Yes, indeed, there is Williams.

17 December 1980 Went to London for another legal
conference on *The Romans*. A great deal of research has
been done and it is clear that we can do nothing at all
to challenge the Attorney General; only Parliament can
do that. However, a completely new approach was
decided upon. Since we can do nothing under the
Theatres Act, I could take a private prosecution against
the director of the play, Michael Bogdanov, under the
Sexual Offences Act which makes it a criminal offence
to procure persons for acts of gross indecency in a
public place. Graham, Jeremy and Helen will go to see
the play on Friday night. Helen will take a flashlight
because she will need to check that the script is
followed! As the scene of homosexual rape, which is the
only part of the play concerned, lasts only a minute or

[1] Report of the Committee on Obscenity and Film Censorship.

two it won't need to be on very long. Graham will ask to speak to Bogdanov and ask him whether or not he directed the play; his name on the programme is not sufficient evidence.

10 January 1981 One of the things that I find myself anxious about from time to time is that people think I'm taking this action against the National Theatre out of spite – 'determined to get them' as it were. But examining my heart as honestly as I can, I don't think there's anything of that in it at all. I realize I'm laying my head on the chopping-block but it all comes back to what God would have me do. All the great reformers – Wilberforce, Shaftesbury and the others – saw and used the law for the maintenance and upholding of God's will. The law is – or should be – the interpretation of that will and without it we are all immensely at risk and so is the cohesion of our society.

11 January 1981 I have felt troubled because I'm lacking in regard to *The Romans* prosecution the same sense of identification with Jesus that I felt in the blasphemy case. That was very personal; this is not. But of course they are quite different by their very nature. Last time it was an expression of love, this time a matter of law. Which brings me to the heart of the matter – how important is it to God that the law is upheld? In that such material on stage degrades not only those who play but those who watch – it *is* important. I need to see this action as one step – even if we lose it will perhaps serve to show the nation how far it has fallen, that it no longer is concerned that such things happen in its midst.

The other thing, and this is central to our decision to take the case, is that by refusing to take action the Attorney General has effectively given the go-ahead to productions of *The Romans* all over the country.

The National Theatre is the *National* theatre. It is financed by our money, therefore we all have a responsibility for what is done on that stage. If no action is taken, without doubt 'the boat' will be pushed even further out. It is our culture as much as our national morality which is at stake, and that is important to us all, whether or not we go anywhere near the theatre.

12 January 1981 By one of those 'happy coincidences' my Bible reading this morning was Joshua 1: 1–9, especially, 'Be strong and very courageous' and 'be careful to obey all the law my servant Moses gave you; do not turn from it to the right or to the left. . . Do not be terrified . . . for the Lord your God will be with you wherever you go'. Just what I needed. And as far as what happened in *The Romans* is concerned – the act of simulated sodomy: 'Do you not know that your body is a temple of the Holy Spirit, who is in you, whom you have received from God?' In this sense such a scene as grossly violates the holiness of God as did the blasphemous poem in *Gay News*. There I must leave it.

29 June 1981 Hearing of our charge before the magistrate at Horseferry Road Court. Had to wait till about 3.30 for any news of the case. Michael Bogdanov defended by Lord Hutchinson, defence lawyer in the *Lady Chatterley's Lover* trial in 1961, who claimed, I gather, that there was no case to answer, that the Theatres Act is meant to cover the theatre and that it was never Parliament's intention that the common law Sexual Offences legislation should be applied to it. Apparently John Smyth challenged that by saying if that is so why did Parliament not say so? Graham was in the witness box for an hour and a quarter – instead of me – having seen the play on my behalf.

Peter Hall appeared for Michael Bogdanov and said *The Romans* was a 'very moral play'. Talked about the anal rape as signifying the 'penetration' of Britain by the Romans. I thought that was incredible! After a couple of thousand years this is apparently the only way the National Theatre in 1981 can make us understand that this happened!

Graham thinks it will finish by lunch-time tomorrow. Covered by radio and TV news – photographs of Bogdanov, John Smyth, Lord Hutchinson and me. Couldn't sleep – 2.30 a.m. before I got off – not worried, just overwhelmed.

30 June 1981 Photographer from London's *New Standard* arrived at the door unheralded early this morning, but I didn't want to see him. ITN and various papers rang: where would I be when the verdict came? Here. Nearly one o'clock when the phone began ringing with the news that Bogdanov had been committed for trial. I gather it had all been very heavy going – press thought it would go the other way because of the brilliance of Jeremy Hutchinson, who tried to turn it into an obscenity trial. But in the event Mr Harrington, the magistrate, was out for only three minutes.

Feel tremendous sense of relief; a very great burden lifted. I think the strain of these events takes more out of me than I realize. I do not consciously worry and I do not think or talk about them beforehand, not least because I am so busy with other things, but I think, deep down, they must take their toll. But so far, so good. Graham says that Jeremy Hutchinson was *very* persuasive and if he was like that in a magistrates' court, one can imagine how he will work on a jury!

Very interested, and encouraged, to read the piece by Fenton Bresler, *The Daily Mail* legal expert, this morning:

'Whatever the outcome of the case may be, Mrs Whitehouse – and/or her legal advisers – have achieved a brilliant legal manoeuvre in persuading a London stipendiary magistrate that there is a case to answer against Mr Bogdanov.

'Most lawyers would have said till now that the Theatres Act of 1968 was designed to cover all possible prosecutions with regard to allegedly obscene or indecent stage performances.

'And the Act, passed during Roy Jenkins's "liberal" regime at the Home Office, requires the consent of either the Director of Public Prosecutions for a State prosecution or the Attorney General for a private prosecution.

'Both Sir Thomas Hetherington QC, the DPP, and Sir Michael Havers QC, the Attorney General, have already declined to act. So Mrs Whitehouse has neatly by-passed theatrical law and has now successfully launched a private prosecution under the ordinary criminal law, invoking Section 13 of the Sexual Offences Act, 1956.

'Unlike the Theatres Act and the 1959 Obscene Publications Act, the claim of "public good" or artistic licence provides no defence.'

2 July 1981 *The Romans* still very much in my mind. I know the trial will be the theatrical trial of the century – bound to put an enormous strain on all involved – not least, I imagine, on Bogdanov himself. I constantly need the assurance that this is what the Lord would have me do and I need to know this, not only intellectually but with deep spiritual conviction, then, whatever happens, my mind will be at peace. But what an extraordinary situation I find myself in! For a woman of 71, mother and grandmother, to challenge an act of simulated buggery at the National Theatre in the full publicity which would attend this trial – *what* a comment on the days in which we live!

4 July 1981 Wimbledon and the garden a great help! Lots of messages of support; everywhere that Ernest goes he brings them back. Charles Oxley rang to say that he spoke at a large Church of England Men's Society meeting yesterday. Tremendous amount of support for our work and the Bishop prayed specially for me at this time. Actually feel more public support – and Christian support – than I did over the blasphemy case. This time, of course, the papers have spelt out exactly what happened on the stage, whereas no one – except Nicolas Walter *et al*! – could print the *Gay News* poem. Funny thing is that *The Times* spelt it out in detail; something unbelievable not so very long ago.

25 February 1982 John Smyth rang today to tell me that he will not be able to conduct our case at *The Romans* trial! As he told me several days ago he is suffering from some kind of virus and has lost over a stone in a month. The consultant and his own GP have now strongly advised against him handling the case and of course I understand. But now the question is who will take his place? How sad I feel, but must trust.

28 February In this morning's post I received a copy of the leaflet issued by the Theatre Defence Fund whose aim is to raise funds for Michael Bogdanov's defence. Although I'd seen it before, this was the first time I'd noticed that one of the signatories was Lady Plowden, DBE, formerly Chairman of the IBA! I really felt as though I had been kicked in the stomach, and my mind went back to the day, not long after her appointment as Chairman of the IBA when we had met privately at a mutual friend's house, and I had come away with the strong impression that she was in many ways sympathetic to our cause. That she should now be prepared to campaign in support of productions like *The Romans in Britain* was to me almost unbelievable. I can't help but think this accounts for a lot!

14 March Arrived back today from the Scilly Isles where Ernest and I have had a week's holiday. My fall, broken rib, and the shock associated with it had really knocked the stuffing out of me. But being away from everything has been very good for us both. Standing by myself one day as force 9–10 gales enraged the ocean in a most spectacular way while the sun shone upon it all – one had the sense that the islands only existed by courtesy of the sea! – I experienced an overwhelming sense of the power of Almighty God, a certainty that everything *is* in his hands, that what he wills, will be. Not only must I trust in him but I must rejoice in him.

My heart was at peace – I don't think that ever before had I experienced such a sense of his power and his caring about our, oh so minute, affairs compared with the mightiness of the universe.

15 March *Romans in Britain* case opened. Ian Kennedy QC who is taking John Smyth's place did very *very* well – emphasized from the start that this 'was not a case about censorship' as had been suggested, that it was very important that we had 'a free theatre to challenge and, if need be shock' but that did not mean that the theatre and those who worked in it should be above the law.

Graham, cross-examined by Lord Hutchinson denied that he had attended the play to look for 'the worst possible things' he could find. He would 'have been much happier if what I had seen of the play had not been sufficient to justify prosecution'.

When Lord Hutchinson later suggested that it was perfectly legitimate nowadays to depict rape on stage, if it was done in one way rather than another, Graham said: 'I would consider that an explicit scene of homosexual rape is grossly indecent.'

Quite a number of journalists rang to ask where I was. 'We've missed you,' one said! I told them, which was true, that I was very anxious that the case should not be presented by the media as a Whitehouse/Bogdanov confrontation. It was also true that Mr Kennedy felt very strongly that I should not be there as the case had moved into the Regina v. Bogdanov sphere.

16 March Very wide coverage in the papers this morning. What the respectable readers of *The Daily Telegraph* thought of the detailed reporting of Ian Kennedy's description of everything that was said and done in that particular scene one can only imagine but, at least, no one who reads it can have any doubt about what happened. All the papers carried the judge's warning that their reporting of the case should not be, in any way, in contempt of court.

Call after call from journalists. *The Daily Express*'s man wanted to come and spend the day with me while I shopped and cooked! 'While I did *what?*' I asked. Shopping and cooking were the last things in my mind!

No news of the case on radio or TV tonight. (I discovered later that this was because the press and the jury were out for most of the day while legal points were being debated.) We've apparently come to crisis point – Lord Hutchinson for the defence is claiming that there's no case to answer. I'm told he put his case very powerfully. Ian Kennedy has begun his contention that there is, and will complete it in the morning and the judge will retire to make his judgement on whether or not the theatre is covered by the Sexual Offences Act. If he finds for the defence, that will be the end of the case.

17 March What a remarkable and memorable day! At around midday Graham rang to tell me that the judge's statement was all we could have desired. He had told Lord Hutchinson that he found his submission that there was no case to answer quite unacceptable, that the existence of the Theatres Act in no way exonerated it from the rest of the law and that the Sexual Offences Act most certainly applied to the theatre. How marvellous: Graham said that we are now faced with a choice: we can either continue with the case or withdraw it. I asked him what the defence, and Bogdanov in particular, thought about the case being withdrawn. 'On, they're very pleased too,' said Graham. 'Then most certainly let's withdraw,' I said. We had established a very important legal verdict and there seemed to me absolutely no point in prolonging Michael Bogdanov's agony. To withdraw seemed advantageous to us all. (I did not know till the following day that in fact the decision to withdraw had already been made by Ian Kennedy. Neither did I know till later that strictly speaking a private prosecution cannot legally be withdrawn by the person initiating it once the judge has ruled that there is a case to answer.)

Later in the evening Graham rang again to tell me the case would finish in the morning and asked me to come to the Old Bailey. He told me something else – a note from Ian Kennedy to Hutchinson crossed with a note from Geoffrey Robertson (Supporting Defence Council) to Kennedy, *both* containing the suggestion that the case should be withdrawn.

18 March Left home this morning feeling very happy, but before long I began to suspect that all was not as simple as it had seemed last night. We were met as expected at the Old Bailey with a barrage of TV cameras and press, but, as agreed, I made no comment. Inside Court No. 1 I exchanged friendly smiles with defence barrister Geoffrey Robertson, John Mortimer's number two in the blasphemy case. I heard afterwards that he was telling his friends in court how he'd nearly knocked me down (a gross exaggeration) when I was picking blackberries in the lane outside our house a year or two ago. 'Imagine what a lot of trouble we'd all have been saved if I had,' he joked.

The atmosphere when the judge started to speak was electric – everyone knew something dramatic was about to happen. He first stated his judgement in the matter of the law, declaring that our claim that the theatre could be covered by the Sexual Offences Act was entirely correct. He then went on to deal with what he termed the 'wholly improper' situation which had arisen as a result of Michael Bogdanov having been informed by Counsel that the case against him was being withdrawn and that he would be discharged. Such an initiative had, the judge said, pre-empted his function as a judge. This had created a unique, indeed unprecedented, situation in which the Attorney General's advice had been sought. The judge made it abundantly clear that if events had taken their proper course he would not have allowed the case to be withdrawn. Now, however, Chief Treasury Counsel had a statement to make on the Attorney General's behalf which was to the effect that the Attorney General had intervened and issued a *nolle prosequi*. Within a few moments – or so it seemed – the case was over.

After the jury left Lord Hutchinson asked for Michael Bogdanov's costs and they were granted. Ian Kennedy did not ask for costs for us. And that was that.

Partly because of the delicacy of the situation which had been created and partly because, having achieved a not inconsiderable success, we felt it would be more becoming, we decided I should go straight home. However I had first to get out of the Old Bailey! The police, about a dozen of them, would not let me leave until they had provided safe conduct for me. Not only, I was told, were there hordes of media people outside but there was also an 'anti-me' demonstration. When my taxi had arrived, its door opened and two of my colleagues already seated inside, I was rushed out at great speed, strong bodies surrounding me and firm hands holding my head down as I was pushed inside. The taxi door was banged to so quickly that Graham was left outside on the pavement! Quickly recovering him, we shot away, cameras following us as fast and far as they could.

I suppose the next forty-eight hours were amongst the most harassing of all my campaigning years. I arrived home to discover that 'the whole world had been on the phone', and indeed it literally never stopped ringing. And what did everyone want to know? 'Why did *I* withdraw my case?' (And this after Ian Kennedy had made it abundantly clear in court that our decision to withdraw was his and his alone.) 'Was I upset about my case "collapsing"?' (And this after the judge had found for us.) 'Hadn't John Smyth pulled out of the case and gone on holiday because he knew we could never win?' (what nonsense) And on and on and on.

I listened to a recording of the feature on the case in *The World at One* in which it was claimed that Mr Kennedy had admitted in court that our case had collapsed. I rang *PM* to ask if I could reply to that travesty of the truth and they interviewed me over the phone. After that David Dimbleby rang to see if there was a chance of me going on *Nationwide* – but I'd just got in and didn't feel I could turn round and travel the 60 miles back again. This meant of course that Michael Bogdanov had it all his own way on the programme. By this time he was 'very angry' that the case had been withdrawn and once again the same false picture of what actually had happened came across, as it did in programme after programme and of course in paper after paper next day.

By this time I'd decided that coming home so quickly after the case had been a mistake, and when both BBC TV news and ITN rang to say that TV crews were on their way, I agreed to be interviewed. But the interviews were inevitably very short and rushed. In the meantime a car had arrived to take me back to London to appear in BBC 2's *Newsnight* – what a drive that was! We became completely lost and were about to turn back when we spotted a stationary taxi and he led us at great speed, over halt signs, even over traffic lights to the Television Centre. I was rushed straight into the studio where the programme was already well advanced (it was now eleven o'clock); no time for make-up, hair do or anything. Everyone said afterwards that I looked awful – strained and lined, and I'm sure I must have done. By the time I finally got to bed I'd had a 21-hour day, from 5.30 a.m. to 2.30 a.m!

After a few hours' sleep the phone began ringing again, only the main question this time was, how was I going to pay my costs? Figures of £20,000, £40,000 even £60,000 were being plucked from the air by the various journalists. Of course 'I did not know' was the honest answer. I did not even know what the costs were. Having been granted costs at the Magistrates' Court, and the case having been sent by the magistrate to the Old Bailey because it was of such public interest, there had seemed little doubt that I would be granted costs at the end of the trial. Now, of course, the case had been stopped in mid-stream, as it were, and a completely new situation had arisen.

However, I told the papers quite simply that in this matter, as in all our work, we trusted that all our needs physical and spiritual and material would be met. 'You're saying that the Lord will provide' said *The Sunday Times'* reporter and that was his headline next day. Many other papers made the same point.

In the meantime the Attorney General had joined in again. This time 'a reliable source' claimed – and he didn't deny it – that he was 'very angry' with me. He said he believed I had never intended to go through with the case. I found that incredible. How on earth could he read my mind? Such a thought, in fact, had never entered into it. But I gather the 'anger' was nothing new. He'd apparently been angry with me for initiating the private prosecution after he had refused to take action. What is more he had, I understand, been asked by the defence to issue a *nolle prosequi* after the magistrate at Horseferry Road court had sent the case for trial at the Old Bailey and he had refused. Now he found himself back in the same situation and being forced by circumstances to do so, and I can understand his annoyance.

In fairness it has to be said that, in the end, he was angry with Michael Bogdanov too! In reply to a question in the House of Commons Sir Michael took issue with Mr Bogdanov over his reported comments that he was 'very angry' that the trial had ended in the way it had, with nothing decided. He went on: 'There was no way that the wish of the prosecution, which I was told had the express agreement of the defendant, could be effected without my intervention and since it could have been oppressive to the defendant to put him again in jeopardy after he had been told that the case was to be stopped at that stage, I thought it right to enter a *nolle prosequi*. I should like to make it clear that this was entered with the express agreement of the accused, in spite of comments in the Press.' He also made it clear that the judge's finding that the theatre *is* liable to prosecution under the Sexual Offences Act 'stands'.

I must say that of all the silly things which were said by what one might call 'the theatre lobby' the silliest surely was Marius Goring's claim that if the judge thought that an act of simulated homosexual rape on stage was the same as actual homosexual rape in the context at point, then *Macbeth* involved a handful of (presumably prosecutable) murders. But that which makes the simulated and actual acts the same in this particular context clearly does not apply in the case of murder. If one were to ask where the gulf lies for an audience when it comes to distinguishing the obscenity of an actual rape on stage and a simulated one, the distinction must be nice indeed. Hardly so between real and simulated murder.

In spite of the incredible hassle which followed immediately on the trial, and exhausted though I certainly was at one point, I never really lost the sense of peace that God gave me on the shore in the Scillies, and the days that followed were rich in experience of how God does indeed honour our faith. During the next week I received over 500 letters, all containing small and large sums towards my costs and towards 'the work' in general. As Luke's Gospel says, 'Give, and it will be given to you. A good measure, pressed down, shaken together and running over.'

What happened the following week was wonderful too! Months before, we had invited Hinson McAuliffe, Solicitor General of Fulton County, Georgia to come to Britain, to speak primarily at National VALA's Annual Convention,[1] on his highly successful drive against pornography. Although we had never met before, we got on 'like a house on fire'! During his short visit he and I appeared on radio and TV, visited New Scotland Yard, and held a most successful press conference. He spoke in the House of Lords, met MPs and sat in the Distinguished Strangers' Gallery as the guest of the Speaker to hear Prime Minister's Question Time. As *The Times* headline had it, he was the 'Man who killed sex shops in Atlanta'. The report went on: 'Once upon a time there were 44 dirty bookshops in the United States city of Atlanta Georgia. Now there is none. It was purely, Mr McAuliffe said, a question of good law, good law enforcement officers, good prosecutors and good judges. The British, he clearly implied, though a fine and good people, were deficient in certain of those respects. But he was far too polite to say so.'

Throughout the week, and whoever he spoke to, his words were startling in their simplicity and in their implicit challenge. With effective law he has broken the back of the trade.

[1] 27 March 1982

And he relies on precisely the type of legislation we have long called for here, in which precise indication is given of what is and is not obscene – using heavy fines, prosecutions for the nuisance, assaults and immoral acts so often connected with the sale of pornography, and involuntary bankruptcy petitions against pornographers, thus forcing them to disclose their assets.

Now there are no sex shops left in his area. In reply to a question about Georgia being in 'the Bible belt' he listed other states, far from the Bible belt, including one area of New York, where legal action has been equally effective. He believed, he said, that if present trends continued there would be no sex shops and virtually no pornography in the United States in five years' time.

The amazing thing was the timing of his visit. It had been arranged for some time that he should address a group of peers and MPs, with Lord Nugent PC as his host. In the event that meeting took place the day before the debate in the House of Lords of a new Bill 'to restrict the dissemination of pornography'. Time and again – as he and I were in the public gallery to hear the debate – speakers referred to him and to his success. When the debate was over one Peer after another gathered round to thank him for coming, 'and the hope' that he had given them. It was a marvellous debate and the Bill was given a second reading with only one dissenting voice, that of the humanist peer Lord Houghton. On the very same day that Hinson McAuliffe was speaking in the House of Lords, the Lord Chief Justice of England, Lord Lane, was making his maiden speech in the great law and order debate. What he had to say hit the headlines the next day.

Lord Lane said that by the time the criminal falls into the hands of the police, and particularly by the time he reaches court, it is too late. The damage has been done. The remedy, if it can be found, must be sought a great deal earlier.

All the old sanctions had gone, said his Lordship – the parental, the religious, the social, the financial and the employment sanction. It was now bad psychology for anyone to have a bad conscience or a guilty conscience, but nothing had been found to replace it.

Apart from those disincentives which had gone, criminals were faced with incentives to commit crime in the shape of violence depicted on screens of all sizes.

Acquisitiveness and greed were depicted and religiously imitated by the youngsters who formed such a large part of the statistics.

One would only have to sit a short time in his court in the Strand to realize the imitative effect of the huge increase in the sale of pornography, Lord Lane said.

> It is traceable to glossy imports which come into the country disguised as Danish bacon or Dutch tomatoes, in large quantities which percolate through various shops to find their way into the hands of young people with inevitable serious results which we see increasing every day.
>
> Those are the areas where the attack should be levelled, rather than too late, at the time when these young people arrive in court or in the hands of the police.

The following day the Prime Minister, also speaking on the law and order issue, called for a counter attack on those who had sought to undermine traditional values.

> We are reaping what was sown in the 60s. The fashionable theories and permissive claptrap set the scene for a society in which the old virtues of discipline and self-restraint were denigrated.

Mrs Thatcher also criticized television's role in declining standards, and said that children were fed on a daily diet of violence unparalleled in the country's history.

And in the very same week the BBC devoted BBC 2's *Newsweek*[1] to looking, really for the first time, at the link

---

[1] 2 April 1982.

between pornography and sex crime – and very powerful and persuasive stuff it was.

I could only marvel at the way in which all these things had happened together – their united impact left us with the happy sense that now at last the tide was turning. The cause to which Ernest and I had devoted so many years of our lives was being taken on by those with far more power than we could ever hope or wish to have. I think it was perhaps because he sensed this that one TV interviewer asked me at the end of that week: 'You are now 71, Mrs Whitehouse. When are you going to retire?'

I laughed, pointed upwards, and said, 'That's in his hands, not mine!'

Index